Inductive Logic Programming

Inductive Logic Programming

From Machine Learning to Software Engineering

Francesco Bergadano and Daniele Gunetti

The MIT Press
Cambridge, Massachusetts
London, England

©1996 Massachusetts Institute of Technology

All rights reserved. No part of this book may be reproduced in any form by any electronic or mechanical means (including photocopying, recording, or information storage and retrieval) without permission in writing from the publisher.

This book was set in LaTeX by the authors and was printed and bound in the United States of America.

Library of Congress Cataloging-in-Publication Data

Bergadano, Francesco, 1963–
   Inductive logic programming: from machine learning to software engineering / Francesco Bergadano and Daniele Gunetti.
     p. cm.—(Logic programming)
   Includes bibliographical references and index.
   ISBN 0-262-02393-8 (hc: alk. paper)
   1. Logic programming. I. Gunetti, Daniele. II. Title.
III. Series.
QA76.63.B47   1995   95-14956
005.1′1—dc20   CIP

Contents

Series Foreword — ix

Preface — xi

1 Introduction — 1

I Fundamentals — 9

2 Problem Statement and Definitions — **11**
  2.1 Logic Programs and Their Examples — 11
  2.2 The ILP Problem — 13
  2.3 Incremental Systems and Queries — 22
  2.4 Identifying Logic Programs in the Limit — 27

3 Bottom-up Methods — **33**
  3.1 Plotkin's Least General Generalization — 34
  3.2 Inverse Resolution — 45
  3.3 Inverse Implication — 60

4 Top-down Methods — **77**
  4.1 Shapiro's Model Inference System — 79
  4.2 FOIL — 85

5 A Unifying Framework — **91**
  5.1 Theorem Proving with Inverse Resolution — 91
  5.2 Extensional Top-Down Methods Revisited — 99
  5.3 Example — 103

II ILP with Strong Bias — 107

6 Inductive Bias — 109
- 6.1 Refinement Operators — 111
- 6.2 Clause Templates — 115
- 6.3 Domain Theories and Grammars — 118
- 6.4 Bias in Bottom-up Systems — 125
- 6.5 Clause Sets — 129

7 Program Induction with Queries — 137
- 7.1 The FILP System — 139
- 7.2 Justification of Extensionality and Problems — 142
- 7.3 Completing Examples before Learning — 144
- 7.4 Discussion — 147

8 Program Induction without Queries — 149
- 8.1 The Induction Procedure — 150
- 8.2 Example — 153
- 8.3 Properties of the Induction Procedure — 154
- 8.4 A Simplified Implementation — 157
- 8.5 Discussion — 163

III Software Engineering Applications — 165

9 Development, Maintenance, and Reuse — 167
- 9.1 Introduction — 169
- 9.2 Inductive Logic Programming Languages — 171
- 9.3 The Inductive Software Process — 174
- 9.4 From Inductive Learning to Inductive Programming — 180

10 Testing — 185
- 10.1 Introduction to Testing — 186
- 10.2 Induction and Testing Compared — 187
- 10.3 Inductive Test Case Generation — 189
- 10.4 Examples — 191

11 A Case Study — 199
- 11.1 Synthesizing *Insert* — 200
- 11.2 Testing *Insert* — 209

A How to FTP Our Software	**217**
Bibliography	**219**
Index	**237**

Series Foreword

The logic programming approach to computing investigates the use of logic as a programming language and explores computational models based on controlled deduction.

The field of logic programming has seen a tremendous growth in the last several years, both in depth and in scope. This growth is reflected in the number of articles, journals, theses, books, workshops, and conferences devoted to the subject. The MIT Press series in logic programming was created to accommodate this development and to nurture it. It is dedicated to the publication of high-quality textbooks, monographs, collections, and proceedings in logic programming.

Ehud Shapiro
The Weizmann Institute of Science
Rehovot, Israel

Preface

Inductive Logic Programming (ILP) has evolved from previous research in Machine Learning, Logic Programming, and Inductive Program Synthesis. Like relational Machine Learning, it deals with the induction of concepts represented in a logical form. Typically, the output of an ILP learner is a set of Horn clauses. However, ILP cannot be just a new name for relational Machine Learning. This book emphasizes this fact by giving special attention to "Programming," less to "Inductive" and "Logic." ILP techniques have the potential to support software development and maintenance. Some of these techniques, developed by the authors, are studied in full detail and their implementations are made available through anonymous ftp. Their Software Engineering applications are then discussed in the context of a relatively complex logic program. However, this book also has the important motivation of providing an up-to-date and extended survey of ILP as a research area. The basic notions, the most common induction operators, and the best-known methods and systems are described and analyzed. Compared with other existing surveys, the present book may be more complete, and includes newer notions, such as inverse implication; newer goals that are important for programming assistants, such as multiple predicate learning; and important topics that are often overlooked, such as declarative bias.

This work is the result of many years of research, and many have directly or indirectly contributed to it. We wish to thank Lorenza Saitta and Attilio Giordana, as well as Gabriele Lolli, for the early joint work that has inspired our more recent perspectives, and for their continuing support. As in all long-term research efforts, an essential contribution is represented by discussions, joint work on related topics, and collaboration in international projects. This kind of support is due to many researchers who cannot all be listed here. However, we would like to mention the Machine Learning and AI group at the University of Turin, the European researchers involved in the ESPRIT ILP project, and Ryszard Michalski and his group at George Mason University. Stan Matwin and Claire Nédellec read and commented on a first draft of the book, that resulted in a number of improvements and changes. The research described in this book was financially supported by the European Union, under contracts 6020 (ESPRIT BRA ILP) and 6156 (ESPRIT BRA DRUMS2); by involvement in the ILPNET PECO network and in the ML-NET network of excellence; and by the Italian CNR, for the bilateral project on Inductive Inference (Italy-USA).

Francesco Bergadano and *Daniele Gunetti*
Turin, January 1996

Inductive Logic Programming

1
Introduction

Inductive Logic Programming is sufficiently new to require starting this book with a definition. A definition that has generated some agreement is found in [62]. It states that Inductive Logic Programming is the research area covering the intersection of Machine Learning and Logic Programming. This is about like saying that it is concerned with Induction and Logic Programming. Indeed: inductive, logic, and programming. Although the authority of this view dates back to Lapalisse, we will risk generating less agreement and propose a more informative notion. Inductive Logic Programming (called ILP in the rest of the book) has been concerned with systems and general methods that are given examples and produce programs. In fact, an ILP system may receive various kinds of information about the desired program as input, but this input always includes examples of the program's input/output behavior. The output that is produced is a logic program that behaves as expected on the given examples, or at least on a high percentage of them. Typically, the obtained programs will then be used on new examples, not given to the ILP system during the learning phase. The above may be an oversimplification, but for a computer scientist, it is just a form of program synthesis from examples. The view presented in this book emphasizes the fact that examples are absolutely not the only input to practical ILP methods. Another important source of information comes from a priori knowledge about the target program, including partially developed software components, and properties of the needed subprocedures, such as the number and the type of the arguments and of the returned values. To stress this observation, and also the fact that practical tools will have to be embedded in more complex environments, we would like to look at ILP as *logic program development with the help of examples*, and not just automatic programming from examples. This book provides an up-to-date and complete survey of ILP as a research area, and then concentrates on methods that are effective for software development.

Although definitions may be useful, and ours also serves the purpose of proposing a particular perspective, a better way to define a research area is to look at the roots of its ideas and at the history of its early developments. In this context, the definition of ILP as the intersection of Machine Learning and Logic Programming loses its tautological strength and seems to suggest that ILP has evolved from both disciplines. But this is not true. Most research and researchers in ILP came from Machine Learning alone, and some of the initial motivations are meaningful if framed in the evolution of inductive reasoning from Pattern Recognition, through initial approaches to symbolic Machine Learning, to more recent techniques for learning relational concepts.

In Pattern Recognition, one obtains the definition of a *class*, a group of objects that are similar or should be grouped together for the purposes of some application. The definition that is learned inductively is usually numeric, or at least contains some numeric parameters. The main purpose of the training phase is the fine-tuning of these numeric parameters. A good example is found in linear discriminants. A class is a set of points in an n-dimensional space. A learned description of a class is a hyperplane in that space: what lies on one side of the plane is classified as belonging to the class. The training phase determines the parameters of the hyperplane.

Early research in symbolic Machine Learning, e.g., [200, 128, 129, 91, 159], pointed out that not all classes can be distinguished on the basis of numeric information alone. For instance, one may describe some disease also by means of nonnumeric features such as the sex and the race of the patient. Treating symbolic features numerically is inefficient and inadequate, and makes it difficult to use prior information and so-called domain knowledge. For instance, the description "*shape*=square and *side*>10" makes the additional constraint "*area*>100" useless. This was considered especially important in the context of Artificial Intelligence applications, where prior knowledge in symbolic form was usually available. To emphasize the difference with respect to previous approaches in Pattern Recognition, "classes" were renamed "concepts," and "training" became "learning."

However, as shown in the shape, side, and area example above, initial work in Machine Learning would produce concept descriptions that were still relatively simple. Examples, in particular, would be described by a list of attribute-value pairs. For instance, an example of basketball player could be:

height=2.10m, *weight*=100kg, *preferred_music*=soul

and an example of a football player could be:

height=1.85m, *weight*=110kg, *preferred_music*=rock.

1. Introduction

As a consequence, concept descriptions would consist of conjunctions or disjunctions of simple propositional literals such as:

weight>100 and (*preferred_music*=rock or *preferred_music*=rap) → football_player.

As a further example, which will be continued below, the concept of a "grandfather" may be described as:

beard=yes and *hair_color*=white and *number_of_descendants*>2

In such concept descriptions there are no variables or quantifiers, and no relations among example components. The concept description languages used are variants or restrictions of propositional logic. Well-known examples of learning systems with these characteristics are Michalski's AQ [132] and Quinlan's ID3 [159].

More recently, more expressive concept description languages were considered in relational Machine Learning methods, e.g., [128, 19, 26]. In this case, examples may contain components, and some attributes may be meaningful only for some of the components. As a consequence, we need a variable size list of attribute-value pairs for each of the components. For instance, one may consider the following example of a family including a "grandfather":

name: dave, *son*: mike, *father*: ron
name: mike, *son*: junior, *father*: dave
name: junior, *father*: mike

Obviously, one could translate this representation into a unique list of attribute-value pairs, where each attribute is indexed with the name of the corresponding component. However, as the number of attributes per component is not always the same, and because the number of components may change from one example to the other, the translation would take away space and might also be harder for the user to understand. More important, the concept descriptions that are obtained in relational learning will not just be propositional sentences, but may contain quantifiers and variables. In other words, relational concept description languages are first-order languages with possible restrictions. For example, a possible description of a family including a grandfather would be:

$\exists$x,y,z (son(x)=y and son(y)=z)

In the early literature on relational learning, quantifiers were usually omitted, and implicitly taken to be existential.

ILP has continued this evolution of Machine Learning research by taking Prolog or a restriction of Prolog as the concept description language. This has brought two advantages with respect to previous research in relational learning. On the one hand, expressive power was increased, mainly by allowing for recursive definitions. This brings the learned concept descriptions much closer to real programs, and opens up the possibility of using inductive learning for software development. On the other hand, the simpler and more standard notation found in Prolog has permitted a substantial clarification and a more rigorous formalization. Examples are no longer described by components, with their attribute-value pairs, but are just written as ground literals, i.e., predicates applied to constant arguments. The previous example for families and grandfathers, would be described by a set of ground literals as follows:

grandfather(dave,junior), father(ron,dave),
father(dave,mike), father(mike,junior)

The the so-called *background knowledge* is now simply a Prolog program, given by the user, that will have to be integrated with the learned concept description. For instance, the user might tell the ILP system that[1]

son(X,Y) :- father(Y,X).

Finally, the learned concept description will also be a Prolog program. A "concept" is now translated into a "Prolog predicate," and we are able to distinguish the following three different descriptions of "grandfather":

grandfather :- father(X,Z), father(Z,Y).
grandfather(X) :- father(X,Z), father(Z,Y).
grandfather(X,Y) :- father(X,Z), father(Z,Y).

where the first identifies a family database containing at least one grandfather, the second defines the requirements for being a grandfather, and the third defines the fact that some specific person X is the grandfather of another specific person Y. In previous relational learning, these three "concepts" would be hard to distinguish, and some confusion has been generated in the Machine Learning literature. This example is about the clarification and formalization issue that has been addressed in ILP. For the increased expressive power, Prolog's Horn clause notation allows

---

[1] Throughout the book, we will use the standard Prolog notation for Horn clauses, with the consequent on the left side of the clause, the body on the right, and ":-" in place of the arrow symbol.

1. Introduction

for concept descriptions such as:

ancestor(X,Y) :- father(X,Z), ancestor(Z,Y).

that had not been considered in previous approaches to relational learning because they were unable to deal with recursion.

Techniques have changed and improved, but for a large part of the ILP applications, the goals have remained the same as in Pattern Recognition and Machine Learning. Positive and negative examples are given, a logic program is learned that should distinguish positive and negative examples. This should happen for a large part of the given examples, and about the same should be observed on new examples not given during the learning phase. This goal has been addressed in Pattern Recognition and Machine Learning with different degrees of success in different applications. The first obvious observation is that when moving from early research in Pattern Recognition and Machine Learning to ILP, the concept description language becomes more expressive, and it becomes easier to separate the given positive and negative examples. However, predictive power is worse when moving to more expressive concept-description languages. ILP systems will then have to expect a serious degradation of performance when moving from given examples to the test data. Nevertheless, if an application does require the expressive power of a Prolog program, this means that simpler formalisms will fail to provide accurate classifications even on the given data. In these cases, ILP methods may turn out to be superior to traditional classification techniques. Impressive results have been obtained for the diagnosis of faults in electromechanical apparatus [78], secondary structure prediction in protein folding [111], drug design [110], finite element mesh [65], and document classification [73]. The expressive power achieved in relational learning is certainly needed in the above-cited applications. It is not always clear whether adding the possibility of recursion really makes a difference. But, with or without recursion, ILP offers a unified framework for relational learning that is effective in many classification problems.

There is, however, another way of looking at the evolution of ILP, and another way of understanding its importance in computer science. In fact, ILP may be seen as a modern and more effective approach to automatic programming, and as a software engineering tool for logic program development. As such, its roots must be found in the program synthesis research that was done, essentially, during the 1970s. A substantial part of that research was devoted to the automatic synthesis of LISP functions from input/output examples (e.g., [187, 25, 115]). This approach was based on the ambitious goal of obtaining programs without a programmer. Although interesting methods and results were reached, this goal was not achieved, criticism was generated, and this type of automatic programming received less attention after 1980. One of the problems consisted in the fact that methods were generally heuristic, and there was no guarantee that an adequate program would be obtained from given examples; it was not easy to determine the type of target programs and examples that would allow the proposed methods to produce a solution. Another problem lay in the fact that learned programs were generally very simple and unrelated to other software components, while development tools were moving toward complex, embedded systems.

Some of the above criticism may still be applicable to some ILP methods, but at least two important differences must be mentioned. First, the choice of Prolog as a programming language for the learned programs was a good one. This was noticed early on by Ehud Shapiro when he developed the first automatic logic programming method, called MIS, during the early 1980s [176]. Prolog's simple syntax identifies procedures with clauses, which can be expanded simply by adding literals to the antecedents. Examples are just predicates applied to constant arguments, and no complicated example specification language is needed (as developed, e.g., in [11]). On the other hand, one is not limited to providing input/output examples for the top-level procedure only. Examples of predicates corresponding to subprocedures will follow the same simple syntax. For instance, for learning multiplication, one may provide:

times(2,3,6), times(1,3,3), add(3,3,6).

Thus, we may give the ILP system information for the main computation (times), and also for the subcalls that are needed (add). Finally, nondeterminism makes the code more concise and substantially shorter than in imperative languages; as a consequence, learning a program may require fewer steps.

Second, examples are no longer considered the only source of information: previous knowledge about parts or properties of the target program may be used by the ILP system. We are no longer interested in programming without a programmer. By contrast, we consider a scenario where a more competent programmer, with a more diverse set of programming tools, will now also consider examples and inductive inference methods as an option. The above differences, together with the fact that more and more diverse methods were subject to extensive theoretical and experimental analysis in ILP, suggest that inductive program synthesis may deserve a second chance and renewed consideration from the software development world.

Assistance during software development is probably the most natural, but certainly not the only, software engineering application of ILP. First of all, it must be noted that the kind of software development that is achieved through ILP techniques includes a simple form of maintenance. After an initial version of a program has been coded or generated automatically, it may be used on specific cases that arise in the end application. If an error is detected, the corresponding and corrected input/output example may be added to the example base, and the program may be corrected automatically, or a new program may be learned from scratch. ILP techniques have been also used for test-case generation [16, 63] by "reversing" the induction process: we go from programs to relevant input values instead of learning a program from some of its input/output examples. If examples are seen as a *specification* of the learned program, this kind of test-case generation may also be viewed as a type of reverse engineering (from existing programs to specifications). Another kind of reverse engineering that is of interest for ILP techniques uses an existing, possibly complex, program to obtain meaningful input/output examples, and then learns a Prolog specification of the given implementation [49]. The obtained Prolog specification may be simpler and easier to use in further analysis, with respect to the initial implementation, which may be given in an imperative language or lack clarity and documentation. Similarly, ILP has been used to induce loop invariants from the observed values of the relevant variables in the loop during program execution [29].

As mentioned earlier, most approaches to ILP are actually derived from previous Machine Learning research, and typically devoted to classification problems. The view of ILP as a source of Software Engineering tools is proposed in this book as an alternative. However, this book also serves as a survey of basic research done in ILP and of more recent developments, as well as an introduction to the field. This tutorial and survey objective is addressed in part I, where terminology and problems are introduced, and well-known program induction operators, methods, and systems are described. This survey does not claim to be exhaustive, but contains a description of basic approaches that have influenced more specialized methods. The presentation is up-to-date, and includes recent relevant topics, such as inverse implication. In parts II and III, the more software-oriented view is considered. Part III presents specific software engineering applications, including test-case generation and a more extensive program development example. Part II presents induction methods that are particularly appropriate for these goals. The main advantage is that these methods guarantee that a program that is consistent with respect to the given examples will be found if it exists. The key notion of *inductive bias* is also introduced in part II as a way of providing an ILP system with prior information about the target program. Only with strong prior information, including partially developed procedures and program skeletons, can ILP methods be effective when developing medium-size subprograms to be embedded in larger systems.

I
Fundamentals

2
Problem Statement and Definitions

Induction and learning are difficult to study under a unified theory, and different views abound. It is not always clear what the goals and the essential techniques are. The motivations, the problems, and the methods of Machine Learning may become clearer if studied from a perspective of inductive program synthesis. For a computer scientist, this is also the most natural way to understand the notion of "learning." Such clarification is possible only after inductive program synthesis has been suitably defined and formalized. This is one of the goals of this chapter. The other goal is to survey some fundamental concepts that have been studied in ILP. This will also provide the basis and the terminology for the more extensive survey of methods and systems that will follow.

2.1 Logic Programs and Their Examples

Inductive Logic Programming is mainly concerned with the problem of learning logic programs from examples. In the rest of the book, we will assume a basic knowledge of predicate logic and Logic Programming. Readers who are not familiar with related concepts and terminology should consult, e.g., [125]. Here, we start by introducing the notion of an *example* of the input-output behavior of a logic program.

Intuitively, an example should describe the input/output behavior of a program in a specific case. For instance, an example for the intersection of two lists could be:

input: [4,2,6],[6,5,2,8]

output: [2,6].

For logic programs, this is easily formalized by requiring examples to be ground literals, i.e., literals that do not contain variables. The above example of intersection would then be written as int([4,2,6],[6,5,2,8],[2,6]).

The possibility of having examples that are not ground is interesting, but not sufficiently well understood in ILP. For instance, one could consider int([],X,[]) as an example of *int*. This actually describes an infinite set of ground examples, obtained by substituting all possible lists to X. The user is then allowed to provide the input to the learning system in a more concise way. Some systems accept input information of this kind, e.g., the ones described in [59, 174], and also the TRACY system, described in part II of this book, but limited to negative examples. However, most approaches only consider ground examples. We will also base our discussion on this assumption.

Examples need not only describe the desired behavior of a program, but can also provide negative information, i.e., things that the program should not compute. In general, inductive learning systems use *positive examples* and *negative examples*. Positive examples are ground literals that are regarded as true by the user, while negative examples are ground literals that the user labels as false. For instance, the ground literal int([4,2,7],[6,5,2,8],[2,6]), could be a negative example for *int*. The learned program should perform computations that do not contradict the examples. If we consider a set E^+ of positive examples and a set E^- of negative examples, this is made precise in the following:

Definition 1 *A logic program P is* complete *(with respect to E^+) if and only if (iff), for all examples $e \in E^+$, $P \vdash e$.*

Definition 2 *A logic program P is* consistent *(with respect to E^-) iff, for no example $e \in E^-$, $P \vdash e$.*

The words *completeness* and *consistency* have been used in Machine Learning with a similar meaning since the works of Michalski (see, e.g., [129]). For instance, if:

E^+ = {int([4,2,7],[4],[4]), int([4,2,7],[],[])},
E^- = {int([4,2,7],[6],[6])}, and
P = int(X,Y,Y).

then P is complete, because it derives both positive examples, but is not consistent, because it derives the negative example. Completeness and consistency are, in a sense, a minimum requirement for inductive program synthesis. At the very least,

the user will want the learned program to be correct for the specific cases that are
described in the given examples. Typically, one would then also use the learned
program on other input values that did not occur in the examples, while still hoping
that an adequate result is produced. This fundamental problem of *predicting* the
truth value of examples never seen by the learning program will be discussed in
greater detail later in this chapter.

2.2 The ILP Problem

We can now define a basic form of ILP problem:

Given:
    a set $\mathcal{P}$ of possible programs
    a set E^+ of positive examples
    a set E^- of negative examples
    a consistent logic program B, such that
        $B \not\vdash e^+$, for at least one $e^+ \in E^+$.

Find:
    a logic program $P \in \mathcal{P}$, such that the program B,P is complete and consistent.

A few technical comments are needed.

- The logic program B, which is given as an input of the learning system, is often referred to as *background knowledge*; it represents a part of the desired program that the user has already available or is willing to program directly.

- The program B,P is obtained by adding the clauses of P after the clauses of B. We could have written $B \cup P$ or $B \wedge P$, but when dealing with Prolog programs, the order of the clauses is also relevant.

- The set $\mathcal{P}$ of the programs that may be learned will be called a *hypothesis space*. These words are more often used to define a set of possible clauses, but our definition (possible programs) is more general. In fact, even if some clauses may be viewed as individually possible, the user might know that no meaningful program could contain all of them at the same time.

Below, an instantiation of this basic ILP problem is given for learning the program
computing the intersection of two lists:

Example 1

Given:

$\mathcal{P}$: all logic programs containing clauses of the type "int(X,Y,Z) :- α,"
where α is a conjunction of literals chosen from among the following:

null(X), null(Y), null(Z), cons(X1,X2,X), int(X2,Y,W),
int(X2,Y,Z), cons(X1,W,Z), member(X1,Y), notmember(X1,Y).

E^+: int([4,2,6],[5,2,8],[2])
E^-: int([4,2,6],[5,2,8],[2,6]), int([4,2,6],[5,2,8],[4,2,6])

B: null([]).
cons(X,Y,[X|Y]).
member(X,[X|Y]).
member(X,[Z|Y]) :- member(X,Y).
notmember(X,[]).
notmember(X,[Z|Y]) :- X$\neq$Z, notmember(X,Y).

Find:

a program P1 for computing intersection that is complete and consistent with respect to E^+ and E^-.

For instance, the following program would be an acceptable solution:

P1:
int(X,Y,Z) :- null(X), null(Z).
int(X,Y,Z) :- cons(X1,X2,X), member(X1,Y), int(X2,Y,W), cons(X1,W,Z).
int(X,Y,Z) :- cons(X1,X2,X), int(X2,Y,Z).

It is easy to verify that the above program is complete and consistent. However, it is not guaranteed to be correct for cases that are not given with the positive and negative examples, and in fact it is not. For instance, it derives the ground literal int([1],[1],[]), which is false. The proposed basic ILP problem statement does not require that the learned program be correct for examples that were not given.

2.2.1 Soundness and completeness

When considering methods and systems for solving the basic ILP problem, the notion of an inductive inference machine (IIM) will be used. An IIM is a formalization of the concept of a learning system. If M is an IIM, then we shall write M($\mathcal{P}$,E^+,E^-,B)=P to indicate that, given a hypothesis space $\mathcal{P}$, positive and negative examples E^+ and E^-, and a background knowledge B, the machine outputs a program P. We shall write M($\mathcal{P}$,E^+,E^-,B)=$\perp$ when M does not produce any

2.2. The ILP Problem

output, either because it does not terminate or because it stops without having found an appropriate program. Saying that an IIM has solved the basic ILP problem will then involve two different requirements: producing only programs that are complete and consistent, and finding one such program when it exists. This is captured by the following definitions:

Definition 3 *An IIM M is* sound *iff*
if M($\mathcal{P}$,E^+,E^-,B)=P,
then P$\in$ $\mathcal{P}$ and P is complete and consistent with respect to E^+ and E^-.

Definition 4 *An IIM M is* complete *iff*
if M($\mathcal{P}$,E^+,E^-,B)=$\bot$,
then there is no P$\in$ $\mathcal{P}$ that is complete and consistent with respect to E^+ and E^-.

It is easy to notice an analogy with deductive inference. Soundness of an IIM is the property of making correct inferences. Completeness is the ability to make correct inferences whenever it is possible. However, it is important to grasp the difference between the completeness of a learned program P and the completeness of an IIM. The former means that P entails all the positive examples used during the learning task. The latter means that the IIM is able to find a complete and consistent program (with respect to the given examples) whenever it exists in $\mathcal{P}$. Before defining and discussing a number of issues and key words that are common in ILP, based on the above framework, a final remark is needed.

A logic program is a collection of Horn clauses and, as a consequence, it may contain arbitrary complex terms built by using any function symbol. For instance, in example 1, the programs in the background knowledge B make an extensive use of functions through the classical list notation of Prolog. However, many ILP systems adopt a *flattened* representation of logic programs. That is, each term $f(X_1, ..., X_n)$ in every clause C of a given program is replaced by a new variable X, and a new predicate $P_f(X_1, ..., X_n, X)$ is added to the body of C. That is, X is the result of applying f to $X_1, ..., X_n$. Then, in the background knowledge, P_f must be defined as follows:

$$P_f(X_1, ..., X_n, f(X_1, ..., X_n))$$

in order to preserve the semantics of the original clause. For example, the clause:

member(car,[car]).

can be flattened to:

member(X,Y) :- cons(X,Z,Y), car(X), null(Z).
car(car).
cons(A,B,[A|B]).
null([]).

Flattening is often used in Machine Learning in order to avoid dealing with function symbols and arbitrary complex terms. In ILP, too, many systems adopt a flattened representation. Flattening and unflattening of a logic program can be done automatically, in linear time, with respect to the size of the input program and preserving the semantics of the program. A final example is the following program to *append* two lists:

append([],Y,Y).
append([H|T],Y,[H|W]) :- append(T,Y,W).

is normally flattened to the equivalent program:

append(X,Y,Z) :- null(X), assign(Y,Z).
append(X,Y,Z) :- head(X,H), tail(X,T), append(T,Y,W), cons(H,W,Z).
null([]).
assign(X,X).
head([H|_],H).
tail([_|T],T).
cons(H,T,[H|T]).

An extended discussion of flattening can be found in [167].

2.2.2 Multiple predicate learning

Early work in Machine Learning used the word "concept" for a class of objects with similar properties that one wishes to distinguish from other classes [130, 131, 133]. For instance, a set of persons having the same disease, a set of speech signals obtained by pronouncing the same word, or a set of different photographs of the same object would be a concept or class. A concept would be "learned" by inferring its definition from examples; then this definition could be used as a classifier.

A similar framework is followed in Pattern Recognition. If there are only two classes, C_1 and C_2, one could learn a description D of just one class, e.g., C_1, and then use it for classification as follows: if $D(e)$ is true, then classify e as belonging to C_1, otherwise classify e as belonging to C_2. Then one is faced with the problem of learning just one concept. If there are $n \geq 2$ classes $C_1, ..., C_n$, it is necessary to

2.2. The ILP Problem

learn a description D_i for every class C_i. The key word "multiple concept learning" has been used in the Machine Learning literature in this sense [19].

In ILP, the notion that naturally corresponds to a "concept" is "predicate." A positive example, $Q(c_1, ..., c_n)$, belongs to a concept associated with the n-ary predicate Q. The key word "multiple predicate learning" has also been used in ILP [61, 21], and can now be formalized with respect to the basic ILP problem defined in this section:

A system performs *multiple predicate learning* whenever the output program P contains clauses that define more than one predicate, i.e., such that the predicate of the head literal is not always the same.

It is essential that definitions for more than one predicate be in the learned program P, and not only in the program obtained by adding to P the background knowledge B. In other words, a learning system that outputs a program P with clauses for just one predicate will be said to perform single predicate learning, even if it uses a background knowledge B that contains definitions for other predicates.

Typically, there will be an adequate number of examples for every predicate to be learned, but this is not required. In particular, only examples of one predicate might be available, yet multiple predicate learning could be observed. With respect to Pattern Recognition methods, a key innovation stems from the fact that the learned predicates may also occur in the antecedents of the learned clauses, or anywhere in the background knowledge B. In other words, the learned concept definitions may be interrelated and depend on one another, either hierarchically (concept/subconcept) or involving some kind of mutual recursion.

In example 1, where the program P1 for the intersection of two lists was given as a solution of the basic ILP problem, we had single predicate learning. In fact, P1 contains three clauses where the head literal is always int(X,Y,Z). By contrast, it would have been possible not to give a definition for *member* in B, and require it to be learned and inserted in the output program P. In order to do this, one might want to provide some examples of *member*, e.g.:

E^+: member(2,[5,2,8])
E^-: member(4,[5,2,8]), member(6,[5,2,8])

In this case of multiple predicate learning, the background knowledge B would then contain only definitions for *cons*, *null*, and *notmember*, and the hypothesis space $\mathcal{P}$ would be augmented with a set of possible clauses for *member*. For instance, we could add to $\mathcal{P}$ all clauses having member(X,Y) as a head literal and an antecedent formed with a conjunction of literals chosen from among the following:

member(X,Z), member(W,Z), null(Y), cons(X,Z,Y), cons(W,Z,Y).

When learning complex classifiers, and especially when learning logic programs for software development applications, multiple predicate learning is essential. In fact, real programs normally contain more than one procedure, and real logic programs contain clauses for more than one predicate. It is true that a logic program for many different predicates may be learned one predicate at a time, by repeating single predicate learning for each predicate that is needed. However, this is possible only when there is a sufficient number of examples for each of these predicates. Moreover, prior knowledge about the way different predicates relate to each other may be lost or more difficult to express. As will be shown later, multiple predicate learning produces a number of problems, especially when the examples are insufficient or not well chosen. In the above example, one may observe that the examples of *member* are chosen also on the basis of the examples of *int*. If we had chosen other unrelated examples, e.g., $member(a, [b, a])$, some learning systems might have been unable to produce a suitable solution.

2.2.3 Predicate invention

Predicate invention is another widely used keyword in ILP which will be made precise based on our problem definition. Again, the topic is best introduced by referring to earlier work in Machine Learning, where the term *constructive learning* was used with a similar meaning [128, 129, 163]. Learning was said to be "constructive" whenever the learned concept definitions contained "descriptors," i.e., predicates, that did not occur anywhere in the examples. Otherwise, we would have *selective learning* [129, 162], because the learned descriptions would be only a selection of some of the features that are present in the examples.

For instance, if e is a positive example described as follows:

train(t), has_cars(t,[c1,c2]), small(c2), closed_top(c1), open_top(c2),

then selective learning could output a concept description such as:

train(T) ∧ has_cars(T,[C1,C2]) ∧ open_top(C2).

However, constructive learning could also output a description where *new* predicates are introduced, e.g.:

train(T) ∧ last_car(T,C) ∧ open_top(C).

The predicate last_car is new, in the sense that it does not occur in the given positive example. In Michalski's systems, the definition of new predicates would

2.2. The ILP Problem

have to be given together with the background knowledge B. In the above example, B would contain:

last_car(T,C) :- has_cars(T,L), append(L1,[C],L).
append([],L,[]).
append([X|Y],Z,[X|W]) :- append(Y,Z,W).

As a consequence, the new predicate is not really invented — it is given, although it is not used in the examples. This form of constructive learning is a first step toward the notion of predicate invention, but is quite common in ILP, as predicates defined in the background knowledge can always be used in the learned clauses. Consider again example 1 for the intersection of two lists, with program P1 as a solution. In the single predicate learning version of the problem, the predicate *member* did not occur in the examples but was defined in the background knowledge B. We will then require the following:

an ILP system performs *predicate invention* whenever the learned program defines at least one predicate that does not occur anywhere in the input, neither in the examples nor in the background knowledge.

However, the learned definition of the new predicate obviously will have to occur in a program belonging to the hypothesis space $\mathcal{P}$, because the learned program P must belong to the hypothesis space. It may happen that the actual description of $\mathcal{P}$ lists the possible programs or the possible clauses explicitly; in this case, the "new" predicate will also be mentioned explicitly to the learning system when defining $\mathcal{P}$. In general, predicate invention is defined to cover this case as well; the only requirement is that the new predicate not be used in the examples and in the background knowledge.

For instance, consider a modified ILP problem for the intersection of two lists:

Example 2

Given:

$\mathcal{P}$: all logic programs containing clauses of the types:
"int(X,Y,Z) :- α." - "p1(X,Y) :- α." - "p2(X,Y) :- α."
where α is a conjunction of literals formed with the variables
X,Y,Z,X1,X2,W and with the predicates: int,p1,p2,cons,null,neq.

E^+: int([4,2,6],[5,2,8],[2])
E^-: int([4,2,6],[5,2,8],[2,6])

int([4,2,6],[4,2,8],[2]), int([4,2,6],[5,2,4],[2])
int([4,2,6],[6,2,8],[2]), int([4,2,6],[5,2,6],[2])

B: null([]).
cons(X,Y,[X|Y]).
neq(X,Y) :- X≠Y.

Find:

a program P2 for computing intersection that is complete and consistent.

The following program would be an acceptable solution:

P2:
int(X,Y,Z) :- null(X), null(Z).
int(X,Y,Z) :- cons(X1,X2,X), p1(X1,Y), int(X2,Y,W), cons(X1,W,Z).
int(X,Y,Z) :- cons(X1,X2,X), p2(X1,Y), int(X2,Y,Z).
p1(X,[X|Y]).
p1(X,[Z|Y]) :- p1(X,Y).
p2(X,[]).
p2(X,[Z|Y]) :- neq(X,Z), p2(X,Y).

Example 2 is a case of predicate invention, where the "invented" predicates are $p1$ and $p2$. P2 is complete and consistent, and, in this case, it also a correct implementation for the intersection of two lists.

The easiest way of implementing predicate invention is to take a group of literals occurring somewhere in the learned program P, substitute them with a new literal, and define the predicate of this new literal accordingly. For instance, if P is:

Q(X) :- A(X,Y), B(Y), C(Y).

then P could be transformed into:

Q(X) :- A(X,Y), N(Y).
N(Y) :- B(Y), C(Y).

where N is the new predicate. This is rather trivial. A more interesting form of predicate invention is an invented predicate that is defined recursively. Example 2 is one such case. This is in fact more interesting, because no correct program for intersection could be learned without introducing a new predicate playing the

2.2. The ILP Problem

role of *member*. As $\mathcal{P}$ is very constrained in example 2, not even a correct and complete program without auxiliary new predicates could be produced. Actually, using $p1$ and $p2$ could be avoided by means of clauses like:

int(X,Y,Z) :- cons(X1,XT1,X), cons(X2,XT2,XT1), cons(X3,XT3,XT2),
              cons(Y1,YT1,Y), cons(X2,YT2,YT1), cons(Y3,YT3,YT2),
              neq(X1,Y1), neq(X1,Y3), neq(X3,Y1), neq(X3,Y3),
              cons(X2,N,Z), null(Z).

But this has too many variables and does not satisfy the definition of the hypothesis space $\mathcal{P}$ in example 2. When the introduction of new predicates is needed for satisfying some given criterion of successful learning, predicate invention is called *necessary*. Ling [122] first introduced this notion, arguing that necessary new predicates have to be recursive when the hypothesis space $\mathcal{P}$ is sufficiently large. In fact, if a new predicate Q is defined by means of a nonrecursive clause Q(Args) :- α, then we could simply splice α wherever Q would be used and avoid the introduction of Q. In order to do this, $\mathcal{P}$ would have to allow for clause antecedents with sufficiently many literals and variables. Typically, "interesting" new predicates will be recursive. More on predicate invention will be said in connection with inverse resolution (Section 3.2), and a brief survey is found in [183].

2.2.4 Theory revision

Prior to learning, a tentative solution may be available that can be considered as close to the final result. Some kind of modification would then be necessary, based on the information coming from the examples. This tentative solution may be called an initial theory or an initial program, and learning in this context is often referred to as *theory revision* [77, 204, 176, 57]. The possibility of providing an initial guess, given a priori by the user, has been investigated before in Machine Learning, e.g., in [129].

With respect to our basic ILP problem, this means that an initial program IP is given as an input to the learning system, and the hypothesis space $\mathcal{P}$ consists of programs that are "close" to IP. In other words, the hypothesis space depends on the initial program IP, and may be indicated as $\mathcal{P}(\text{IP})$. If IP is complete and consistent with respect to the given examples, then it is not modified, and P=IP is output. Otherwise, IP is specialized so that negative examples are no longer derived, or is generalized until all positive examples are derived.

For instance, consider example 1 with IP=P1 and an additional negative example, namely, int([1],[1],[]). Moreover, suppose that $\mathcal{P}(\text{IP})$ contains all programs P' satisfying the following property: if C′ is a clause of P′, then C′ is obtained from a clause IC of IP by either adding or removing one literal. Obviously, many other ways of defining $\mathcal{P}(\text{IP})$ have been proposed. Here, we also require that P′∈ $\mathcal{P}$, with $\mathcal{P}$ defined as in example 1. In this case, the following program P3 would be an acceptable (complete and consistent) solution of the theory revision problem:

P3:
int(X,Y,Z) :- null(X), null(Z).
int(X,Y,Z) :- cons(X1,X2,X), member(X1,Y), int(X2,Y,W), cons(X1,W,Z).
int(X,Y,Z) :- cons(X1,X2,X), **notmember(X1,Y)**, int(X2,Y,Z).

where the literal in bold has been added to IP. In fact, IP=P1 would derive the added negative example int([1],[1],[]), and the new literal would avoid this problem. Finally, P3∈ $\mathcal{P}$(P1) because all clauses are the same, except for the last one, where a single literal has been added.

Theory revision is normally easier than learning from scratch, because the hypothesis space $\mathcal{P}(\text{IP})$ tends to be smaller than $\mathcal{P}$ would be in the general case. The reason is that $\mathcal{P}(\text{IP})$ usually consists of a limited number of programs that are syntactically similar to IP. This immediately suggests a natural learning strategy: start from an arbitrary initial program IP, then read new examples and refine IP when necessary, until a suitable solution is found. This brings us to the discussion of incremental systems, which is considered in the next section.

2.3 Incremental Systems and Queries

In general, a learning system has been defined as *incremental* if it reads examples one at a time, and after each new example, produces an inductive hypothesis. Some incremental systems read a *group* of new examples at each cycle, and not necessarily just one new example every time. By contrast, *one-step* methods want all examples to be given at the beginning, and then produce an inductive hypothesis on the basis of all those examples [129]. When the inductive hypothesis is a logic program, and the learning procedure is one-step, the notation $M(\mathcal{P},E^+,E^-,B)=P$ is used to indicate that P is produced based on all the given examples E^+ and E^-. An incremental system, instead, performs some loop of this type:

initialize the accumulated information I to empty
repeat
       read a batch of positive and negative examples E^+ and E^-
       let $P=M(I,\mathcal{P},E^+,E^-,B)$
       update the accumulated information I

2.3. Incremental Systems and Queries

until no more examples or P is accepted by the user

where the inductive inference machine M now has an additional input — the accumulated information I — that should be used effectively for producing a higher-quality program P. The accumulated information could be of different kinds [69]:

1. Some of the examples seen previously, which will be used by M by adding them to the next batch of examples E^+ and E^-. For instance, we could keep one example for every clause in the current program P, so that such clauses may be kept afterward, unless disconfirmed by negative examples. As an extreme case, if all examples are always kept in I, only the last step through the loop matters, and it is the same as a one-step method.

2. The program P that was learned from the previous examples. This program may actually be seen as a compressed description of previous examples, and M would use the accumulated information I=P as a theory revision system. In other words, M would use the previous program P as a meaningful tentative solution, to be modified only slightly in order to make it consistent with the information coming from the new examples.

3. Similarly, but more generally, the accumulated information could consist of an annotation of the hypothesis space that would exclude some clauses or some programs, or make some programs in the hypothesis space preferred, according to some heuristic measure. This is a generalization of the previous criterion that leads to preferring programs that are close to the program P learned during the previous cycle. Mitchell's version space approach [135] also falls under this type of incremental system: the hypotheses that do not lie in the version space are excluded, and the version space is updated incrementally as new examples are seen.

There has been substantial work on incremental learning (e.g., the works in [69]), and many ILP systems are, in fact, incremental. However, one could wonder if and why incrementality is necessary or useful. There are a number of justifications. First, having all examples at once may be impossible, while a learned program may be required before all examples are seen. This is the case when the learning system interacts with an external environment, and the learned program must operate in that same environment. For instance, a robot learning problem has these characteristics. The robot must act and solve problems when the system is still learning, and the mistakes of the robot represent a main source of new examples. Second, storing all examples may be impossible, and most examples seen in the past must be compressed in the current inductive hypothesis, which is modified incrementally. Third, even if it would be technically possible to store all examples, it might be more efficient, for the learning procedure, not to do so. Fourth, incrementality is necessary in formalizations where the number of examples needed is not known, as in identification in the limit, which will be discussed shortly. Finally, systems that ask queries tend to be incremental.

In fact, the issue of incrementality is closely related to the fact that additional data is input upon the system's request. Many ILP systems (e.g., [176, 57, 21]), after receiving in input an initial set of positive and negative examples E^+ and E^-, need other examples before an acceptable solution can be produced. More generally, the system is allowed to interact with the user and ask questions of restricted kinds, called *queries*. In this case, the notation $M(\mathcal{P},E^+,E^-,B)=<P,Q>$ is used, to indicate that the induction procedure M has output program P, and has asked the queries in Q during this learning process. As every query $q \in Q$ has an answer given by the user, the set of such answers is implicitly considered as another input to the inductive inference machine M.

The simplest kind of query consists in asking whether a given example is positive or negative, e.g., asking whether member(a,[b,a]) is true or false. These have been called *membership queries* in the computational learning theory literature, but usually in connection with automata [5, 24] or Boolean formulas [105]. When learning logic programs, and for such kinds of queries, the formula passed to the user in order to obtain its truth value is a ground atom. We shall then call these membership queries for logic program *ground queries*.

Ground queries are questions without quantifiers. With existential quantifiers in queries, questions are of the type "which instantiations of these variables would make this atom a positive example?" For instance, for the query ($\exists$X) append(X,[1,2],[0,1,2]), the answer X=[0] would be appropriate. The atom append([0],[1,2],[0,1,2]) would then be used as a positive example. Existential queries need not have unique answers — for instance, ($\exists$X,Y) append(X,Y,[0,1,2]), has four correct answers. Such questions have been called *existential queries* [57, 21]. We will distinguish between existential queries that simply require a yes/no answer (type I) and existential queries that also require the instantiations of the variables that make the formula true (type II). For instance, a correct answer for the type I existential query ($\exists$X) append(X,[1,2],[0,1,2]) is "yes," while an acceptable answer for the type II existential query ($\exists$X) append(X,[1,2],[0,1,2]) is "X=[0]."

Both ground and existential queries force the system to be incremental. The reason is obvious: after the initial sets E^+ and E^- of examples are given, the learning process will start but a number of queries may be asked. Every query will obtain an answer, and one or more positive or negative examples must be added. Learning must then proceed by taking the new examples into consideration. The soundness requirement of definition 3 must then be modified as follows:

Definition 5 *An IIM with queries M is* sound *iff*

2.3. Incremental Systems and Queries

if $M(\mathcal{P},E^+,E^-,B)=<P,Q>$, then $P\in \mathcal{P}$ and P is complete and consistent with respect to E^+, E^-, and the examples obtained from the queries in Q and from their answers.

Definition 4, for completeness, needs no modification. This is because the system must be able to find a solution when there is one. If the particular queries asked by the system make it impossible to find a complete and consistent solution, this is the system's fault. The user would have been happy with a solution that is acceptable with respect to the examples given initially. By contrast, soundness was changed because, after the user has indeed answered a query, she or he will want the output program to behave as specified in that answer.

Ground and existential queries are questions about examples. In computational learning theory, questions about the current inductive hypothesis also have been studied. Such questions are called *equivalence queries*: the system gives the user an inductive hypothesis H and asks whether it is correct or not. Such queries are essential, for instance, for the exact identification of deterministic finite-state automata [5].

In ILP, these kinds of queries have been used less, perhaps only as part of some user-guided stopping criterion. However, the issue is of interest for at least two reasons. First, we must consider not only the correctness of the current inductive hypothesis (a Prolog program) but also the correctness of parts of it (a clause). We may then speak of *clause equivalence queries* and *program equivalence queries*. Clause equivalence queries may be easier to answer. Second, there is a continuum from membership to equivalence queries, easily formalized by the kind of quantifiers that occur. We have seen that ground queries have no quantifiers, and existential queries have existential quantifiers. A clause equivalence query has a series of universal quantifiers, followed by a series of existential quantifiers. For instance, knowing whether the clause p(X) :- r(X,Y) is correct amounts to answering the query $(\forall X)\, (\exists Y)\, r(X,Y) \rightarrow p(X)$.

We would like to conclude this section with an important consideration that also introduces the remaining two sections in this chapter. By analyzing the ILP framework described thus far, and in particular the crucial requirements of correctness and consistency, the average Machine Learning reader might have the impression that something is missing. We require that the learned program be complete and consistent (soundness), and we want one such program to be found when there is one (completeness), but this always means complete and consistent *with respect to the given examples*. What about accuracy measured on new data? If soundness and completeness is the only requirement, it is easily achieved: just learn a program that is the conjunction of the positive examples. This will be obviously complete and, in a deterministic setting with no overlapping among classes, also consistent. As a summary: where is generalization, in this understanding of learning?

The answer is that the requirement of generalization, as well as the concerns of predictive accuracy, are hidden in the fact that the learned program P must belong to the hypothesis space $\mathcal{P}$. For example, the hypothesis space will normally exclude a conjunction of positive examples as an acceptable inductive hypothesis. More essentially, in program synthesis applications the hypothesis space will be small and well chosen by a programmer, and the inductive use of the examples will lead to choosing a subset of possible clauses that are already meaningful and sufficiently general.

This view may be biased toward an understanding of ILP as mainly a Software Engineering tool. More generally, the issue of correctness on new examples has been addressed in a number of different ways. On the experimental side of Machine Learning and Pattern Recognition, the performance on unseen data is estimated by means of cross-validation procedures. Basically, the learned program would have to be tested on separate and independent examples. Such an approach has also been followed in ILP-related research; for instance, new ILP methods are typically compared to more established systems, such as FOIL [160], on the basis of their cross-validation accuracy as measured in some application domain. An extensive discussion of this experimental view of ILP is found in [117].

However, this perspective may be adequate for classification tasks but questionable in program synthesis applications. In this case, a more valuable evaluation of the learned program would come from sophisticated program testing techniques, while cross-validation would correspond to some kind of brute-force random testing. Important, although rare, errors may be hidden in the structure of the generated program, and accuracy is not always the only relevant parameter.

From a more theoretical perspective, the issue of prediction has been addressed in ILP mainly from two points of view: identification in the limit and PAC-learning. In the first case, we aim at the exact identification of a program that is correct for all possible examples, but an unbounded stream of input examples is needed. In the second case, a limited (actually, a polynomial) number of examples is required, but we get an output program that is only approximately correct on new examples. Moreover, the success of learning is required only to be highly probable, not certain. In both cases, results have been obtained for the problem of learning restricted classes of logic programs that relate the ILP framework defined in this chapter to the problem of predictive accuracy. Readers who are mainly interested in practical aspects and in software development applications can skip the next section, where we deal with identification in the limit. For PAC-learning results related to ILP, see [67, 106, 60, 46].

2.4 Identifying Logic Programs in the Limit

One thing is clear: from finite information and no other assumptions there is no guarantee of prediction. If we play a two-person game where player 1 picks an arbitrary function, and player 2 tries to guess the function from a finite sequence of examples, then player 2 is bound to lose. For instance, from the examples p(2,4) and p(0,0) one could guess that p(X,Y) computes Y=X+X or Y=X*X, and there is no objective reason to prefer one choice over the other. For any finite set of examples, there is an infinite number of recursive functions that are equally plausible and equally correct for those examples. Gold [79] was the first to formalize a notion of program induction that makes the above game more meaningful. Under this notion, player 1 picks a recursive function in a set H and passes to player 2 an infinite list where every input/output pair for that function would eventually occur. Player 2 makes a guess after every new input/output pair. Player 2 wins if, after a finite number of guesses, he produces a correct guess and never changes it. In this case we say that player 2 has identified the function *in the limit*. There are cases, i.e. classes H of recursive functions, where the game can be won by player 2 and cases where it cannot. More formally,

Definition 6 *Let f be a total recursive function and E an infinite list containing all the pairs <i,f(i)>. Let E_n be the list of the first n input/output pairs in E. An inductive inference machine M* EX-identifies[1] *f if there is an n such that, for all $m \geq n$, $M(E_n)=i$, and i is an index of a recursive function equivalent to f.*

Definition 7 *An IIM M EX-identifies a class H of recursive function iff it EX-identifies every function in that class.*

Definition 8 *A class H of recursive functions is* EX-identifiable *iff there is an IIM that EX-identifies it.*

The above notion of identification in the limit is obviously related to prediction: once the IIM has made its final guess, this guess will be correct for all remaining examples and can be used for "predicting" correct output values. If we have an IIM for learning Prolog programs, as defined in section 2.2, we can use it for solving the ILP problem and learn a program that is consistent with given examples. But if this IIM can identify some class of programs in the limit, then, at some point, the learned program will also be correct on unseen examples. Unfortunately, the machine is not required to know when such a point has been reached. The machine will only output guesses, it will not say when such guesses will stop changing. It is in this precise sense that the identification is exact, but only in the limit.

---

[1] EX stands for "explanatory" identification, which is one possible formalization of identification in the limit. There are many others; a good survey can be found in [149].

Although EX-identification seems quite a strong requirement, there are large classes of functions that are identifiable in this sense. For example, the primitive recursive functions are identifiable by the following simple procedure (identification by enumeration):

Consider an enumeration f_1, f_2, ... of the primitive recursive functions
Examples := $\emptyset$
loop
    read the next input/output pair and add it to Examples
    output the first f_j such that for all <i,o>$\in$Examples, f_j(i)=o.
goto loop

Let f_k be the first function in the enumeration that is equivalent to f. There must be one such function as f is primitive recursive. All functions f_m with m<k will eventually be discarded when an example $<i,o>$ is considered such that $f_m(i) \neq o$. At this point, the guess will stabilize on f_k.

There are larger classes of functions that are EX-identifiable, in particular EX-identifiable classes that are not identifiable by enumeration [27]. Wiehagen [199] provides a characterization of EX-identifiable classes of functions.

It is also interesting to note that there are important classes of functions that are not EX-identifiable. For instance, the total recursive functions are not EX-identifiable [79]. In particular, they cannot be identified by enumeration as above, because they are not enumerable. The partial recursive functions cannot be identified by enumeration because it is impossible to decide if f_j(i)=o.

When learning logic programs, the above definitions need to be adapted, as we are not dealing with one function but rather with a set of relations. The following formalization follows that of Shapiro [176]. Instead of considering an unknown function f, an unknown interpretation M for a first-order language L is of interest. Instead of considering input/output pairs for the function f, a *presentation* S of M is given:

Definition 9 *A* presentation *for an interpretation M for a language L is a sequence S of ground literals in the Herbrand base of L, such that if A is true in M, then A occurs in S, and if A is false in A, then $\neg A$ occurs in S.*

Intuitively, the presentation lists all the facts that are true and false in some actual state of the world. This is more informative than just input-output pairs for a target function. In fact, requiring all ground atoms to occur in the presentation with their truth value amounts to asking for input-output pairs not only for the top-level target function but also for its subprocedures and for all other functions that may be relevant to the overall computation done by the unknown program to be identified. Moreover, the information contained in the ground atoms that are true is relational, e.g., one may have both p(a,b) and p(a,c) true in M, while there is only one output per input in the recursive function formalization.

The notion of identification in the limit does not substantially change for logic programs with respect to the above definition of EX-identification[176]:

Definition 10 *A program P is totally correct with respect to an interpretation M iff it succeeds on every goal that is true in M and finitely fails on every goal that is false in M.*

Definition 11 *An IIM identifies an interpretation M in the limit iff given a presentation S for M, after a finite number of guesses, the IIM stabilizes to a program P that is totally correct with respect to M.*

The main result of Shapiro [176] was that his system MIS (described in section 4.1) identifies in the limit interpretations M that have *h-easy* programs that are totally correct. A program P is h-easy iff for any goal A in the Herbrand base of P, the depth of any deduction of A with P is at most h(A). This result, from the point of view of theoretical inductive inference, is not impressive. In fact, identification in the limit could be obtained, under these assumptions, by the following enumerative procedure:

Consider an enumeration $p_1, p_2, ...$ of all logic programs
Examples := $\emptyset$
loop
read the next ground literal L and add it to Examples
output the first p_j such that
    for all A $\in$Examples, p_j succeeds on A with a deduction of depth less than h(A)
    for all $\neg$A $\in$Examples, p_j fails on A with a deduction of depth less than h(A)
goto loop

The bound on the depth of the computation makes success and finite failure decidable, and therefore all nonterminating or otherwise wrong programs will be excluded until a totally correct program in the enumeration is reached. At this point the interpretation will have been identified.

What is interesting in Shapiro's result is that MIS is not purely enumerative, but intrinsically more efficient while still preserving the identification in the limit property. Along this line of reasoning, other results of EX-identification have been obtained in ILP. DeRaedt's system Clint [57] is shown to identify a target logic program in the limit under similar definitions. It should be noted that the system might output programs that are not consistent with facts that were already considered before it converges. After convergence, it will of course have to output a program that is correct with respect to all examples. DeRaedt calls this *postponed* identification in the limit, and related notions have been analyzed in the inductive inference literature (e.g., [149, 76, 196]). Arikawa et al. [7] adapt the MIS system to the problem of identifying elementary formal systems in the limit, with applications to the learning of context-free languages.

In [59] a simple modification of MIS is presented that identifies restricted logic programs in the limit. The main innovation is that the input presentation is more general that just a stream of examples; it contains all integrity constraints that are satisfied by the target program. An integrity constraint is defined in that context as a range-restricted[2] clause without functors. Integrity constraints need not be Horn clauses. From this kind of presentation, the proposed algorithm identifies in the limit any program P that consists of Horn clauses that are linked,[3] range-restricted, and without functors.

Most work on identification in the limit has been done in a recursion-theoretic framework. In ILP, this issue has been studied mainly in connection with Shapiro's system MIS. However, further research might lead to interesting results. As a first observation to this end, consider Gold's original definition of EX-identification and Shapiro's modified setting for identifying logic programs. With recursive functions, the input to the inductive inference machine is a stream of input/output pairs. With logic programs a *presentation*, i.e., a stream of ground facts with their truth values, is given. Suppose we wanted to learn a program for the multiplication of integers. In Gold's setting we would have in input an infinite list <0*0=0,0*1=0,1*1=1,...>, where every possible multiplication would eventually occur. For ILP, we would have a stream of all the facts that are true in one possible implementation of the target programs, e.g., <3*2=6,3*1=3,2-1=1,3+3=6,...>, and a stream of all facts that are false. The presentation of true and false facts used for ILP learning is of course more informative (and also more difficult to provide for the user). It is possible that, in this setting, larger classes of functions may be identifiable, or that the same classes may be identified more efficiently.

In the inductive inference literature, the above issue has been considered in [6], where the notions of *sequence* and *parallel* EX-identification are analyzed.

Definition 12 *A sequence $< f_1, ..., f_n >$ of recursive functions is $S^n EX$-identified by an IIM M iff $\forall i \in [0..1]$ M EX-identifies f_i, given $f_1, ..., f_{i-1}$ and a stream of input/output pairs for f_i.*

---

[2] A clause is range-restricted if all variables in the head also occur in the body.
[3] A clause is linked iff all of its variables are linked, and a variable is linked iff it occurs in the head of the clause or in a literal that contains a linked variable.

2.4. Identifying Logic Programs in the Limit

In other words, an IIM identifies a sequence of functions under this notion if it can identify every function after having identified the previous ones in the sequence. In [6] it is shown that for all n, there are sequences that can be S^nEX-identified, such that no subsequence of n-1 functions can be S^{n-1}EX-identified. In particular, there are functions that can be identified given other (previously identified) functions but cannot be EX-identified alone. In ILP, this could correspond to learning some predicates first, and then using the result as part of the background knowledge when learning other, more difficult concepts. Unfortunately, the proof techniques in [6] are based on coding mechanisms that do not naturally correspond to this notion. The same is true for parallel learning:

Definition 13 *A sequence $< f_1, ..., f_n >$ of recursive functions is P^nEX-identified by an IIM M iff M EX-identifies $f_1, ..., f_n$, given simultaneously n streams of input/output pairs, one for each f_i.*

In [6], it is shown that parallel EX-identification is strictly easier than sequence EX-identification, in the sense that any sequence $< f_1, ..., f_n >$ that can be S^nEX-identified can also be P^nEX-identified, while the converse is not always true. Parallel learning would correspond in ILP to multiple predicate learning as defined in section 2.2.2. Parallel learning is also closer to Shapiro's notion of identification in the limit of an unknown interpretation from a presentation of the facts that are true and false in that interpretation.

The same type of presentation used by Shapiro and adopted for ILP above is considered by [151] in the context of first-order logic. Again, we have an interpretation M, unknown to the learning procedure, and a presentation with all the ground literals that are true in M. However, in [151] the goal is not to induce a program P that is totally correct with respect to M, as is the case for Shapiro's and other formalizations related to ILP. By contrast, a first-order formula ϕ is given, and the goal is to identify in the limit its truth value in M. If this is possible, ϕ is said to be *detectable*. Previous work by the same authors [153] shows that there are formulas that are not detectable. In [151] and in the related exposition of [152] an important result is established: there is a universal inductive inference machine for this problem, i.e., a machine M_U such that if a first-order formula ϕ is detectable, then M_U can identify its truth value in the limit. The same is not true for natural extensions of first-order logic, e.g., it is not true for second-order logic. This problem can be related to the usual framework of identifying a totally correct program P as follows. Suppose a finite number n of examples has been seen. Suppose also that we are interested in a current hypothesis P for a totally correct program with respect to the unknown interpretation M. The universal IIM M_U can be used to simulate P on specific inputs: to run P in order to obtain the output X such that Q(i,X) is true, dovetail M_U on all formulas Q(i,0), Q(i,1), ..., Q(i,n) and produce the first output o such that Q(i,o) is true according to M_U. If there is no such output from 0 to n, answer "no," meaning that $(\exists X)Q(i,X)$ is false. After some point, this output will be correct because (1) all truth values for Q(i,0), ..., Q(i,n) will be correct with respect to M and (2) a sufficiently large n will have been reached. If no output is ever found, then there is no such output and the program's behavior is correct. As a consequence, in the detectability paradigm of [151], the goal is not to learn an unknown program but to correctly simulate the unknown program on given inputs. A similar relation exists between EX-identification and next value, or NV-identification [10, 27]. A comprehensive treatment of such issues in ILP is still lacking.

3
Bottom-up Methods

A classical key word in Machine Learning is *generalization*. Even if there is not a total agreement in the Machine Learning community on the meaning of generalization, it is often intended as the task of building a general description from a set of (positive) examples, such that the description can be used to predict the classification of new data [129]. In other words, we look for a compressed description of the data that, after some initial effort to build it, could be used without further changes.

Intuitively, we say that a statement S_1 is a generalization of a statement S_2 if whatever is true on the basis of S_2 is also true for S_1, but not vice versa. In a logical framework, this may be made precise in a number of different ways, such as $S_1 \models S_2$ or $S_1 \rightarrow S_2$. In other words, S_1 is more general than S_2 if everything that can be derived by using S_2 can also be derived by using S_1. As a consequence, here, the notion of generalization corresponds to the notion of logical implication. Generalization is normally intended as a "specific to general" task, Being the examples the ("specific" or "bottom") starting point, and the learned description the ("general" or "top") ending point: a set of rules entailing those, and perhaps other, examples. Bottom-up methods, all based on the generalization of a set of positive examples, fit perfectly into the notion of generalization, no matter which generalizing operation is in use.

Bottom-up methods can be conveniently classified with respect to the way they perform generalization. Classical generalization operators are well represented by such rules as *dropping condition*, *turning constants into variables*, and *turning conjunction into disjunction*, which have been extensively used in Machine Learning [129]. However, all of the above are heuristic rules, and can fail to give a correct generalization. In ILP inductive operators have been developed by inverting well formalized deductive rules, namely, unification, resolution, and implication. As a consequence, inversion of these rules has led to the construction of learning systems with a strong theoretical basis. These bottom-up approaches to the ILP problem will be discussed in the next sections.

The task of generalization is quite common in everyday life, and fundamental in the process of human learning. However, it requires attention, in order to avoid mistakes. For example, suppose a child living in a city sees a sparrow flying, and then a dove flying. As a consequence he may think that everything having wings can fly. He has to see a negative example, e.g., a man with two artificial wings, as in the famous drawings by Leonardo da Vinci, to convince himself that not everything with wings can fly. In general, it seems quite intuitive that we need some negative examples of a concept that we want to learn, in order to limit the generalization process. However, Plotkin showed that we can limit the generalization of a set of positive examples, without using negative examples, by computing their *least general generalization*.

3.1 Plotkin's Least General Generalization

Plotkin [158, 156, 157] was the first to rigorously analyze the notion of generalization as an automatization of the process of inductive inference. He did not restrict himself to Horn clause logic; in fact, Logic Programming did not yet exist at that time.

As a first example of generalization, consider the following clauses:

C_1: has_wings(tweety) :- bird(tweety).
C_2: has_wings(birdy) :- bird(birdy).

If we apply the dropping condition rule (i.e., if we drop a literal in the body of a given clause) and the turning constants into variables rule to the above clauses, we get the generalization (see also subsection 3.2.3):

C_3: has_wings(X).

that can be read as "everything has wings," and is clearly wrong. In fact, clause C_3 is overgeneral, and an adequate counterexample can be used to notice the error. An alternative solution is looking for the *minimal* possible generalization, under some generality relation between clauses. This solution was investigated by Plotkin [156, 157], and led to the following notion of least general generalization under θ-subsumption:

Definition 14 *Clause C θ-subsumes (or is a generalization of) a clause D, if there exists a substitution θ such that $C\theta \subseteq D$. Usually this is written $C \preceq D$. C is the*

3.1. Plotkin's Least General Generalization

least general generalization *(lgg) of D under θ-subsumption if $C \preceq D$ and, for every other E such that $E \preceq D$, it is also the case that $E \preceq C$.*

The definition extends immediately to the notion of least general generalization of a set of clauses: clause C is the lgg of a set of clauses S if C is the lgg of each clause in S.

By using the above definition, it is easy to see that C_3 is a generalization of C_1 and C_2, but not a least general generalization. The correct lgg for C_1 and C_2 is:

C_4: has_wings(X) :- bird(X).

We are clearly dealing with a syntactic notion of generality, which is, however, correct: if $C \preceq D$ then $C \models D$. On the other hand, the converse is not always true. As a consequence, the relation based on θ-subsumption is weaker than implication. For example, consider the two clauses:

C: even(X) :- even(half(X)).
D: even(X) :- even(half(half(X))).

Then, clearly C implies D (for example, we get D by resolving C against itself), but $C \not\preceq D$. In fact, there is no substitution θ such that $C\theta \subseteq D$. Plotkin [158] made precise the relationship between implication and θ-subsumption:

Theorem 1 *$C \preceq D$ iff D is a tautology or C is used exactly once in a resolution proof of $\Sigma \vdash C \rightarrow D$, where Σ is an arbitrary set of clauses.*

In particular, C cannot be applied to itself directly or indirectly during the proof.

However, the choice of generalization under θ-subsumption is justified by the fact that θ-subsumption between clauses is decidable, and relatively easy to compute (although it is NP-complete). In general, there may be no least general generalization of two clauses, but if two Horn clauses have a common predicate symbol with the same sign, then they have an lgg under θ-subsumption. Conversely, as opposed to [148], implication between Horn clauses is undecidable [127], and there is not always a least generalization under implication of two Horn clauses.

3.1.1 Computation of least general generalizations

When restricted to atoms with the same sign and predicative symbol, least general generalization is exactly the dual of unification. That is, given two terms f_1 and f_2 and the ordering imposed by $\preceq$, then the lgg of f_1 and f_2 is their greatest lower bound (glb) and the most general unification of f_1 and f_2 is their least upper bound (lub).

To compute the lgg of two examples (clauses), we need to compute the lgg of two literals and hence the lgg of two terms.

The lgg of two terms $f_1(l_1, ..., l_n)$ and $f_2(m_1, ..., m_n)$ is a new variable v if $f_1 \neq f_2$ and is defined[1] as $f_1(lgg(l_1, m_1), ..., lgg(l_n, m_n))$ if $f_1 = f_2$.

The lgg of two literals $L_1 = (\neg)p(t_1, ..., t_n)$ and $L_2 = (\neg)q(s_1, ..., s_n)$ is undefined if L_1 and L_2 do not have the same predicative symbol and sign; otherwise it is defined as:

$$\text{lgg}(L_1, L_2) = (\neg)\text{p}(\text{lgg}(t_1, s_1), ..., \text{lgg}(t_n, s_n)).$$

The lgg of two clauses $C_1 = \{l_1, ..., l_k\}$ and $C_2 = \{m_1, ..., m_n\}$ is defined as:

$$\text{lgg}(C_1, C_2) = \{\text{lgg}(l, m) \mid l \in C_1 \wedge m \in C_2 \wedge \text{lgg}(l, m) \text{ is defined}\}.$$

As a consequence we note that the length of the lgg of two clauses C_1 and C_2 can be at most $|C_1| \times |C_2|$. The above definitions are easily extended to sets of terms, literals, or clauses, since lgg is associative. In particular, the lgg of a set of clauses always exists (even though it can be the empty clause), and the lgg of a set of Horn clauses is always a Horn clause. However, while the lgg of a set of literals is unique up to renaming of variables, this is not necessarily true for a set of clauses. For example, $C_1 = $ "q(b)$\wedge$ p(y)" and $C_2 = $ "q(b)" can be two different lggs for the set of clauses {"q(b)$\wedge$ p(x)," "q(b)"}. If C_1 and C_2 are lggs of a set of clauses, it is always the case that $C_1 \preceq C_2$ and $C_2 \preceq C_1$. This defines an equivalence relation under *theta*-subsumption $\equiv_\theta$. To represent the corresponding equivalence class, the shortest of all $\equiv_\theta$-equivalent clauses is chosen. It is possible to prove that such a clause is unique up to variable renaming [156]. This clause is *reduced*, in the sense that it does not contain redundant literals under θ-subsumption (a literal l occurring in C is *redundant* under θ-subsumption if $C - \{l\} \equiv_\theta C$). Reduced clauses are important, since inferred clauses often contain redundant literals that should be removed to get more compact and/or efficient theories. Plotkin proposed an algorithm to reduce clauses. Unfortunately, this algorithm was NP-complete. A more recent study of reduction under θ-subsumption can be found in [83].

As a final example [156], consider the following two ground clauses:

---

[1]When computing the lgg of two terms, it is important to use the same new variable for all possible occurrences of the lggs of subterms. For example, lgg(q(a,a), q(b,b)) = q(lgg(a,b), lgg(a,b)) is q(v,v), and not q(u,v).

3.1. Plotkin's Least General Generalization

C_1 = win(conf1) :- occ(place1,x,conf1),occ(place2,o,conf1).
C_2 = win(conf2) :- occ(place1,x,conf2),occ(place2,x,conf2).

representing two winning configurations in a two-person game with two places that can be occupied by an "x" or an "o." The lgg of the two clauses turns out to be:

lgg(C_1,C_2) = win(Conf) :- occ(place1,x,Conf), occ(L,x,Conf),
    occ(M,Y,Conf), occ(place2,Y,Conf).

After the elimination of redundant literals, we get:

lgg(C_1,C_2) = win(Conf) :- occ(place1,x,Conf),occ(place2,Y,Conf).

meaning that a position is winning if it contains a "x" in the first place and something in the second.

3.1.2 Relative least general generalization

In the ILP setting, least general generalization can provide a theoretical basis for generalization. However, the simple lgg of a set of clauses cannot be very useful for the ILP problem. For example, given the two clauses:

C_1 = uncle(X,Y) :- brother(X, father(Y)).
C_2 = uncle(X,Y) :- brother(X, mother(Y)).

the corresponding lgg is:

lgg(C_1, C_2) = uncle(X,Y) :- brother(X,Z).

which is not very informative to define the *uncle* relationship. In fact, we are mostly interested to find the generalization of a set of examples in relation to a background knowledge or theory. So, if in the above example we also know that parent(father(X),X) is true and parent(mother(X),X) is true, then the least general generalization of C_1 and C_2 relative to this knowledge turns out to be:

C = uncle(X,Y) :- brother(X,U), parent(U,Y).

In general, a clause C is more general than a clause D with respect to a theory T if $T \land C \vdash D$. As a special case, T can be a set of Horn clauses. This case is important for ILP, because we may have available a partial logic program B, and need to refine it by adding other clauses that would allow us to derive new examples. This partial logic program is usually known as the *background knowledge*, as discussed in chapter 2.

The notion of generalization relative to a given theory was studied and defined by Plotkin as an extension of least general generalization under θ-subsumption:

Definition 15 *An atom A is an lgg of an atom B with respect to a theory Σ, if there is a unifier σ such that $\Sigma \vdash A\sigma \equiv B$. We write $A \preceq_\Sigma B$. A clause C is an lgg of a clause D with respect to theory Σ, if $\Sigma \vdash C\theta \rightarrow D$ for some substitution θ. We say that C is the least general generalization of D relative to Σ (rlgg). This is equivalent to saying that $C \wedge \Sigma \vdash D'$ where D' subsumes D and C is used only once in the derivation of D'.*

The extension to sets of clauses is straightforward: the rlgg of clauses C_1 and C_2 with respect to Σ is the lgg of D_1 and D_2, if D_1 and D_2 are respectively the rlgg of C_1 and C_2 relative to Σ.

The (nondeterministic) algorithm proposed by Plotkin to compute the rlgg of a set of clauses relative to a background theory is in fact a systematic search for lggs interleaved with reductions and consistency tests. Clearly, such an algorithm was, in practice, unfeasible, and hence useless for the ILP problem. Moreover, Plotkin showed that, in general, there may be no least general generalization of a set of clauses relative to a given theory. This is also true for sets of Horn clauses. For example [148], given clauses $C_1 = $ q(f(a)) and $C_2 = $ q(g(a)) and the background theory $\Sigma = \{$p(f(X),Y), p(g(X),Y)$\}$, there is no rlgg of C_1 and C_2 with respect to Σ. In fact, each clause of the type:

$$C = q(X) :\text{-} p(X, g_1(X)), ..., p(X, g_n(X)).$$

is a possible generalization of C_1 and C_2 with respect to Σ. But we can always build more and more specific generalizations by adding to the body of C literals of the type p(X,g_i(X)), the g_i(X)s being more and more complex terms.

However, Plotkin also showed that there are least general generalizations relative to ground theories (even if they can still be highly impractical to compute and can also have infinite length — Muggleton and Feng [145] report the example of an rlgg for the quicksort program that could have a length of 13,869,455,043 literals). In particular, if Σ is a finite set of ground literals, then the rlgg of two clauses C_1 and C_2 with respect to Σ is the lgg of $\Sigma \rightarrow C_1$ and $\Sigma \rightarrow C_2$. This property is at the basis of the ILP learning system GOLEM [145]. GOLEM is the only learning system explicitly based on the notion of relative least general generalization.

3.1. Plotkin's Least General Generalization

The GOLEM system

Suppose we are given a logic program P (i.e., a background knowledge) and two examples (two ground atoms) E_1 and E_2 such that $P \not\vdash E_1$ and $P \not\vdash E_2$. We want to build the lgg C of E_1 and E_2 relative to the program P. That is, we look for a clause C such that $P \wedge C \vdash E_1 \wedge E_2$ and C is used only once in the derivation of both E_1 and E_2. Following the GOLEM approach, we can proceed as follows [145]:

$P \wedge C \vdash E_1$
$C \vdash P \to E_1$
$\vdash C \to (\neg P \vee E_1)$
$\vdash C \to ((\neg p_1 \vee \neg p_2 \vee \ldots) \vee E_1)$

where, in the last step, P is replaced by the ground atoms p_1, p_2, ..., representing a (partial) model of P. Similar steps can be done for E_2. Now, if we put:

$C_1 = ((\neg p_1 \vee \neg p_2 \vee \ldots) \vee E_1)$
$C_2 = ((\neg p_1 \vee \neg p_2 \vee \ldots) \vee E_2)$

it follows that $\vdash C \to lgg(C_1, C_2)$. This can be obtained by letting $C = lgg(C_1, C_2)$.

As an example, suppose we are given the following logic program P:

A: bird(tweety).
B: bird(birdy).

and the two examples (not entailed by P):

E_1: has_wings(tweety).
E_2: has_wings(birdy).

Atoms A and B represent a ground model for P. From the above reasoning we have:

C_1 = has_wings(tweety) :- bird(tweety), bird(birdy).
C_2 = has_wings(birdy) :- bird(tweety), bird(birdy).

Now, the lgg of C_1 and C_2 turns out to be:

lgg(C_1,C_2) = has_wings(X) :- bird(tweety), bird(birdy), bird(X).

And by removing redundant literals we get:

$C = $ has_wings(X) :- bird(X).

which is the lgg of examples E_1 and E_2 with respect to P. Clearly, $P \wedge C \vdash E_1 \wedge E_2$.

This approach requires the choice of a model for P. P being a logic program, we could use the *minimal Herbrand model* M_P of P. In this case, it can be proved that the rlgg of n examples is finite and at most has length $|M_P|^n + 1$. Unfortunately, M_P may be infinite. As a consequence, we must choose a finite subset of M_P, possibly with some well-defined properties.

Restrictions of the background knowledge

Muggleton and Feng suggest first considering only ground instantiations of atoms derivable from P in at most h resolution steps. This set, called the *Herbrand h-easy model of P* ($M_h(P)$), is clearly a subset of M_P. However, $M_h(P)$ can still be infinite. If $P = \{member(X,[X|Y]).\}$, then there is trivially only one atom derivable from P, but there are infinite ground instantiations, such as $member([],[[]])$, $member([],[[],[]])$, ...

A stronger constraint is to require all clauses in P to be *syntactically generative*. A clause is said to be syntactically generative if the variables in its head are a subset of the variables in its body. It can be proved [145] that for every syntactically generative set of clauses P and for every h, $M_h(P)$ is finite.

Even using a finite Herbrand model $M_h(P)$, the length of the lggs is exponential in the number of given examples. As a consequence, further restrictions must be imposed on the hypothesized clauses.

Restrictions on the hypotheses

When building lggs, many literals are produced that contain variables not occurring in the head of the clause. In fact, these literals are interesting only if they "produce" values for new variables by directly or indirectly using variables in the head of the clause. Intuitively, this means that when a clause head is instantiated against an example, the computation must flow from left to right in the body, and variables are instantiated only on the basis of variables instantiated previously. Moreover, we can require that there be only one possible instantiation. For example [145], consider the following clause:

3.1. Plotkin's Least General Generalization

C_1 = multiply(A,B,C) :- decrement(B,D), multiply(A,D,E), plus(A,E,C).

where *decrement* and *plus* have the obvious meanings. Then, the value of D depends on the value of variable B in the head of C_1 and the value of E depends on the value of D and of A. Given the example multiply(l,m,n), there is only one valid ground substitution θ_1 such that decrement(m,D)θ_1 is true. The valid substitutions for D depend only on the substitutions applied to one term, B. As a consequence, we say that literal decrement(B,D) has *degree* 1 with respect to D. Since there is only one ground substitution θ_1 making decrement(m,D)θ_1 true, we say that D is *determinate* in decrement(B,D). In the literal multiply(A,D,E), the value of E depends on the values of both A and D, and hence this literal has degree 2 with respect to E. Hence, a literal L is determinate if all its variables not appearing in preceding literals are determinate (i.e., there must be only one possible ground substitution making L true, given the bindings of the variables of L appearing in preceding literals). A clause is determinate if all of its literals are determinate. A possible restriction on hypothesized clauses can be obtained by using only determinate clauses, and imposing a limit j on the maximum degree of any literal in the clause with respect to any determinate term in that literal. A clause is *j-determinate* if it is determinate with a maximum degree j for each literal in the clause.

Moreover, the dependencies between variables in a clause can be used to define a partial ordering over the literals of that clause. We say that a literal L has *depth* 1 if its determinate terms depend on variables occurring in the head of the clause. In general, a literal has depth $n + 1$ if its determinate terms depend on variables whose values are determined in literals of depth no greater than n. Hence, the literal decrement(B,D) has depth 1 in clause C_1, while multiply(A,D,E) has depth 2, since the value of E depends on the value of D, which is determined in a literal of depth 1. A restriction can be obtained by placing a limit i on the maximum depth of each literal in a hypothesized clause. A clause is *i-determinate* if it is determinate with a maximum depth i for each literal in the clause.

By combining parameters i and j we get the *ij-determinism* restriction: a clause C is ij-determinate if it is determinate and each literal in the body of C has maximum depth i and maximum degree j [145, 67]. When building the rlgg of a set of examples, GOLEM considers only ij-determinate clauses.

It is worth noting that many classical logic programs (such as *quicksort*, *reverse*, and so forth) are made up of ij-determinate clauses only, and with very small values (i=2, j=2, at most) for i and j. Moreover, clauses that are not ij-determinate can often be restated in terms of semantically equivalent ij-determinate clauses.

It is also worth noting that, by using ij-determinism and syntactically generative background clauses only, the length of the lgg of a set of examples no longer depends on the number of examples:

Theorem 2 [145] *Let there be given a syntactically generative set of clauses P and a set of examples $e_1, \ldots, e_n$. If t is the number of terms in $lgg(e_1, \ldots, e_n)$, and m is the number of distinct predicative symbols in $M_h(P)$, then the number of literals in the body of the ij-determinate rlgg of $e_1, \ldots, e_n$ with respect to $M_h(P)$ is at most $\mathcal{O}((t\ m\ h)^{i^j})$.*

Since ij-determinism does not completely avoid redundant literals in learned clauses, GOLEM uses negative examples and input-output mode of variables (see chapter 6) as a post-processing step. Let there be given a learned clause C = "A :- $B_1, ..., B_n$." First, literals B_i are removed from C one after the other, as long as C does not derive any negative example. Second, if the output variables of the head of C can be computed in different ways by a subset of the literals in the body of C, a different clause is produced for each subset. The preferred clause can then be chosen by the user or by the system itself (see [145] for the details of these clause reduction techniques).

GOLEM takes in input a set of positive E^+ and negative E^- examples of the target concept, an h-easy model of a background knowledge P, and outputs a set of clauses that, together with P, derive all examples in E^+. A "greedy" search is adopted by looking for an ij-determinate clause that is the rlgg of the maximum number of positive examples without covering any negative examples. Covered examples are removed from E^+ and the procedure is iterated until no uncovered positive example remains.

GOLEM is able to learn classical logic programs in a few seconds, from randomly chosen positive and negative examples. It has been successfully used to learn rules for predicting the secondary structure of proteins from their amino acid sequence [112, 111], for predicting structure-activity relationships in drug design [110], and for learning temporal diagnostic rules for physical systems [75].

However, a strong limitation of GOLEM is the need to find a suitable h-easy model of P ($M_h(P)$). Normally, this is done by providing all the examples of maximum depth h. These examples are not always available, unless the clause to be learned is known in advance. Moreover, GOLEM cannot learn multiple predicates, and it is not sound, since clauses are learned independently of each other. Because of the use of a partial model of P, GOLEM is also, in general, not complete. In particular, soundness is not guaranteed because, even if two learned clauses C and D independently do not cover any negative example, their conjunction can cover some of these examples.

3.1.3 Buntine's generalization

Relative least general generalization can be seen as a way of avoiding some meaningless results of least general generalization by using background knowledge. However, even the notion of rlgg can lead to some counterintuitive conclusions. For example [37], according to definition 15, it is easy to check that the clause:

$C = $ small(X) :- cat(X).

is more general than the clause:

$D = $ cuddly_pet(X) :- fluffy(X), cat(X).

with respect to the program P:

pet(X) :- cat(X).
cuddly_pet(X) :- small(X), fluffy(X), pet(X).

But let us assume a clause C to be more general than a clause D if any interpretation of C can be used to draw at least the same conclusions as D [135]. Then, clauses C and D above are not in a generality relationship, since they define different concepts.

To avoid such anomalies of relative subsumption, Buntine [37] introduced the notion of *generalized subsumption* as a special case of relative least general generalization, restricted to definite clauses. In the generalized subsumption framework, a clause C is more general than a clause D with respect to a (consistent) program P if, whenever D can be used (together with P) to explain some example, C can be used as well. That is, C will apply in any situation where D is applicable. A model-theoretic formalization of such a notion of generality is given by the following:

Definition 16 *Clause C is more general than clause D with respect to a program P iff, for any Herbrand interpretation I (over the language of at least P, C, D) being a model for P, then $T_{\{D\}}(I) \subseteq T_{\{C\}}(I)$. This is written as $C \preceq_P^B D$ (the B is for Buntine).*[2]

Following this definition, clearly clauses C and D of the previous example cannot be compared, since they have different heads. Definition 16 leads also to a natural

---

[2]We recall that the *immediate consequence operator* T is defined with respect to a program P over the Herbrand interpretations of P as [72]:
$T_P(I) = \{A \mid $ there exists a clause $C = C_{head}$:- $C_{body} \in P$ and a ground substitution θ such that $C_{head}\theta = A$ and $C_{body}\theta$ belongs to (or is true in) $I.\}$.

notion of equivalence between clauses. We write $C \equiv_P^B D$ if $C \preceq_P^B D$ and $D \preceq_P^B C$. This allows for the formulation of clause hierarchy and redundancy with respect to a given program. All of these concepts extend naturally to sets of clauses.

But Buntine also gives an operational view of generalized subsumption [37]:

Theorem 3 *Let C and D be clauses with disjoint variables and let P be a logic program. Let θ be a substitution grounding the variables in D to new constants not in C, D, P. Then $C \preceq_P^B D$ if and only if there exists a substitution σ such that:*

$$C_{head}\sigma = D_{head} \text{ and } P \cup D_{body}\theta \models \exists (C_{body}\sigma\theta).$$

Theorem 3 immediately suggests a way of testing for generalized subsumption: just run the logic program $P \cup D_{body}\theta$ against the query :-$C_{body}\sigma\theta$. Obviously, such a test is only semi-decidable, as it is guaranteed to terminate only when $C \preceq_P^B D$. But this can also be reinterpreted as follows: C is more general than D with respect to P if C can be converted to D by repeatedly:

1. turning variables to constants or other terms,
2. adding atoms to the body,
3. partially evaluating the body by resolving clauses in P against an atom in the body.

But theorem 3 also determines the precise relation between generalized subsumption and logical implication [37]:

Theorem 4 *Let D be any clause not tautologically true and P be a logic program. Then (1) $P \models \forall D$ if and only if $\exists C \in P$ such that $C \preceq_P^B D$; (2) if $C \preceq_P^B D$, then $(P \cup \forall C) \models (P \cup \forall D)$.*

Intuitively, this means that whenever a clause in a logic program is replaced by a more general clause, at least the same goals will succeed with the resulting program.

What is the relationship between generalized subsumption and Plotkin's generalization? In fact, generalized subsumption degenerates to θ-subsumption when the background knowledge is absent (i.e., when P is empty). That is, $C \preceq_\emptyset^B D$ if and only if $C \preceq D$. Hence, θ-subsumption can be seen as a special case of generalized subsumption.

More interesting is the relationship with relative least general generalization. As a consequence of theorems 3 and 4 (first part), it turns out that $C \preceq_P^B D$ if and only if C occurs at most once at the root of a refutation proving $P \models (C \rightarrow D)$. But this is a special case of the notion of rlgg (see definition 15). As a consequence, generalized subsumption turns out to be a special case of relative least general generalization. The distinction between the two notions of generality comes out when the two involved clauses have different predicative symbols in the head.

On the basis of the notion of the $\preceq_P^B$ relation, Buntine defines a space of possible inductive hypotheses, where each point corresponds to an equivalence class with respect to the equivalence relation $\equiv_P^B$ derived from $\preceq_P^B$. If compared with the analogous space built up from the relation based on θ-subsumption, this space is much smaller, since many clauses that do not subsume each other collapse to the same class under $\equiv_P^B$. Hence, we have a restriction of the search space, but in practice this is not very useful, since the relations $\preceq_P^B$ and $\equiv_P^B$ are harder to compute than those based on θ-subsumption. To this end, Buntine introduces the notion of *most specific generalization*, which is the analogue of the notion of lgg with respect to θ-subsumption. Also proposed is a method to compute most specific generalizations that is essentially the one used in GOLEM and is based on a subset of M_P. Buntine also defines a set of *relevant constraints* [36] to allow the induction algorithm to focus on relevant information.

Despite the advantages of generalized subsumption over θ-subsumption, the approach has not led to any solution to the ILP problem that is of practical interest, and remains mainly of theoretical importance.

3.2 Inverse Resolution

The notion of inverse resolution was introduced for the first time in the seminal work by Muggleton and Buntine [144]. However, some previous works [172, 141] used essentially a simplified form of inverse resolution. Since the first paper on inverse resolution, many different approaches have been presented, involving different representational languages and learning procedures [121, 169, 9], but it has been shown that these works are essentially a special form of the general theory of inverse resolution [124]. Moreover, Muggleton [142] has described a unified perspective for inverse resolution and the notion of relative least general generalization, which will be presented in the next section. We start by recalling the resolution rule and the needed notation.

Given two clauses C_1 and C_2, the resolution rule [165] allows one to deduce a new clause as follows. Assume the two clauses are variable disjoint, and let literals l_1 and l_2 belong to C_1 and C_2, respectively. Let θ be the most general unifier of l_1 and l_2 such that $\neg l_1 \theta = l_2 \theta$. Since l_1 and l_2 are variable disjoint, this can be rewritten as $\neg l_1 \theta_1 = l_2 \theta_2$, with $\theta = \theta_1 \theta_2$. Then, applying the resolution rule to *parent* clauses C_1 and C_2, the *resolvent* C is:

$$C = (C_1 - \{l_1\})\theta_1 \cup (C_2 - \{l_2\})\theta_2 \tag{3.1}$$

This operation is also indicated as $C = C_1 \cdot C_2$ and is usually depicted as in figure 3.1.

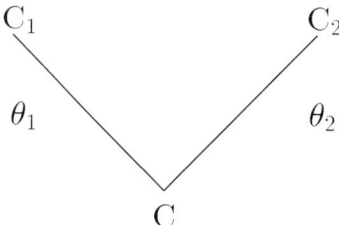

Figure 3.1: The resolution rule

A clause C is a consequence of a theory T if and only if the empty clause can be derived from $\{T \wedge \neg C\}$ by (repeated) application of resolution. An example of derivation of the empty clause at the propositional level can be found in figure 5.1b.

As resolution is the basis for deductive systems, inversion of resolution can become the basis to build inductive systems. That is, if a correct hypothesis, together with background knowledge, can be used in a resolution proof of some examples, then that hypothesis can be induced from the background knowledge and the examples by inverting the resolution process.

However, some problems arise when inverting resolution. Suppose we have the following three clauses, where C is the resolvent of C_1 and C_2:

C_1 = A :- B,C,D.
C_2 = B :- E,F.
C = A :- E,F,C,D.

Now, if we are given only C and C_1, then C_2 is clearly a legal solution to the problem of finding a parent clause producing C when resolved against C_1. However, the following clauses would also be a correct solution to the same problem:

C_2' = A :- B,C,D,E.
C_2'' = A :- B,C,D,F.
C_2''' = A :- B,C,D,E,F.

That is, in general we do not have a unique solution unless we assume C_1 and C_2 to be literal disjoint. The problem gets even worse if we have to deal with first-order clauses. Consider this other example [144]. Given:

3.2. Inverse Resolution

C_1 = :- heavier(hammer,feather).
C = :- denser(hammer,feather), larger(hammer,feather).

very many solutions for C_2 are possible, from the most specific:

C_2' = heavier(hammer,feather) :- denser(hammer,feather), larger(hammer,feather).

to the most general:

C_2 = heavier(A,B) :- denser(C,D), larger(E,F).

In fact, to generate C_2 we have to decide if and how to turn terms involved in the resolution operation into variables.

These problems were explicitly faced for the first time in the learning system CIGOL [144]. CIGOL uses three operators to build clauses from given examples and a background theory (that can also be empty). Invented clauses are presented to the user to determine whether they should be accepted and put in the background theory, or rejected.

3.2.1 The "V" operators

Proof trees, like the one of figure 5.1b, can be seen as made up of a number of connected "V"s, where each "V" represents a single resolution step, as in figure 3.1. Resolution is able to derive the clause at the base of the "V" (the resolvent), given the parent clauses labeling the arms. By contrast, inverse resolution is able to build one of the two parent clauses given the other parent clause and the resolvent. Let us first introduce informally the two operators that carry out inverse resolution, and that go under the common name of "V" operators, namely, *absorption* and *identification*.

Absorption

Let C_2 be the parent clause containing the negated literal in equation 3.1. The *absorption* operator builds C_2, given the resolvent C and the parent clause C_1. The use of the term *absorption* is clear if we deal with Horn clauses: the body of C_1 is *absorbed* into the body of C (after the application of a suitable unification) and replaced with its head. For example, given:

C = bird(tweety) :- feathered(tweety), has_wings(tweety), has_beak(tweety).
C_1 = fly(X) :- feathered(X), has_wings(X).

the body of C_1 {feathered(X), has_wings(X)} is absorbed into the body of C after the substitution $\theta = \{X/\text{tweety}\}$ and replaced with its head "fly(X)θ," giving, as a possible solution:

$C_2 = $ bird(tweety) :- fly(tweety), has_beak(tweety).

Clearly, $C = C_1 \cdot C_2$. Other inverse resolution based systems use terms such as *generalize* [9] or *saturation* [169, 166] (see below) to indicate similar operations.

Identification

Let C_1 be the parent clause containing the positive literal in equation 3.1. The *identification* operator builds C_1, given the resolvent C and the parent clause C_2. The idea is to *identify* part of the body of C_2 in the body of C through a suitable substitution θ. Then, suppose the heads of C and C_2 are unifiable through θ, and exactly one literal l in the body of C_2 does not occur in the body of C. Identification can build C_1 by using as head l and as body the part of C not found in C_2. For example, given clauses C and C_2 as in the previous example, we have $l = $ fly(tweety), and $C - C_2 = $ {feathered(tweety), has_wings(tweety)}. Hence, we have:

$C_1 = $ fly(tweety) :- feathered(tweety), has_wings(tweety).

which is a possible solution for $C = C_1 \cdot C_2$.

Actually, only the absorption operator is implemented in the CIGOL system. The same is in general true for other ILP systems. In fact, we are mostly interested in building a generalization (clause C_2) of the concept at the base of the V (clause C), while clause C_1 is normally part of the background knowledge.

Now, if C_2 contains the negated literal, then $l_2 = \neg l_1 \theta_1 \theta_2^{-1}$, and by manipulating equation 3.1 we get a formal definition of the absorption operator:

$$C_2 = (C - (C_1 - \{l_1\})\theta_1)\theta_2^{-1} \cup \{\neg l_1\}\theta_1\theta_2^{-1} \tag{3.2}$$

Here, an inverse substitution θ^{-1} is the process of replacing terms by variables, such that for every literal L, it is the case that $L\theta\theta^{-1} = L$. For example, if $L = $ P(X,Y) and $\theta = \{X/a, Y/b\}$, then $\theta^{-1} = \{a/X, b/Y\}$. To compute an inverse substitution it must be decided which terms and subterms must be replaced by the same variable, and which by different variables. As a consequence, this can lead to

3.2. Inverse Resolution

a combinatorial explosion. We will not go through a formal discussion of inverse substitution. The reader can refer to [144] for a thorough treatment. Finally, we note again that C_1 and C_2 are considered to be variable disjoint.

Equation 3.2 synthesizes a range of possible solutions for C_2, all of them satisfying $C = C_1 \cdot C_2$. Different solutions depend on the choice of θ_1, θ_2^{-1}, and on the literals not shared between C_1 and C_2. On the other hand, if we limit ourselves to Horn clauses, then the choice of l_1 is unique, since it must be the positive literal. In order to restrict the number of possible solutions of equation 3.2, some syntactic constraints must be imposed on the form of the involved clauses.

In CIGOL, the two constraints are that (1) the clauses $(C_1 - \{l_1\})\theta_1$ and $(C_2 - \{l_2\})\theta_2$ must not contain common literals — this is called the *separability assumption*; and (2) C_1 must be a unit clause (i.e., $C_1 = \{l_1\}$) — this is called the *unit clause assumption*. In fact, the second constraint includes the first.

As a consequence of the constraints, equation 3.2 simplifies to:

$$C_2 = (C \cup \{\neg l_1\}\theta_1)\theta_2^{-1} \qquad (3.3)$$

Now, only θ_1 and θ_2^{-1} are unknown. The major problem here is to build θ_2^{-1} by choosing which terms within $(C \cup \{\neg l_1\}\theta_1)$ must be replaced by common variables in C_2. This can lead to a combinatorial explosion. CIGOL uses a nondeterministic algorithm rewritten in terms of a best-first search. Moreover, note that if C_1 is a ground clause (that is, a positive example), then θ_1 is empty.

Clearly, the unit clause assumption strongly limits the kind of theories that can be learned. In fact, only resolution steps where at least one of the parent clauses is a unit clause can be inverted. More recent systems (such as IRES [169] and LFP2 [202]) can avoid such a restriction.

As an example of inverse resolution (adapted from [144]), suppose we have the following clauses:

C = less(A, succ(succ(A))),
C_1 = less(B,succ(B)).

Then, if we set $\theta_1 = \{B/\text{succ}(A)\}$, we have:

$(C \cup \{\neg l_1\}\theta_1)$ = (less(A,succ(succ(A))) :- less(succ(A),succ(succ(A)))))

Now, to compute θ_2^{-1}, we must decide how to turn the two occurrences of term succ(succ(A)) into variables. Suppose we decide to map both occurrences to the same new variable D. We get:

$C_2 = (C \cup \{\neg l_1\}\theta_1)\theta_2^{-1}$ = less(A,D) :- less(succ(A),D)

satisfying the relation $C = C_1 \cdot C_2$.

Incompleteness of absorption and a possible solution: Saturation

Recall the notion of a complete inductive inference machine (definition 4). Can we achieve completeness for a learning system using inverse resolution as an inductive operator? To answer this question, let us first introduce the following definition (adapted from [166]). Let there be given a background theory P and an input clause $C = C_{head}$:- C_{body}, such that $P \not\models C$:

Definition 17 *An inductive rule is* inversion complete *iff, given P and C as above, repeated applications of the inductive rule produce all the clauses $D = D_{head}$:- D_{body} such that $P \cup D \models C$. This is equivalent to saying that $C_{head}\theta = D_{head}\theta \wedge \{P \cup C_{body}\theta\} \models D_{body}\theta$, for some substitution θ.*

A possible situation grasped by the above definition is when C is a positive example not entailed by P, and we are looking for a clause D such that $P \cup D$ entails C. Now, recalling the definition of absorption, a main problem comes out when dealing with nonunit clauses: absorption is destructive, in the sense that replaced literals are lost and cannot be used for further generalizations with absorption. This happens when the bodies of some given clauses partially overlap, thus competing for generalization.

As an example, consider the following clauses, where C_1 and C_2 are the background theory and C_3 is an input clause:

C_1 = P :- Q,R.
C_2 = S :- R,T.
C_3 = V :- Q,R,T,W.

We note that C_1 and C_2 share a literal in their body, and that both could be used to perform absorption with respect to C_3. Suppose C_1 is selected. Absorption of C_3 with C_1 gives C_4 = V :- P,T,W. But now, absorption of C_4 with C_2 is no longer possible, since the literal R has been removed. This results in a form of incompleteness for absorption with respect to definition 17: given a background theory and an input clause, not all possible generalizations can be found by applying absorption, since allowed generalizations depend on the order in which absorption operations are done.

To avoid this problem, two independent solution have been proposed in [166, 169] and in [142]. We will discuss this second solution in the next section. In [169]

3.2. Inverse Resolution

the inverse resolution operator called *saturation* is introduced. From an operational point of view, the essential difference between absorption and saturation is that saturation keeps replaced literals while performing absorption, enclosing them within brackets. Literals within brackets are those already used for an absorption step, and therefore they are optional. However, they can be used in the subsequent steps, thus allowing alternative solutions to be discovered later.

Referring to the clauses C_1, C_2, and C_3 above, the saturation of C_1 and C_3 would be C_4 = V :- [Q,R],T,W,P. Now we can apply saturation to C_4 and C_2, obtaining C_5 = V :- [Q,R,T],W,P,S. Clause C_5 represents in a compact way all possible generalizations of clause C_3. These clauses can be obtained by dropping some of the literals in brackets, by means of the truncation operator (subsection 3.2.3).

From a theoretical point of view, absorption and saturation are quite different, since with saturation no generalization is achieved until the application of truncation. In fact, a logical analysis ([169]) shows that saturation works by performing all possible deductions on the (skolemized) body of the input clause, using the background theory. However, resolved literals are not removed but kept within brackets. This points out a close relationship between inductive and deductive inference.[3] We will show a tighter relationship in chapter 5. Strictly speaking, literals in brackets are redundant [166]. In fact, they are useful to perform further saturation steps, but can result in very large saturated clauses. For this reason, systems employing saturation (such as IRES [169] and ITOU [166]) use various constraints (mainly syntactic) to limit the possible generalizations.

As a consequence of keeping all replaced literals, we have the following result [166]:

Theorem 5 *Saturation is inversion complete.*

3.2.2 Predicate invention: The "W" operators

Predicate invention is the ability of a system to enrich its vocabulary by introducing new terms. A more precise definition is given in chapter 2. According to [122], a new term can be classified as *useful* if its invention and use do not affect the learnability of a theory. A new term is *necessary* if, without it, the theory is not learnable according to some criterion of successful learning.

Even if the introduction of new predicates does not produce any form of generalization, we discuss predicate invention here because this issue can be easily formalized in the framework of inverse resolution. In practice, predicate invention

---

[3] A strong similarity may be also noticed between the approach and notation adopted for the saturation operator and ordered linear deduction [40] (also called model elimination deduction [126]) used in automatic theorem proving.

is normally used to build compact theories (e.g., shorter than the whole length of the conjunction of the provided examples). This can be achieved by (a) rewriting a (partial) theory in a more concise way if that theory already exists[4] or (b) keeping a theory that is being built below a given size. These two approaches have been called, respectively, the *reformulation approach* and the *demand-driven approach* [183].

As a general form of the reformulation approach [122], suppose the following theory has been learned:

$C_1 = P\theta_1 \text{ :- } \alpha\theta_1, \beta.$
$C_2 = P\theta_2 \text{ :- } \alpha\theta_2, \gamma.$

where α, β and γ are conjunctions of literals. Then the common part of the two clauses is extracted and a new predicate can be introduced. The theory is rewritten as:

$D_1 = P \text{ :- } \alpha, N.$
$D_2 = N\theta_1 \text{ :- } \beta.$
$D_3 = N\theta_2 \text{ :- } \gamma.$

Obviously, this invention can be extended to a set of clauses. Note that if the theory must cover a finite number of examples (that is, a finite number of examples is given to the learning system), then N does not need to be a recursive predicate. The demand-driven approach behaves similarly, but it is activated only if the clause that is being learned grows beyond a predefined size.

Predicate invention is formalized in the so-called "W" operators. The "W" operator is obtained by combining two "V"s, as in figure 3.2.

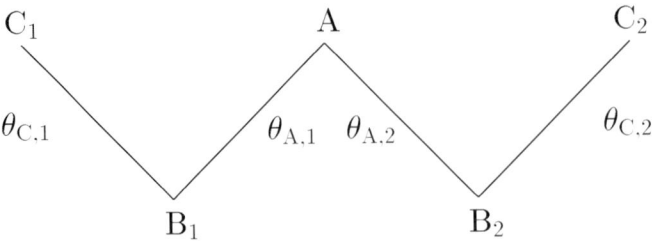

Figure 3.2: A "W" operator

---

[4]This can also be seen as a form of *theory restructuring*, as in [180] and [181].

3.2. Inverse Resolution

Assume clauses C_1 and C_2 resolve on a common literal l within clause A to obtain clauses B_1 and B_2. Then the "W" operator builds clauses A, C_1 and C_2 given B_1 and B_2. In particular when l is negative, this operation is called *intraconstruction*, and *interconstruction* when it is positive. A similar operation is found in [9] as *dream* and is implemented in the procedure *create* in [121]. Since literal l in A is resolved away and is not found in B_1 and B_2, in order to build A, C_1, and C_2 a new predicate must be *invented* by the "W" operator. From figure 3.2 and equation 3.1 we get:

$$B_1 = (A - \{l\})\theta_{A,1} \cup (C_1 - \{l_1\})\theta_{C,1} \qquad (3.4)$$
$$B_2 = (A - \{l\})\theta_{A,2} \cup (C_2 - \{l_2\})\theta_{C,2}$$

Again assuming C_1 and C_2 to be unit clauses, from 3.4 we get:

$$A = B_1\theta_{A,1}^{-1} \cup \{l\} = B_2\theta_{A,2}^{-1} \cup \{l\} = B \cup \{l\} \qquad (3.5)$$

where B is a common generalization of clauses B_1 and B_2. In CIGOL, in order to determine the arguments of the new predicate, substitutions $\theta_{A,i}$ are considered. All substitutions for a variable in $\theta_{A,i}$ having no variables in common with substitutions for other variables in $\theta_{A,i}$ are *irrelevant* and will not appear as an argument of the new predicate. See [124] and [185] for a general discussion on how to choose variables for an invented predicate, and [184] for a thorough discussion on the utility of predicate invention in ILP.

Other learning systems ([169, 9]) are able to drop the unit restriction for clauses C_1 and C_2. For example, in IRES and ITOU this is achieved through a flattened representation of clauses (see section 2.2). In this case, intraconstruction of clauses C_1 and C_2 can occur if they have a nonempty common generalization. Such a generalization must cover the heads of C_1 and C_2 and at least one literal in their bodies. As in the last example, first a generalization of the heads of C_1 and C_2, and a generalization C of the bodies of C_1 and C_2 are found. Second, a new concept *newp* is introduced. *Newp* is defined by means of two new clauses built by using the leftover literals of C_1 and C_2. The arguments of *newp* are chosen in order to avoid undesired generalizations with respect to the initial clauses. For example [169], from the clauses:

C_1 = grandfather(X,Z) :- father(X,Y), father(Y,Z).
C_2 = grandfather(A,C) :- father(A,B), mother(B,C).

IRES is able to build:

$C = $ grandfather(L,N) :- father(L,M), $newp$(M,N).
$C_3 = newp$(Y,Z) :- father(Y,Z).
$C_4 = newp$(B,C) :- mother(B,C).

3.2.3 The truncation operator

The special case when A, C_1, and C_2 are unit clauses (that is, B_1 and B_2 are the empty clause) in equations 3.4 and 3.5 is handled by the *truncation* operator. This term is used because, in a flattened representation of clauses, saturation can be performed by dropping literals, so that clauses appear to be truncated. In CIGOL, truncation is implemented by computing the least general generalization of C_1 and C_2. Clearly, lgg(C_1, C_2) subsumes both C_1 and C_2. IRES and ITOU work with a flattened representation of clauses. As a consequence, in these systems, truncation is performed by dropping literals. The dropped literals can be those introduced during the flattening step[5] or the literals within brackets produced by saturation. Actually, the truncation operator used in IRES and ITOU is more general, because any literal can be dropped. This can also bring generalization outside the scope of SLD resolution. In fact, from the clause $C_1 = $ "V :- W,P,S" we can get the clause "$C_2 = $ 'V :- W,P" by means of truncation. However, this is no longer an inverse resolution step. In fact, it is not possible to get clause C_1 from clause C_2 by means of SLD resolution. Nevertheless, we note that still $C_2 \models C_1$. That is, truncation as a dropping rule accounts for a more general form of generalization ([169]. See also section 3.3 and definition 18).

3.2.4 The learning task

Inverse resolution based systems are mainly interactive systems. They rely heavily on positive examples and on the interaction with an oracle (normally the user), that has to decide whether to accept or reject the result of the application of each operator. In other words, clause equivalence queries (section 2.3) are made to the user during the learning task.

Consider CIGOL. The system starts by taking as input a set of positive examples of the target concept[6] and a background theory, which can also be empty. Pairs of positive examples are selected and generalized by using truncation. The result of each truncation step is presented to the user to be accepted (and put in the background theory) or rejected. If a clause is rejected, the user can input

---

[5]In fact, in an unflattened representation this corresponds to generalizing a clause by turning some terms into variables.

[6]In general, clauses in input to CIGOL are not required to be ground unit clauses. Arbitrary Horn clauses can be given, representing a partial description of the target concept.

3.2. Inverse Resolution

a counterexample.[7] Rejected clauses are recorded, and thus they will never be generated again.

When truncation has been exhaustively applied to new examples, the system applies absorption and intraconstruction to the examples and the background theory, resulting in nonunit clauses that are presented to the user. Since CIGOL builds proof trees in reverse order, only clauses at the leaves, if accepted by the user, are added to the background theory. Clauses at the intermediate nodes of the proof are deleted from the theory, since they are redundant. If intraconstruction is used, the user is also required to name the new invented predicate. To this aim, the system also presents to the user a set of possible instances of the predicate. Referring to figure 3.2, the instances are built by matching the head of A with the positive examples, and then propagating the instantiations to the body, and hence also to the literal made up with the new predicate. Instances of the new concept will help the user to identify the "meaning" of the invented predicate and to choose a meaningful name.

Finally, the resulting theory is processed by using Buntine's redundancy algorithm [37], in order to remove any remaining redundant clauses. The above steps are repeated by adding new examples, accepting or rejecting guessed clauses until a satisfactory theory (from the point of view of the user) is found. A learning session of CIGOL (adapted from [144]) is reported below. The system is trying to learn the concept of an *arch* (see also [172], where the same problem is faced by the MARVIN system). User input is reported in bold, and comments are in italics.

Initially, few examples of arch are given in input to CIGOL:

arch([],beam,[]).
arch([block],beam,[block]).
arch([brick],beam,[brick]).
arch([block,brick],beam,[block,brick]).

CIGOL starts to apply truncation to the given examples, presenting the result of each generalization to the user:

Is arch(A,beam,A) always true? **no.**
Is arch([A|B],beam,[A|B]) always true? **no.**
Is arch([block|A],beam,[block|A]) always true? **no.**

Note that all the proposed generalizations are wrong and hence are rejected by the

---

[7]This negative example could be used, together with a depth-bounded SLD theorem prover, to check the correctness of a theory that is being learned.

user. Then, CIGOL applies intraconstruction to the examples, inventing a new predicate. Instances of the predicate are presented to the user, in order to recognize its meaning:

arch(A,beam,A) :- *newpred*(A).
newpred([]).
newpred([block]).
newpred([block,brick]).
newpred([brick]).
what shall I call *newpred*? **column.**

Now, CIGOL applies absorption to the clauses "column([])." and "column([block])." A new clause is built and proposed to the user:

New clause: column([block|A]) :- column(A).
Is the new clause always true? **yes.**

Since the proposed clause is accepted, CIGOL tries to continue along this path by further generalizing the recursive clause:

New clause: column([A|B]) :- column([A,brick]),column(B).
Is the new clause always true? **ignore.**

Note that the proposed generalization is correct but redundant. Hence, the user tells the system to ignore such a clause. As a consequence, no further generalization will be attempted along this path. Then, another absorption is tried, using the first and fourth atom clauses for column:

New clause: column([brick|A]) :- column(A).
Is the new clause always true? **yes.**

Now intraconstruction can be applied to the two discovered recursive clauses, yielding:

column([A|B]) :- *newpred*(A),column(B).
newpred(brick).
newpred(block).
what shall I call *newpred*? **brick_or_block.**

The final set of learned clauses, together with some of the ground atoms, represents

3.2. Inverse Resolution

a possible description of the concept of arch:

arch(A,beam,A) :- column(A).
column([A|B]) :- brick_or_block(A),column(B).
brick_or_block(brick).
brick_or_block(block).
column([]).

Other systems may apply the various steps in a different order. For example, IRES and ITOU first apply saturation to the input examples, using the background theory. Since ground examples are flattened, even at this step nonunit clauses are involved. The saturated input is then undergone to intraconstruction and truncation, to achieve generalization. The result of these operators is presented to the user and, if accepted, is added to the background theory. Since saturation can produces very large clauses, the application of intraconstruction and truncation after saturation also has a compaction effect on the theory being learned.

A similar approach[8] is taken in CLINT [58]. Given an uncovered positive example e, first, a completion procedure is performed by computing the set of most specific clauses with respect to the uncovered example, the background theory, and the hypothesis language that cover e. The produced clauses that do not cover any negative example are then generalized by using the dropping condition rule (i.e., by dropping literals from the body of the starting clause). The result of each generalization is presented to the user to be accepted or rejected. If accepted, a clause may be undergone to further generalization.

3.2.5 A unifying perspective

Besides the solution based on saturation, another one, involving *most specific V operators*, was proposed by Muggleton ([142]) in order to overcome the incompleteness of absorption. However, these new operators also provide a theoretical link between inverse resolution and relative least general generalization: the rlgg of a set of clauses can be built by means of repeated applications of the most specific V operators. In this section we outline the main points of such a unifying perspective.

Consider again the resolution equation 3.1, but now let us avoid the separability assumption. That is, now the parent clauses C_1 and C_2 can contain common literals. Let D be the literals of C occurring in C_1 but not in C_2 (i.e., $D = (C_1 - \{l_1\})\theta_1 - (C_2 - \{l_2\})\theta_2$). From equation 3.1, and because $\neg l_1\theta_1 = l_2\theta_2$, we get:

---

[8] A comparison of different approaches to generalization adopted in bottom-up systems can be found in [168].

$$C_2 = ((C - D) \cup \{\neg l_1\}\theta_1)\theta_2^{-1} \qquad (3.6)$$

We know that such an equation has a whole range of solutions, depending on the choices of θ_1 and θ_2^{-1}, and now also on the choice of D, with $\emptyset \subseteq D \subseteq (C_1 - \{l_1\})\theta_1$. The most specific of such solutions for the absorption operator is given by $D = \emptyset$ and $\theta_2^{-1} = \{\}$. This is denoted with $C_2\!\downarrow$ as:

$$C_2\!\downarrow = (C \cup \{\neg l_1\}\theta_1) \qquad (3.7)$$

Via a similar reasoning, the most specific solution for the identification operator turns out to be:

$$C_1\!\downarrow = (C \cup \{\neg l_2\}\theta_2) \qquad (3.8)$$

Now, in equation 3.7, θ_1 remains to be determined. Clearly, part of θ_1 (say θ_1') can be determined by matching literals in C and C_1, but what about variables occurring in l_1 and not affected by θ_1'? In fact, any substitution would be plausible for such variables. This problem can be avoided by requiring each variable in C to occur in at least two literals of C. Then, each variable in l_1 (i.e., the head of C_1) will also occur in some other literal of $(C_1 - \{l_1\})$ (i.e., the body of C_1), and hence $\theta_1' = \theta_1$.

Clauses respecting such a constraint are called *strongly generative*. Note that this is a reinforcement of the notion of syntactically generative clauses used in the GOLEM system (section 3.1.2). For the sake of brevity, in the following by a "generative clause" we mean a "strongly generative clause."

By using most specific V operators, we may obtain a restricted form of completeness for inverse resolution similar to the one stated for saturation. This is achieved by means of the $\mathcal{V}$ function, returning the set of most specific clauses that can be constructed by repeated applications of most specific V operators. The function

$\mathcal{V}$: *Generative_Logic_Programs* $\times$ *Clauses* $\rightarrow$ *Clause_Theories*

represents the (restricted) counterpart of Robinson's function[9] $\mathcal{R}(P)$ [165] for inverse resolution, and is defined as follows:

$$\mathcal{V}^0(P, C) = \{C\}$$
$$\mathcal{V}^n(P, C) = \mathcal{V}^{n-1}(P, C) \cup \{(C' \cup \{\neg l\}\theta) : l \in C_{1,2} \in P \text{ and}$$
$$C' \in \mathcal{V}^{n-1}(P, C) \text{ and } (C_{1,2} - \{l\})\theta \subseteq C'\}$$

---

[9]The function $\mathcal{R}$: *Set_of_clauses* $\rightarrow$ *Set_of_clauses* is defined as follows:
$\mathcal{R}^0(P) = P$
$\mathcal{R}^n(P) = \mathcal{R}^{n-1}(P) \cup \{R \mid C, D \in \mathcal{R}^{n-1}(P) \text{ and } R \text{ is a resolvent of } C \text{ and } D\}$ for $n > 0$.

3.2. Inverse Resolution

The closure of $\mathcal{V}^n(P,C)$ is denoted by $\mathcal{V}^*(P,C)$. It is clear from the above definition that $\mathcal{V}^n(P,C)$ contains, besides the most specific absorptions up to depth n, the most specific identifications to depth n. Also note that $\mathcal{V}^n(P,C)$ can contain non-Horn clauses. In fact, the above definition does not require P to be a logic program.

The most important property of the $\mathcal{V}^n(P,C)$ function is the following [142]:

Theorem 6 *Let P be a strongly generative logic program, and $\{D_1, ..., D_{k-1}\}$ be a subset of P. Let C be the last center clause of the linear derivation $(D_1 \cdot (D_2 \cdot ...(D_{k-1} \cdot C_k))$, with $C_k \notin P$. For every such derivation $\exists\, C_k\!\!\downarrow \in \mathcal{V}^n(P,C)$ such that $C_k \preceq C_k\!\!\downarrow$.*

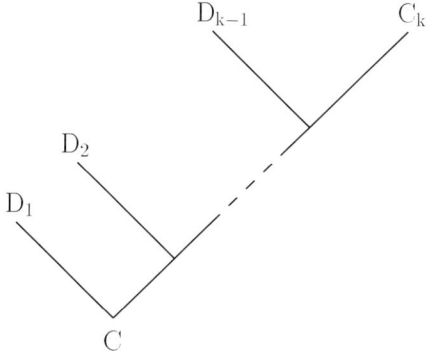

Figure 3.3: Linear derivation of C

Figure 3.3 illustrates the theorem. From the point of view of learning logic programs, the practical meaning of theorem 6 is the following. Suppose we are given a background knowledge P such that each clause in P is a strongly generative Horn clause, and an example C such that $P \nvdash C$. Moreover, there exists a clause C' such that $P \cup C' \vdash C$ in a linear derivation with top clause C' that is used exactly once in the derivation. Then, for some value k, $\mathcal{V}^k(P,C)$ contains a clause $C_k\!\!\downarrow$ such that $C' \preceq C_k\!\!\downarrow$, and such that clause $C_k\!\!\downarrow$ could be used in place of C' to derive C. Hence, the $\mathcal{V}$ function can be used to learn such a clause $C_k\!\!\downarrow$ from P and C. Moreover, note that C does not need to be a ground or atomic clause. It is worth noting, as the learnability of $C_k\!\!\downarrow$ is not assured if the general absorption operator is used in place of the most specific operator. Also, it is clear from theorem 6 that $C_k \preceq \bigcup \mathcal{V}^k(P,C)$. As a consequence of theorem 6, $\bigcup^* \mathcal{V}^k(P,C)$ contains all the generalizations of the initial clause C from P. Hence, $\bigcup^* \mathcal{V}^k(P,C)$ can also be seen as a formalization of the saturation operator.

Now, consider two clauses C and D and a clause $C_k \notin P$ such that there exists a linear derivation of depth at most k from C_k and P of both C and D. Then, $C_k \preceq \bigcup \mathcal{V}^k(P,C)$ and $C_k \preceq \bigcup \mathcal{V}^k(P,D)$ and, recalling the definition of least general generalization, $C_k \preceq \text{lgg}(\bigcup \mathcal{V}^k(P,C), \bigcup \mathcal{V}^k(P,D))$. But then, the least solution for C_k is also the least general generalization of $\bigcup \mathcal{V}^k(P,C)$ and $\bigcup \mathcal{V}^k(P,D)$. This situation is depicted in figure 3.4:

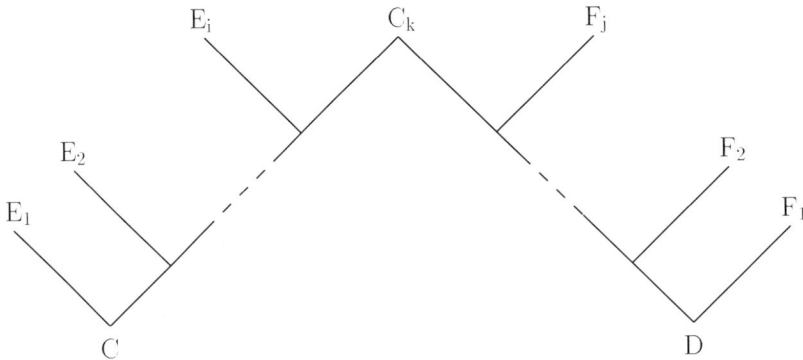

Figure 3.4: Linear derivations of C and D from C_k and P

Now, suppose that clause C_k of figure 3.4 is the least general possible solution, i.e., $C_k \equiv_\theta \text{lgg}(\bigcup \mathcal{V}^k(P,C), \bigcup \mathcal{V}^k(P,D))$. By the construction of figure 3.4, it is the case that $P \cup \text{lgg}(\bigcup \mathcal{V}^k(P,C), \bigcup \mathcal{V}^k(P,D)) \vdash C \wedge D$. But then, recalling the definition of rlgg of two clauses with respect to a background knowledge, we have the following:

Theorem 7 *Let P be a logic program and let C and D be Horn clauses. Then, $rlgg_P(C,D) = lgg(\bigcup \mathcal{V}^k(P,C), \bigcup \mathcal{V}^k(P,D))$.*

We note that the parameter k, limiting the depth of linear derivations, has the same meaning as the parameter h of the GOLEM system.

Theorem 7 is the link between Plotkin's rlgg and inverse resolution: the rlgg of clauses can be built by computing the lgg of inverse linear derivations — a procedural approach — or by adopting the model-based approach followed by GOLEM.

3.3 Inverse Implication

At the beginning of this chapter, we observed that the notion of generalization could be related to the notion of logical implication. The precise relationship be-

3.3. Inverse Implication

tween implication and logical consequence, adapted to our framework, is commonly defined thus:

Definition 18 *Let C and D be clauses. We say that C implies D, or $C \to D$, if and only if every model for C is also a model for D, i.e., iff $C \models D$. We say that C is a* generalization (under implication) *of D.*

Definition 18 provides a precise (and complete) notion of a clause C *being more general than* clause D in a logical framework. It is well known that if $C \preceq D$, then $C \to D$, but the converse is not necessarily true (an example was given in section 3.1). Practically, this amounts to the incompleteness of generalization under θ-subsumption since, by definition 18, it can be the case that $C \models D$ but $C \not\preceq D$. That is, if we perform generalization under θ-subsumption of a set of clauses S, we can fail to find a suitable explanation, even if there exists a clause C such that $C \models S$.

Due to the tight connection between θ-subsumption and inverse resolution shown in the previous section, a similar problem also holds for inverse resolution. For example, Lapointe and Matwin [116] point out that inverse resolution cannot reverse SLD derivations when the clause to be synthesized is used more than once (e.g., a self-recursive clause repeatedly applied to itself). Recall that theorem 1 and definition 15, on least general generalization and relative least general generalization, respectively, require clause C to be used only once in the involved derivation.

Hence, why not invert implication to get a complete form of generalization? The first reason is that, in general, implication is undecidable. In other words, a procedure to check whether $C \to D$ does not exist [173]. This is a consequence of the undecidability of first-order logic, and this is true also for Horn clauses [127]. The second reason is that inverting implication can be computationally very expensive, unless we impose some constraints that can limit the kind of clauses that can be learned.

Despite these problems, one of the most recent trends in Machine Learning and ILP is the study of inverse implication, since this kind of generalization is fundamental to inducing self recursive clauses, which play a basic role in logic programming. In fact, the true difference between implication and θ-subsumption concerns only the so-called *ambivalent* clauses [82]:

Definition 19 *A clause is* ambivalent *iff it contains a pair $(C, \neg D)$ of ambivalent literals. A pair $(C, \neg D)$ of literals is ambivalent if C and D have the same predicative symbol and sign.*

Theorem 8 [82] *Let C and D be nonambivalent clauses. Then $C \to D$ if and only if $C \preceq D$.*

Ambivalent clauses need not be recursive (for example, q(a) :- q(s(s(a))) is ambivalent and not recursive), but recursive clauses are ambivalent.

A more operational view of the distinction between implication and θ-subsumption can be found by studying the relationship between implication and resolution [143].

Definition 20 [143] *If T is a set of clauses, then the nth linear resolution of T, denoted $\mathcal{L}^n(T)$, is defined as:*

$$\mathcal{L}^0(T) = T$$
$$\mathcal{L}^n(T) = \{R \mid C_1 \in \mathcal{L}^{n-1}(T), C_2 \in T \text{ and } R \text{ is the resolvent of } C_1 \text{ and } C_2\}$$

The function $\mathcal{L}$ contains only the linear derivations of Robinson's $\mathcal{R}$ function, but its closure is equivalent, since linear derivation is complete.

Theorem 9 (Subsumption theorem) [120, 8] *If T is a set of clauses and D is a nontautological clause, then $T \models D$ iff $\exists C \in \mathcal{L}^n(T)$ such that $C \preceq D$ for some $n \geq 1$.*

We can apply the subsumption theorem to implication by letting T be a single clause.

Corollary 1 [143] *Let C be a clause and D a nontautological clause. Then $C \rightarrow D$ iff $\exists E \in \mathcal{L}^n(\{C\})$ such that $E \preceq D$ for some $n \geq 1$.*

This corollary restates implication in terms of self-resolution and θ-subsumption. $C \rightarrow D$ whenever (1) D is a tautology, or (2) $C \preceq D$, or (3) $E \preceq D$ and E is built by repeatedly self-resolving C. Whereas the first two conditions are, in some way, trivial, the third shows the significance of self-recursive clauses in inverting implication.

So far, there have been three independent approaches to inverting implication. However, they are closely related to each other, as they work by finding regularities in the terms and in the literals of the input clauses. In the rest of this section we will briefly sketch these three approaches.[10]

3.3.1 Finding structural regularities of terms

The first implemented attempt to (partially) invert implication was presented in the LOPSTER system [116], later improved in the CRUSTACEAN system [2, 3].

---

[10] We will give here a somewhat simplified description of these approaches. See the references for details.

3.3. Inverse Implication

Consider a recursive clause C of the following form:

$$C = \text{p}(T_1, ..., T_n) \text{ :- } \text{p}(V_1, ..., V_n).$$

where T_i is a term and V_i is a variable, and for $1 \leq i \leq n$ the variable V_i occurs in term T_i. Consider also a derivation tree as in figure 3.5, where C is a recursive clause as above, D is the (atomic) base clause of the recursive relation, and E is an atom derivable from C and D (E is normally a positive example, but it need not be ground). Clearly, the structure of the terms occurring in E depends on (1) the structure of the terms in D, (2) the structure of the terms in C, and (3) the number of recursive applications of C. All this is in some way "embedded" in E. Given E and D, LOPSTER is able to identify the structural regularities of terms in E in order to rebuild clause C, by performing the following steps.

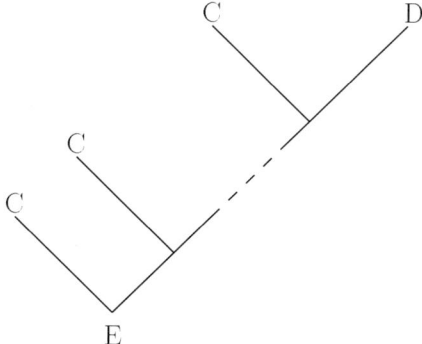

Figure 3.5: A (linear) derivation involving a recursive clause

First, the contribution of D must be identified. When D is resolved against C, it turns variables in C into other terms (possibly ground) through a suitable unifier, and these terms must be found at the end of the derivation as subterms[11] of E. Hence, terms in D must be unifiable with subterms in E. For example, suppose we are given:

$D = \text{p}(\text{s}(X), \text{f}(Y)).$ $E = \text{p}(\text{s}^4(0), \text{f}^7(0)).$
$t_1^D = \text{s}(X),$ $t_2^D = \text{f}(Y),$ $t_1^E = \text{s}^4(0),$ $t_2^E = \text{f}^7(0)$

---

[11] A *subterm* s of a term t is a term occurring somewhere in t. In general, terms from D can be instantiated further during the repeated applications of C.

where p is a predicate symbol, s and f are functors, and $s^n(X)$ means s(s(....s(X))), where "s" is repeated n times. Then t_1^D is unifiable with a subterm of t_1^E (namely, s(0)), through the substitution $\sigma = \{X/0\}$ (i.e., $t_1^D \sigma = s(0)\sigma$). We say that σ is a *subunifier* of term t_1^D in t_1^E. In general, given two terms t_1 and t_2, there can be an infinite number of subunifiers of t_1 in t_2, so LOPSTER considers only the *most general subunifiers*, which are defined similarly to most general unifiers. The notion of subunification is naturally extended to literals. Given the clauses D = p(t_1, ..., t_n) and E = p(s_1, ..., s_n), θ is a subunifier of D in E if it is a subunifier of t_i in s_i for $1 \leq i \leq n$. In our example, the most general subunifier of D in E is $\theta = \{X/0, Y/0\}$.

As a second step, after having identified the effect of D on E, this effect is removed by turning the subterms in E unified with the terms in D into a new variable. In our example, the subterm s(0) of term t_1^E (which unifies with t_1^D) is turned into the new variable "X," obtaining the so-called *embedding term* t_1^X = $s^3(X)$. Similarly, from the term t_2^E we get the embedding term t_2^X = $f^6(X)$. Intuitively, an embedding term can be seen as the result of repeatedly resolving a recursive clause against itself, thus generating more and more complex terms.

The third step is to decompose the embedding term t^X, in order to find a substitution σ and a new term gt^X such that:

$$gt_1^X \ \{X/gt_2^X\} \ \{X/gt_3^X\} \ ... \ \{X/gt_n^X\}\sigma = t^X.$$

(where each gt_i^X is gt^X with all of its variables, except for X, renamed to new variables). The term gt^X is called *generating term* of depth n of the embedding term t^X, since it can be used to generate that term. The intuitive meaning of this step is that when the head of clause C is repeatedly resolved against its body, the terms of C_{head} are repeatedly unified with the variables of C_{body}, producing more and more complex terms. These terms are the embedding terms whose generating terms are the terms of C_{head}. In our example, one possible generating term of the embedding term t_1^X = $s^3(X)$ is gt_1^X = s(X), with depth 3. In fact, we have that $gt_1^X \cdot \{X/gt_2^X\} \cdot \{X/gt_3^X\}\sigma = t_1^X$ (where σ is the empty substitution, and gt_i^X = gt^X for all i, since gt^X has only one variable, X). An embedding term can have generating terms of different depths. As an example, for the embedding term $s^4(X)$ we have a generating term of depth 4, which is s(X), and one of depth 2, which is $s^2(X)$ (for any embedding term, there is also a trivial generating term, of depth 1, which is the embedding term itself. This term is useless, and it is never taken into consideration).

The notion of generating term is easily extended to a tuple of generating terms. Given a tuple of embedding terms et = <t_1^X, ..., t_m^X>, a *tuple of generating terms of depth n* of et is a tuple gt = <gt_1^X, ..., gt_m^X> such that each gt_i^X is a generating

3.3. Inverse Implication

term of depth n for t_i^X. It is important to note that all generating terms must have the same depth. In practice, a tuple of generating terms represents the terms in the head of a recursive clause. When this clause is repeatedly self-resolved, a set of embedding terms is produced, all of them having at least one generating term with the same depth. This depth is the number of self-resolutions plus one. For example, the pair of embedding terms $<s^6(X), s^4(X)>$, has only one possible pair of generating terms. It is $<s^3(X), s^2(X)>$, with depth 2. However, the two embedding terms each have other generating terms of different depths. If there are more tuples of generating terms for a given tuple of embedding terms, LOPSTER chooses the one with maximum n, in order to build the deepest (and hence the most general) induced clauses with respect to D and E. The pair of generating terms for our example is $<s(X), f^2(X)>$, with depth 3.

As a last step, we have to build the recursive clause C by using the discovered (tuple of) generating terms. This is done as follows: each variable X in gt_i^X is renamed X_i. Then gt_i^X becomes the i-th argument in the head of C, and X_i becomes the i-th argument in the body of C. The predicate symbol used in the head and in the body of C is the same as in clauses D and E. As a consequence, the general form of C turns out to be:

$$C = p(gt_1^X\{X/X_1\}, ..., gt_n^X\{X/X_n\}) \text{:-} p(X_1, ..., X_n).$$

In our example, the induced clause will be C = "p(s(X), f^2(Y)) :- p(X, Y)," which, in fact, can be used to derive E = p($s^4(0)$, f$^7(0)$) using D = p(s(X), f(Y)).

As a further step, the induced clause C can be specialized by finding common variables among literals in C_{head}. C is used to deductively reduce E to (an instance of) D. If, during the proof, two variables in C_{head} are found to have the same sequence of instantiations, they are turned into the same variable.

Logic programs whose recursive clause follows the same pattern, as in the general form of C above, are called *purely recursive*. It is often possible to rewrite logic programs by means of purely recursive clauses. In this case, LOPSTER will succeed in finding an acceptable solution. For example, classical logic programs such as *member, append, reverse,* and *factorial*, are normally written by using purely recursive clauses.

Beside purely recursive programs, LOPSTER is also able to learn with the same technique another class of logic programs: left-recursive programs, i.e., programs whose recursive clause has the following structure:

$$p(T_1, ..., T_m, X_1, ..., X_n) \text{:-} p(Y_1, ..., Y_m, Z_1, ..., Z_n), L_1, ..., L_k.$$

Where $X_1, ..., X_n, Z_1, ..., Z_n$ are variables, for $1 \leq i \leq m$ variable Y_i occurs in term T_i, and L_1, ..., L_k are literals (usually given as background knowledge). A classical left-recursive program is, for example, *multiply*, whose recursive clause is "multiply(X,s(Y),Z) :- multiply(X,Y,W), plus(X,W,Z)." Literals L_1, ..., L_k are added in order to bind unbound variables in the recursive literal ("W" in the case of *multiply*), until a consistent clause is found.

LOPSTER takes as input a set of positive and negative examples, and a set of background Horn clauses. First it selects a pair of positive examples $<E_1,E_2>$ such that the arguments of E_1 are subunifiable with those of E_2, and the destructuring procedure as described above can be performed, in order to get a tuple of generating terms. Then a purely recursive clause is induced and tested against the negative examples. If it is not consistent, another tuple of generating terms is sought. If no consistent clause can be found, the system tries to induce a left-recursive clause in the same way. If also this fails, another pair of positive examples, if any, is taken into consideration.

LOPSTER is very efficient, compared with other learning systems (classical purely recursive programs can be learned in a few hundredths of seconds) and it requires in input just two (well-chosen) positive examples. However, the approach has some drawbacks.

First, the class of programs that can be learned is restricted, and there is no evidence that the technique is easily applicable to other classes of logic programs, preserving efficiency.

Second, by finding generating terms of maximum depth, LOPSTER can sometimes induce overgeneral clauses. For example [100], given the pair of examples $<$even(0), even(s^4(0))$>$, LOPSTER induces the clause:

$C = $ even(s(X)) :- even(X).

instead of the correct one:

$C' = $ even(s^2(X)) :- even(X).

Obviously, clause C can be found wrong by providing a suitable negative example.

Third, the two positive examples in the pair $<E_1,E_2>$ must lie along the same inverse resolution chain, and one of the two examples must be the base clause of the target recursive relation (the clause D of figure 3.5). Sometimes, this requires some knowledge of that relation. When arbitrary examples are provided, LOPSTER normally fails or performs poorly.

This last problem has been overcome in the CRUSTACEAN system [2, 3]. CRUSTACEAN can work with randomly selected and completely independent examples, a strong improvement with respect to LOPSTER, since the user is not re-

3.3. Inverse Implication

quired to have any knowledge about the program to be learned. As in LOPSTER, the class of purely recursive programs is considered. Suppose CRUSTACEAN is given in input the two positive examples E_1 and E_2, such that E_1 is proved by using D_1 and C, and E_2 is proved by using D_2 and C. D_1 and D_2 are (in general different) specializations of D, so that E_1 and E_2 lie on different chains of recursive calls of C. To illustrate the technique, let us use the examples $E_1 = p(s^4(0), f^7(0))$ (that is, the same recursive example as before) and $E_2 = p(s^3(1), f^5(1))$.

In short,[12] the base clause D must be identified. Its arguments must be unifiable with subterms of E_1 and E_2. Hence, for each argument of E_1 its subterms and the corresponding embedding terms are first computed. For each tuple of embedding terms, the corresponding tuple of generating terms is then found. The same is done for E_2. In our examples, suppose the following subterms, embedding and generating terms have been found, from among the other possible:

E_1:
$st_1 = $ <s(0), f(0)>, $et_1 = $ <s^3(X), f^6(X)>, $gt_1 = $ <s(X), f^2(X)> (depth 3)
E_2:
$st_2 = $ <s(1), f(1)>, $et_2 = $ <s^2(X), f^4(X)>, $gt_2 = $ <s(X), f^2(X)> (depth 2)

Then, subterms of the arguments of E_1 and E_2 are paired. A pair is legal if the corresponding generating terms are the same (however, these generating terms may have different depths, as the corresponding examples can require different numbers of recursive calls to be proved). A legal pair in fact represents a pair of possible instances of the arguments of D. As a consequence, the arguments of D are computed as the least general generalization of each legal pair. In our example, s(0) can be paired with s(1), because the two subterms have the same generating term, s(X). The same is true for f(0) and f(1). As a consequence, a possible solution for clause D is computed as:

$D = $ p(lgg(s(0),s(1)), lgg(f(0),f(1))) = p(s(X), f(Y)).

The induced clause is checked against the provided negative examples and, if consistent, is used to learn the recursive clause C, as in LOPSTER.

CRUSTACEAN is less efficient than LOPSTER, since it must also learn the base clause of the target relation. It is proved to be complete with respect to the class of purely recursive logic programs [3].

An approach close to the technique illustrated in this section is the so-called *BMWk methodology*,[13] developed in [103] in the framework of the LISP notation

---

[12]The details can be found in [2] and in [3].
[13]BMWk stands for Boyer, Moore, Wegbreit, and Kodratoff.

([187]), and later readapted to the ILP setting ([119]). As in LOPSTER, within BMWk too sequences of terms are compared in order to discover recursive relations among them and to build functions accounting for the term sequence. Although developed independently, the BMWk methodology can be seen as an extension of the LOPSTER approach, since the class of functions BMWk can synthesize is larger. However, no implementation of BMWk in the ILP framework has been available until now.

We conclude with some remarks on the examples used in this section. Let C^2 = "p(s^2(X), f^4(Y)) :- p(X, Y)" be the self-resolvent of C = "p(s(X), f^2(Y)) :- p(X, Y)." First, clearly $C \to C^2$ but $C \npreceq C^2$. Following definition 19, we note that C is ambivalent. Second, By resolving C^2 and D = "p(s(X), f(Y))" we get F = p(s^3(X), f^5(Y)). It is easy to see that $F \preceq E_2$ = "p(s^3(1), f^5(1))." Moreover, $C \to E_2$, but $C \npreceq E_2$.

3.3.2 Finding structural regularities of literals

An approach in some way complementary to LOPSTER can be obtained by flattening clauses and then finding structural regularities of literals. This is Muggleton's approach to inverting implication [143]. First we introduce some notation.

Definition 21 *Given clauses C and D, D is an* nth power *of C iff D is an alphabetic variant of a clause in $\mathcal{L}^n(\{C\})$ for $n \geq 1$. We say that C is an* nth root *of D.*

We will also need the following:

Definition 22 *Given clauses C and D, D is an* indirect nth power *of clause C iff there exists a clause E such that E is an nth power of C and $E \preceq D$. We say that C is an* indirect nth root *of D.*

Definition 23 *Given clauses C and D such that D is an indirect nth power of C, we say that D is a* proper indirect nth power *of C iff $C \npreceq D$. We say that C is a* proper indirect nth root *of D.*

From the above definitions it follows that a root of a clause is also an indirect root of that clause. Moreover, by corollary 1, it follows that $C \to D$ if and only if C is an indirect root of D. For example, clause C^2 at the end of the previous section is a (proper indirect) second power of C, and C is a (proper indirect) second root of C^2.

Now, suppose we are given a clause D, and we want to find the nth root C of D, for some value n.

3.3. Inverse Implication

The first step is to flatten D in order to remove functional terms from the recursing literals. For each term, this is done by introducing a new variable and an equality literal for the new variable and the replaced term. For example, the clause:

$D =$ "p(s(s(s(X)))) :- p(X)."

is flattened to:

$D_f =$ "p(Y) :- Y = s(Z), Z = s(W), W = s(X), p(X)."

By using the equality axiom "X = X," clauses D and D_f are equivalent.

As a consequence of this transformation, structural regularities of terms that are the result of repeatedly self-resolving the sought clause C, are turned into structural regularities of literals that can now be investigated.[14] Moreover, it can be proved [143] that the most general unifier involved in self-resolving a flattened clause is just a renaming substitution, and that the composition of renaming substitutions is still a renaming substitution. As a consequence, the inversion of such a unifier is straightforward.

Let C_f be the flattened nth root of a given recursive clause D. The general structure of C_f is:

$C_f = l : -l', B, E.$

Where $|l|$ and $|l'|$ can be unified through the most general unifier $\theta_1 \theta_2$ (for simplicity, l and l' are taken to be variable disjoint), B is an arbitrary conjunction of literals and E is the conjunction of equality literals introduced in the flattening step.[15] Self-resolving C_f with respect to l and $\neg l'$ results in the second power (or the square) of C_f, whose form is the following:

$C_f^2 = l\theta_2 :- l'\theta_1, B\theta_1, B\theta_2, E\theta_1, E\theta_2.$

Self-resolving C_f^2 with C_f with respect to $l\theta_2$ and $\neg l'$ through the most general unifier $\sigma_1 \sigma_2$ gives the third power of C_f:

$C_f^3 = l\sigma_2 :- l'\theta_1\sigma_1, B\theta_1\sigma_1, B\theta_2\sigma_1, B\sigma_2, E\theta_1\sigma_1, E\theta_2\sigma_1, E\sigma_2.$

---

[14] However, it must be noted that this approach is more general than the one of the previous section, since handled clauses are not requested to be purely or left-recursive. For example, a clause D as "p(f(L,M),N,P) :- p(M,f(L,N),P)" can be handled by this approach, but not by LOPSTER.

[15] We recall that if l is a literal, then $|l|$ denotes the atom of literal l.

And so on for the other powers of C_f. Now, clause D_f being the nth power of C_f (i.e., $D_f = C_f^n$) for some n, the literals in D_f must follow some structural regularity, as C_f^2 and C_f^3 above. In fact, D_f (or C_f^n) must contain a pair of ambivalent literals, and the number of B and E literals must be a multiple of n. Suppose we know the value of n, and let B be empty for sake of simplicity. Then clause C_f can be built by:

1. identifying the pair of recursing literals $\{l\beta, \neg l'\alpha\}$ (the ambivalent pair);

2. finding two conjunctions of literals $E\alpha$ and $E\beta$ in $H = \{D_f - \{l\beta, \neg l'\alpha\}\}$, where $|E\alpha| = |E\beta| = |H|/n$, for some number n;

3. constructing E as the lgg of $E\alpha$ and $E\beta$, which are alphabetic variants;

4. constructing α and β by matching E to $E\alpha$ and $E\beta$;

5. applying β^{-1} and α^{-1} to $l\beta$ and $l'\alpha$, respectively, to get l and l';

6. returning $C_f = $ "l :- l', E."

Instead of going into the details of this procedure, we illustrate it on the clause $D_f = $ "p(Y) :- Y = s(Z), Z = s(W), W = s(X), p(X)." Let $n = 3$.

1. Let the chosen pair of ambivalent literals be $l\alpha = $ p(Y) and $l'\beta = $ p(X).

2. Let $E\alpha = \{$"Y = s(Z)"$\}$ and $E\beta = \{$"W = s(X)"$\}$. Note that the cardinality of $E\alpha$ is one-third of the cardinality of $\{D_f - \{l\beta, \neg l'\alpha\}\}$. The same is true for $E\beta$.

3. Let $E = \text{lgg}(E\alpha, E\beta) = $ "M = s(N)."

4. Let $\alpha = \{M/Y, N/Z\}$ and $\beta = \{M/W, N/X\}$. As a consequence, we have $\alpha^{-1} = \{Y/M, Z/N\}$ and $\beta^{-1} = \{W/M, X/N\}$.

5. Let $l = l\alpha\alpha^{-1} = $ p(M) and $l' = l\beta\beta^{-1} = $ p(N).

6. Let $C_f = $ "p(M) :- M = s(N), p(N)," whose unflattened version is $C = $ "p(s(N)) :- p(N)."

It is easy to see that C_f (C) is a third root of D_f (D).

Despite the simplicity of the above example, Muggleton's approach to inverting implication has some drawbacks. First, given a clause D_f that is an nth power, the value n is unknown, and must be guessed. Since $H = \{D_f - \{l\beta, \neg l'\alpha\}\}$ contains n instances of E, the number of occurrences of predicates and function symbols must be a multiple of n. Normally, this results in a small number of candidate values

3.3. Inverse Implication

for n that must be tested. However, the problem gets worse if B is not empty, and can also become unsolvable if some pairs of literals in "$B \wedge E$" become equivalent after some self-resolution, and therefore only one instance will appear in D_f.

Second, the proposed algorithm for computing nth roots of a clause is non-deterministic, and there is no evidence that it could be turned into a feasible deterministic implementation.

Third, as we saw for the LOPSTER system, which looks for generating terms of maximum depth, an overgeneral root can be found by guessing a too large (although legal) value for n.

Finally, when looking for a nth root "l :- l', B" of a given clause D, the algorithm assumes that D has been obtained by always resolving instances of the same pair of ambivalent literals l and l'. Clearly, this simplifying assumption can sometimes be wrong.

The kind of self-recursive clauses that this approach can handle is much more general than in LOPSTER. In principle, almost all (direct) roots of a given recursive clause can be found,[16] but dealing with proper indirect roots appears to be much more problematic. In fact, from corollary 1 we see that in order to find C, given D, we have first to build E such that $E \preceq D$. Muggleton suggests dropping literals from the canonical flattening of D until an appropriate number of occurrences of predicates and function symbols remains in E. Then compute the nth root of E. It is clear that this "generate and test" procedure is likely to be unfeasible or misleading: a wrong (but legal) clause could be learned by dropping the wrong literals. In particular, in order to deal only with renaming substitutions, E must be uninstantiated. This requires D itself to be uninstantiated; otherwise, "grounding" equality literals such as "X = a" must be dropped in the flattened version of D. This may result in a wrong generalization.

It must also be noted that this approach concerns the generalization of recursive clauses, and then has to be fitted into the usual ILP setting, i.e., when a background knowledge P is present and a positive example e^+ not entailed by P is given. By assuming that there is a single recursive clause C such that $P \wedge C \vdash e^+$, Muggleton suggests proceeding as in the GOLEM system:

$P \wedge C \vdash e^+$
$C \vdash P \rightarrow e^+$
$\vdash C \rightarrow (P \rightarrow e^+)$
$\vdash C \rightarrow \neg(P \wedge \neg e^+)$
$\vdash C \rightarrow \neg(l_1 \wedge \neg l_2 \wedge \ldots)$

---

[16] See [99] for an example of roots that cannot be handled by this technique.

Where $(l_1 \land \neg l_2 \land \ldots)$ is a conjunction of ground literals that can be derived from $(P \land \neg e^+)$, the clause $\neg(l_1 \land \neg l_2 \land \ldots)$ can then be used to construct C. Clearly, such a solution will suffer from the same problems as GOLEM.

Because of all the above problems and limitations, and since the technique has not been implemented nor tested in any system, the effectiveness of this approach for the ILP problem is still to be proved.

3.3.3 Finding internal and external connections

The most thorough work on generalization under implication is probably found in [99] (see also [102, 101, 100]). In this section we outline the generalization technique that is of interest for ILP: the so-called *generalization under recursive anti-unification*. This technique is concerned with finding indirect roots of clauses and *minimally general generalizations under implication*:

Definition 24 [99] *A Horn clause C is a* minimally general generalization under implication (MinGGI) *of clauses D and E iff:*
1) $C \to D$ and $C \to E$, and
2) for each Horn clause F such that $F \to D$, $F \to E$ and $C \to F$, then also $F \to C$.

The approach can be regarded as a development of the ideas in the LOPSTER system. It combines the techniques of the previous two subsections, and avoids most of their limitations.

Internal connections

An internal connection is (roughly) a relationship that can be found between two terms s and t occurring in the same *position*[17] in an ambivalent pair of literals[18] of a recursive clause C. Such a connection takes place when:

1. s is a subterm of t;

2. there is a sequence of terms $\sigma = [s_0, \ldots, s_n]$ such that $s_0 = s$, $s_n = t$, and s_i is a subterm of s_{i+1} for $0 \leq i \leq n\text{-}1$;

3. for each pair of terms (s_i, s_{i+1}) of σ, for $0 \leq i \leq n\text{-}1$, s_i is found in the same position in s_{i+1}.

---

[17]We will not go through a formalization of the notion of position. It will be clarified through some examples. See [99, 102, 100] for the precise definition.

[18]As a simplifying assumption, in the following, s and t will be taken to be the ith arguments of the two ambivalent literals, respectively.

3.3. Inverse Implication

For example [99], consider the following clause:

$C = p(a,b) \text{ :- } q(b,c), q(c,d), p(f^4(a),d).$

There is an internal connection between the first arguments of p(a,b) and p(f^4(a),d). We note that a is a subterm of f^4(a). In the sequence of terms $\sigma_1 = $ [a, f(a), f^2(a), f^3(a), f^4(a)] each term is a subterm of the next term. Finally, each term occurs in the same position as a subterm of the next term. This position is indicated as (f, 1). As a consequence, the complete sequence of positions for σ is $\pi_1 = $ [(f, 1), (f, 1), (f, 1), (f, 1)]. We note that a sequence of positions can itself be regarded as a position. In fact, π_1 is the position of a in f^4(a), since (f, 1) is the position of f^3(a) in f^4(a), (f, 1) is the position of f^2(a) in f^3(a), (f, 1) is the position of f(a) in f^2(a), and (f, 1) is the position of a in f(a). Thus, the internal connection from the term a to the term f^4(a) is indicated by the pair (σ_1, π_1).

It is easy to notice a regularity in the above (sequence of) position(s), since (f, 1) occurs four times in π_1. As a consequence, internal connections can be used to identify structural regularities of terms, in the spirit of the LOPSTER system.

External connections

An external connection is (roughly) another kind of relationship that can be found between two terms s and t occurring in the same position in an ambivalent pair of literals of a recursive clause C and such that:

1. there is a sequence of terms $\sigma = [s_0, \ldots, s_n]$ such that $s_0 = s$, $s_n = t$ and

2. there is a sequence of pairs of positions $\pi = [(p_1, q_1), \ldots, (p_n, q_n)]$ such that s_i is found in position p_{i+1} in L_i and s_{i+1} is found in position q_{i+1} in L_i for some literal $L_i \in C$ and for every $0 \leq i \leq$ n-1.

Consider again the clause C of the last example. There is an external connection between the arguments b and d of the ambivalent literals. In fact, the sequence of terms $\sigma_2 = $ [b, c, d] is such that the terms b and c are found in positions ($\neg$q, 1) and ($\neg$q, 2) in the literal $\neg$q(b, c). The term c is also found in position ($\neg$q, 1) in the literal $\neg$q(c, d), and in that literal, the term d is found in position ($\neg$q, 2). The resulting sequence of pairs of positions is $\pi_2 = $ [<($\neg$q, 1), ($\neg$q, 2)>, <($\neg$q, 1), ($\neg$q, 2)>]. This external connection can be indicated with (σ_2, π_2).

Here, too, we notice a regularity in this sequence of pairs of positions, since the pair <($\neg$q, 1), ($\neg$q, 2)> occurs twice in π_2. As a consequence, external connections can be used to identify structural regularities among literals,[19] in the spirit

---
[19]However, it must be noted that not all external connections lead to a structural regularity among literals. The same is true for internal connections.

of Muggleton's approach [143]. For example, it is not difficult to notice an external connection between the terms Y and X of the ambivalent literals in clause D_f of the example of subsection 3.3.2.

Recursive anti-unification

When a clause is repeatedly self-resolved, pairs of terms occurring in the same position in the recursing literals are repeatedly unified, resulting in more and more specific terms. The initial terms can be reconstructed by repeatedly *anti-unifying* the pairs of terms that were unified in each resolution step. Since unification is the dual of least general generalization for terms, recursive anti-unification can be performed as a repeated computation of the lgg of pairs of terms.[20]

Clearly, the number of anti-unifications to apply must be equal to the number of performed self-resolutions. As we saw in the previous approaches to inverse implication, this number can be identified by analyzing the sequence of positions of internal and external connections, in order to find common factors. Consider π_1 above. It can be factorized by 4, getting the divisor $<(f, 1)>$, or by 2, with divisor $<(f, 1), (f, 1)>$ (as we saw previously, the factor 1 is trivial and is not considered). Similarly, π_2 can be factorized by 2, with divisor $<(\neg q, 1), (\neg q, 2)>$. Only one factor, 2, is common to π_1 and π_2. This indicates that we are looking for a second indirect root E of C, with respect to the connections (σ_1, π_1) and (σ_2, π_2).

Now, an identified sequence of terms $\sigma = [s_0, ..., s_n]$ is the result of the sequence of unifications applied when the sought clause E is repeatedly self-resolved. Hence, repeated anti-unifications must be performed backward on σ, in order to retrieve the original pair of terms that produced σ. It is important to notice that in σ, only some of the terms are meaningful and must be taken into consideration. Roughly speaking, these are the i terms that are found at regular intervals between s_1 and s_n, where i is the identified factor for σ. Intuitively, (only) these terms are the intermediate result of unifications due to repeated self-resolutions. In our example, only the terms $f^2(a)$ and $f^4(a)$ are meaningful in the sequence σ_1 (apart from a), because of the identified factor 2, indicating that E is self-resolved once to get C. On the other hand, all the terms of σ_1 would have been considered for the factor 4.

The meaningful terms are then recursively anti-unified. This is done by anti-unifying the first elements of the last two pairs of terms. The same is done for the second elements of the two pairs, resulting in a new pair of terms.[21] This pair is then used to anti-unify the last but two pairs of terms, and so on until the first

---

[20]In fact, "anti-unification" is the term used in Idestam-Almquist's approach for least general generalization when applied to terms and atoms.

[21]Pairs of terms must overlap. Given the sequence of terms $[t_1, ..., t_n]$, the last pair is (t_{n-1}, t_n), the last but one pair is (t_{n-2}, t_{n-1}), the last but two is (t_{n-3}, t_{n-2}), and so on.

3.3. Inverse Implication

pair of (the sequence of meaningful) terms is reached. We illustrate the technique with an example. A formal definition of recursive anti-unification can be found in [99, 102, 100].

Consider the sequence σ_1 and the factor 2. The meaningful terms are a, $f^2(a)$, $f^4(a)$. The anti-unification of the pair (a, $f^2(a)$) (that is, computing the lgg of the two terms) and the anti-unification of the pair ($f^2(a)$, $f^4(a)$) produces the pair (X, $f^2(X)$). This is the result of the recursive anti-unification of the pair of terms (a, $f^4(a)$) relative to the connection (σ_1, π_1) and the factor 2. Moreover, consider the substitution of terms with variables occurred in the two anti-unifications. The terms a and $f^2(a)$ are replaced by X. This is indicated as $\tau_1 = \{(a, f^2(a))/X\}$, and is called a *term substitution*.[22]

We also report the recursive anti-unification of the pair of terms (a, $f^4(a)$) relative to the connection (σ_1, π_1) and the factor 4. First, the two pairs ($f^2(a)$, $f^3(a)$) and ($f^3(a)$, $f^4(a)$) are anti-unified, producing $\alpha_1 = (f^2(X), f^3(X))$. Second, the pair (f(a), $f^2(a)$) is anti-unified with α_1, producing $\alpha_2 = (f(Y), f^2(Y))$. Third, the pair (a, f(a)) is anti-unified with α_2, producing the final anti-unification $\alpha_3 = (Z, f(Z))$. The resulting term substitution is $\{(a, f(a))/X, (a, f(X))/Y, (a, f(Y))/Z\}$. This is obtained as the composition of the term substitutions of each anti-unification.

Finally, we compute the recursive anti-unification of the pair of terms (b, d) relative to the connection (σ_2, π_2) and the factor 2. It is (Y, Z), and is achieved by the anti-unification of the pairs (b, c) and (c, d), with the term substitution $\tau_2 = \{(b, c)/Y, (c, d)/Z\}$.

Computing indirect roots and MinGGIs

Indirect nth roots of a given clause C can be computed by replacing connected pairs of terms by their respective recursive anti-unifications. In our example, we have seen that the recursive anti-unification of (a, $f^4(a)$) relative to (σ_1, π_1) and the factor 2 is (X, $f^2(X)$), with the term substitution $\tau_1 = \{(a, f^2(a))/X\}$. The recursive anti-unification of (b, d) relative to (σ_2, π_2) and the factor 2 is (Y, Z), with the term substitution $\tau_2 = \{(b, c)/Y, (c, d)/Z\}$. We can build a second indirect root of C by replacing a by X and b by Y in the literal p(a,b), and replacing $f^4(a)$ by $f^2(X)$ and d by Z in the literal p($f^4(a)$, d). We obtain the clause:

D = p(X, Y) :- q(b, c), q(c, d), p($f^2(X)$, Z).

---

[22]Formally, $\tau = \{(s_1,t_1)/X_1, ..., (s_n,t_n)/X_n\}$ is the *term substitution* of the anti-unification (or lgg) G of two terms E and F if and only if $G\{X_1/s_1, ..., X_n/s_n\} = E$ and $G\{X_1/t_1, ..., X_n/t_n\} = F$.

There is also an external connection from b to d in C, and so there must be an external connection from Y to Z in D. To get a connection between Y and Z we must anti-unify q(b, c) and q(c, d) using the term substitution τ_2, yielding q(Y, Z). As a consequence, we get the indirect root:

$$E = \text{p(X, Y)} :\!\!- \text{q(Y, Z), p(f}^2\text{(X), Z)}.$$

The clause E includes all found connections between the terms of the clause C.

Minimally general generalizations under implication of two clauses C and D are computed following the same procedure as above, but two extra conditions are required: (1) the recursive pairs of terms of each clause must be found in the same positions; (2) the divisors of the corresponding connections in each clause must be equal. If these conditions are met, a MinGGI of C and D is computed by (a) taking the *greatest common divisor* of the connections of C and D; (b) computing the indirect roots C_{ir} and D_{ir} of C and D, respectively, relative to the greatest common divisor; and (c) computing the least general generalization of C_{ir} and D_{ir}. Examples of computation of MinGGIs can be found in [99], [102], and [100].

The computation of MinGGIs of sets of clauses helps to avoid the overgeneralization problems of the previously described approaches to inverse implication, which concentrate on finding "typical" roots. Also, the use of background knowledge (a set of recursive clauses) is allowed and important.

Recursive anti-unification can compute almost every indirect root of clauses. The only kind of clauses it cannot deal with are those involving the so-called *cross connections*, such as, for example, "married(X, Y) :- married(Y, X)." This clause is recursive, but the position of X in married(X, Y) is not a subposition of the position of X in married(Y, X), nor vice versa. Fortunately, such clauses are rarely used.

The efficiency of the technique is polynomial if limited to internal connections, but becomes exponential with the size of the input clauses, when external connections must be computed. This happens because different ordering of literals must be considered, in order to find a suitable external connection. In some way, this agrees with the efficiency of the LOPSTER system and the (apparent) inefficiency of Muggleton's approach.

Recursive anti-unification must still be fitted in the classical ILP framework. However, its generality, the ability to deal with background knowledge, and its (partial) efficiency are promising features.

4

Top-down Methods

Top-down ILP methods learn programs by generating clauses one after the other, and generate clauses by means of specialization. If we are willing to accept a great deal of approximation and simplification, this is, in general, what they do:

while some positive example is not covered by C∈P **do**
        Generate one clause C
        Remove positive examples covered by C
        add C to P

where the generation of a clause C is as follows:

Select a predicate P that must be learned
C ← $P(\vec{X})$:- true.
while C covers some negative example **do**
        Select a literal L
        Add L to the antecedent of C
        if C does not cover any positive example **then**
            backtrack to different choices for L
return C (or fail if backtracking exhausts all choices for L).

The refinement phase of the MIS system presented in the next section is based on similar principles, and the FOIL system presented in Section 4.2 matches quite closely the above algorithm.

    Most top-down systems (e.g. FOIL[160], ML-SMART[17], FOCL[155], MIS[176], FILP[21]) use an *extensional criterion* for verifying whether a clause

$P(\vec{X}) \text{ :- } \alpha(\vec{X}, \vec{Y}), Q(\vec{X}, \vec{Y}, \vec{Z}), \gamma.$

"covers" an example $P(\vec{a})$. If we suppose that α and γ are defined in the background knowledge BK, whereas Q is a predicate that we want to learn (e.g. P=Q), extensional evaluation works as follows:

1. Obtain $\vec{b}$ such that $BK \vdash \alpha(\vec{a}, \vec{b})$.

2. Ask a type II existential query $\exists \vec{Z}\ Q(\vec{a}, \vec{b}, \vec{Z})$, obtaining, e.g., $\vec{Z}=\vec{c}$. Alternatively, just check whether there is a tuple $\vec{c}$ of constants such that $Q(\vec{a}, \vec{b}, \vec{c})$, is a positive example of Q.

3. Check whether $BK \vdash \gamma[\vec{X}/\vec{a},\ \vec{Y}/\vec{b},\ \vec{Z}/\vec{c}]$.

More formally, if E^+ is the set of positive examples, be they given initially or queried later, a clause $P(\vec{X})$:- α is said to *extensionally cover* an example $P(\vec{a})$ if BK, E^+ is $\vdash \alpha[\vec{X}/\vec{a}]$. A similar notion of extensional coverage for functional logic programs is defined in chapter 7 and is used in the FILP system.

As an example, if the following knowledge is given:

E^+:
$e_1 = $ append([a,b],[c,d],[a,b,c,d])
$e_2 = $ append([b],[c,d],[b,c,d])
$e_3 = $ tail([a,b],[b])

BK:
head([A|_],A).
cons(C,D,[C|D]).

then the clause:

C= append(X,Y,Z) :- head(X,H), tail(X,T), append(T,Y,W), cons(H,W,Z).

extensionally covers e_1. In fact, $BK \vdash $ head([a,b],H), with H = a; if T gets the value [b], then tail([a,b],[b]) is a positive example of *tail*; append([b],[c,d],[b,c,d]) is a positive example of *append*; and $BK \vdash $ cons(a,[b,c,d],Z), with Z = [a,b,c,d].

One should note that with extensional coverage, the evaluation of a clause requires consideration only of that particular clause, of the positive examples, and of the background knowledge. We do not need to worry about the other clauses in the final learned program. On the positive side, clause evaluations are thus independent, the generation of a clause does not influence the evaluation of others, and no backtracking is required at this level. On the negative side, we must realize that the final use of the learned program will not be extensional, and clause antecedents will be evaluated by subcalls to other clauses, not by looking at the positive examples. As a consequence, unexpected results may be observed and the behavior of the learned program may differ from learning time to run time. This issue is analyzed in detail in chapter 7. For the time being, we study two well-known learning systems, MIS and FOIL, that use extensional evaluation and top-down specialization as an essential part of their algorithms.

4.1 Shapiro's Model Inference System

In the early 1980s, Ehud Shapiro developed the Model Inference System (MIS). This represents the first explicit approach to the inductive synthesis of logic programs after Logic Programming had become an established discipline and more people became interested in Prolog as a programming language. The Model Inference System is so called because it infers a finite axiomatization of an unknown model M from the ground facts that are true and false in M. This finite axiomatization is described by means of Horn clauses. The method is *incremental*, in the sense discussed in section 2.3: it maintains a current inductive hypothesis (a logic program P) and modifies it as new examples are provided. The hypothesized program P may have to be modified for two reasons: (1) $P \vdash e$ but e is false in M, (2) $P \nvdash e$ but e is true in M. In case (1) P must be made weaker, and in case (2) it must be strengthened.

P can be weakened either by removing one of its clauses (as done in MIS) or by making a clause weaker, e.g., by adding literals to its body. P can be strengthened either by adding a new clause (as done in MIS) or by making one of its clauses more general, e.g., by removing literals from its body. MIS keeps doing modifications of type (1) or (2) until a complete and consistent program is obtained; then it will be ready to read a new example. Here is the basic scheme of the algorithm:

P ← the program containing only the empty clause
repeat
read a new example
while P is not consistent with the available examples **do**
        if $P \vdash e$ and e is a negative example, **then**
           make P weaker
        if $P \nvdash e$ and e is a positive example, **then**
           make P stronger
forever
Exception: if checking whether $P \vdash e$ requires a number of resolution steps greater

than h(e), call a *divergence check* procedure that will remove a clause from P.

The function h returns an upper bound for the computational effort required when calling the target program P on a given goal. More precisely, a program P, intended to axiomatize an unknown model M, is said to be h-easy when:
(1) if e is true in M, P $\vdash$ e, and the depth of the corresponding SLD proof tree is at most h(e) and
(2) if e is false in M, P $\nvdash$ e, with a finitely failed proof tree of maximum depth h(e). A model M is said to be h-easy if it may be axiomatized by an h-easy program. Related notions were discussed in subsection 3.1.2.

Making P weaker or stronger could, in principle, require a search in the space of all possible logic programs. MIS avoids this by querying the user for the truth value of particular atoms, i.e., it is based on an extensional evaluation of clauses. As a result, the weakening of P has a complexity that is proportional to the depth of the proof tree for P $\vdash$ e, and making P stronger requires only a search in the space of all possible Horn clauses.

Weakening P is accomplished by means of a "contradiction backtracing" algorithm. If e is a negative example, it will be represented as :-e. From this and P, we obtain the empty clause, since P $\vdash$ e. The proof tree for the empty clause is then processed as follows:

start from the root (the empty clause);
at any node, query the user for the truth value of the atom resolved upon
      (a type I existential query);
if it is true, move to the clause containing the atom in the body,
      otherwise move to the clause having the atom as its head;
repeat the above until a leaf is reached;
remove the corresponding clause from P.

The rationale for this procedure is that if the atom resolved upon is true, then the clause having this atom as its head is not necessarily wrong. By contrast, as the resolvent is wrong, the clause using this true atom in its body must be wrong. If it is a leaf, it must be removed; otherwise, the mistake must be found higher up in the proof tree leading to this clause.

For example, suppose MIS has seen the following examples of *member*:

member(2,[4,3,2]). member(2,[2,3]). :-member(2,[4]).

The first two are positive and the third is negative. Suppose also that MIS's current hypothesis is:

4.1. Shapiro's Model Inference System

member(X,[Y|Z]) :- Y=2.
member(X,[Y|Z]) :- member(X,Z).

The above program is consistent with the examples, but if the new negative example member(3,[4,2]) is input, a contradiction is obtained with the proof tree of figure 4.1. As a consequence, the contradiction backtracing algorithm is called:

member(3,[4,2]) is resolved at the root, and is false; we move right,
member(3,[2]) is resolved, and the user marks it as false; we move right,
"2 is 2" is resolved, and the user marks it as true; we move left,
a leaf is reached, and the clause "member(X,[Y|Z]) :- Y=2." is removed.

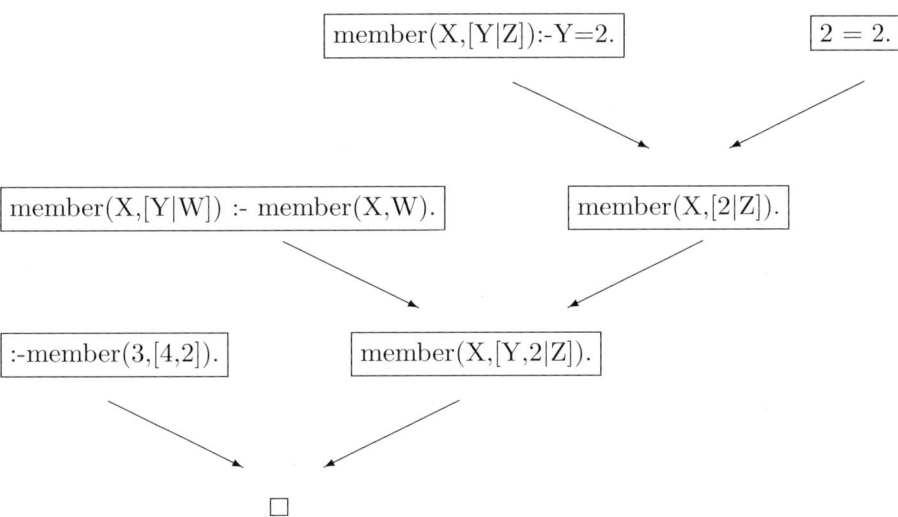

Figure 4.1: A proof tree for contradiction backtracing

Existential queries of type I are all ground in the example of figure 4.1, i.e., they reduce to membership queries. In general, existential variables may occur.

Suppose that the current hypothesis P consists of the following clauses:

r(X,2,T) :- s(X).
s(1).
p(X,Y) :- r(X,Y,Z).

After the negative example p(1,2) is seen, the contradiction backtracing algorithm would be called as $P \vdash p(1,2)$. Which existential query of type I would be asked? What are the possible answers to the query and what is their effect?

Strengthening P may be done by searching a "refinement graph" of clauses. If $P \not\vdash Q(c_1, ..., c_n)$ and $Q(c_1, ..., c_n)$ is a positive example, then the refining process is triggered. MIS starts this process from the empty clause. Here, for simplicity, we may suppose that we begin with the clause $Q(X_1, ..., X_n)$, which as an empty body. Clauses are refined by means of repeated specialization steps that make them weaker. As the ways to do that are many, MIS requires a "refinement operator" that can be changed by the user. The refinement operator outputs a list of clauses that are immediate specializations of the given clause. Here is an example:

Refinement Operator R1:
Let the input clause C be "$Q(X_1, ..., X_n) :- \alpha(X_1, ..., X_n, Y_1, ..., Y_m).$," where α is a (possibly empty) conjunction of literals.
Then, refinements of C are obtained by adding to its body a literal $R(Z_1, ..., Z_p)$, where Z_i is either X_j, Y_k, or a new variable, for $1 \leq i \leq p$, $1 \leq j \leq n$ and $1 \leq k \leq m$. Moreover, we require that the predicate Q be defined by the user as "depending"[1] on the predicate R.

Suppose, for instance, that we define *member* as depending on the predicate *cons* (defined by cons(X,Y,[X|Y])) and on itself. Then the above operator is adequate for MIS to learn a logic program for *member*.

The refinement operator determines a search graph of Horn clauses, the refinement graph. MIS will explore this graph. As in most top-down systems, some kind of pruning is obtained, based on the following simple observation: if a clause C does not cover the positive example, its more specific refinements will also fail to cover that example, and the refinement graph below C can be ignored. Breadth-first search guarantees that solutions are not lost. The first clause that covers the new positive example and was not previously removed by contradiction backtracing is output and added to the current hypothesis. The added clause, if wrong, may be removed by a later call of the contradiction backtracing algorithm.

---

[1] This notion of dependency is related to later work on determinations [170], graphs of predicates [107, 190], and Clause Sets (section 6.5)

4.1. Shapiro's Model Inference System

In order to check whether a clause $Q(X_1, ..., X_n) \text{ :- } \alpha(X_1, ..., X_n, Y_1, ..., Y_m)$ covers the example $Q(c_1, ..., c_n)$, MIS has to evaluate the clause body after substituting $c_1, ..., c_n$ for $X_1, ..., X_n$. The most powerful method adopted by MIS for this purpose is called the *eager* strategy [176] and asks the user for the truth value of each literal occurring in the antecedent after the substitution. Existential variables need to be instantiated, and therefore we need existential queries of type II. If all literals are marked as true, then the example is covered. Alternatively, MIS can use the *lazy* strategy: a literal in the body of the clause is considered to be true only when it matches a positive example that was previously given by the user. The advantage of the lazy strategy is that it does not bother the user with queries. However, it may lead to errors: a clause may be considered to cover some example although it does not, or vice versa. As a consequence, it may happen more frequently that wrong clauses are added to the program P that is being developed, or correct clauses may fail to be considered. Only after a sufficient number of examples are input to the system, will MIS be able to recover from such errors. An intermediate choice consists in the *adaptive* strategy: as in the lazy strategy, a literal is marked as true if it matches a given positive example, but in this case, also when it may be deduced from the current hypothesis P. More precisely, let E^+ be the set of positive examples given up to the evaluation moment: a literal is considered to be true if it may be deduced from $P \cup E^+$. As in the lazy strategy, the covering test may give wrong results, but errors may be less frequent when the current program P starts to be a good approximation of the desired program.

As an example, consider again the above problem of learning *member*. The clause "member(X,[Y|Z]) :- Y=2." was removed by the contradiction backtracking algorithm. Let us rewrite this clause in its equivalent flattened form, so that the above refinement operator **R1** can be used without complicated changes:

member(X,T) :- cons(Y,Z,T), two(Y).

where two(2) is a given initial clause of P. After removing the flattened clause for *member*, the example member(2,[2,3]) is no longer covered. Below are some refinements of the clause produced with the above operator:

(1) member(X,T) :- cons(Y,Z,T), two(Y), member(X,Z).
(2) member(X,T) :- cons(Y,Z,T), two(Y), member(Y,Z).
(3) member(X,T) :- cons(Y,Z,T), two(Y), cons(X,Z,T).

The first and second clauses, if the *eager* strategy is used, produce the query "member(2,[3])." The user will answer that this atom is false, and the clauses are discarded because they do not cover the example. The third clause is immediately found to cover the example, as all the predicates in the body are predefined list-structure descriptors. If it was not previously marked by contradiction backtracing, the third clause would then be added to the program P (in fact, it could not possibly be marked, as it is true in the unknown model M for *member*, and there would be no counterexamples). It should be noted that the added clause is not wrong, but is not sufficient for defining *member*. Moreover, after the correct clause "member(X,[X|_])." is found, the above refined clause will become redundant. This minor problem can be solved only with a postprocessing step that looks for subsets of the generated clauses that are still sufficient to derive the positive examples. The system MARKUS [84], an improved implementation of MIS, does this redundancy check every time a new clause is added.

We still need to discuss the *divergence check* procedure that is called by the main loop in MIS whenever checking whether $P \vdash e$ exceeds the resource bound $h(e)$. This happens when a clause

C = p(X,Y) :- α(X,Y,Z), q(X,Y,Z,W), β.

is called, in the following circumstances:

(1) we are trying, for example, to prove p(a,Y),
(2) the subcall to α(a,Y,Z) succeeds, e.g., for Z=b.
(3) q(a,Y,b,W) is called and $h(p(a,Y)) \leq h(q(a,Y,b,W))$.

In other words, the application of this clause did not bring us one step closer to termination. This may happen for two reasons: (1) the value Z=b computed by the subcall to α is wrong, or (2) clause C is the cause of the resource bound $h(e)$ being exceeded. In case (1), there is a wrong output for some input, and we may simply call the contradiction backtracing procedure to remove some other clause that is responsible for this. In case (2) we remove clause C. In order to discriminate between case (1) and case (2), we do a number of type I existential queries, yielding a truth value for α(a,Y,b). A more extensive treatment of divergence check and termination diagnosis is found in [176].

We conclude by summarizing the identification in the limit results for MIS. Suppose the model M to be identified is h-easy, i.e., suppose that there is a complete and consistent program P that is h-easy. Suppose also that one such program P contains clauses that may be generated by successive refinements of the empty clause, i.e., that P is contained in the space $\mathcal{P}$ of possible programs. Under the above assumptions, we have:

(1) MIS, equipped with the eager strategy, identifies M in the limit.

(2) MIS, equipped with the lazy strategy, or with the adaptive strategy, will identify M in the limit if the presentation of M "conforms" with h: whenever e_1 is an example given before e_2, then $h(e_1) \leq h(e_2)$.

The discussion of divergence check and of identification in the limit may be made more general by replacing the use of the resource bound function h with an arbitrary well-order relation between goals. An extensive discussion of identification in the limit in MIS is found in [175]. In the same work, there is a definition of a general refinement operator that may produce all possible clauses with given function and predicate symbols. This eliminates, from a theoretical perspective, the requirement that the h-easy program P belong to the space $\mathcal{P}$ of possible programs, the programs containing clauses that may be generated in the refinement graph.

4.2 FOIL

The FOIL learning system [160, 161] has been widely used in the ILP community and even by Machine Learning researchers at large. Its efficient implementation is distributed worldwide, and the performance of any new ILP system has been typically compared against the one of FOIL in a number of typical application domains. The method is purely top-down and follows closely the algorithm given at the very beginning of this chapter. The only difference is that in the generation of a new clause, there is no backtracking: once a literal L is added to the antecedent of the clause being generated, it will be kept there, and no alternative choice will be considered. In order to further describe the method, we will use the example given in [160] while abstracting from some low-level implementation details.

Consider the directed graph in figure 4.2.

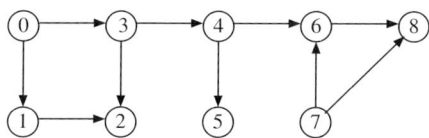

Figure 4.2: A directed graph

This graph may also be described in symbolic form by listing all its arcs as part of a relation called *link*. The tuple $<n, m>$ belongs to the relation *link* if there is a directed arc from node n to node m. The following symbolic description is obtained:

link: = <0,1>,<0,3>,<1,2>,<3,2>,<3,4>,<4,5>,<4,6>,<6,8>,<7,6>,<7,8>.

The above *link* relation, when translated into Prolog facts of the type link(n,m), may be seen as a simple form of background knowledge. We would now like to learn, with FOIL, the concept of reachability in this graph, i.e., a relation called *can-reach*, with the following positive and negative examples:

E^+ can-reach(0,1), can-reach(0,2),
         can-reach(0,3), ... (19 examples)
E^- can-reach(0,0), can-reach(0,7),
         can-reach(1,0), ... (6? examples)

FOIL is able to produce the following correct Prolog definition of *can-reach*:

can-reach(X,Y) :- link(X,Y).
can-reach(X,Y) :- link(X,Z), can-reach(Z,Y).

Below, we will see how this is done. As detailed in the beginning of this chapter, clauses will be generated one at a time. Let us start with the first clause, then. Initially, the clause body is empty, and we have to add the first literal. This situation may be pictured as follows:

can-reach(X,Y) :- ?.

FOIL only considers predicates that occur in the examples or in the background knowledge. Then the literals that may be added are listed below, together with some related information:

link(X,Y)	covers 10 positive, 0 negative
link(Y,X)	covers 0 positive, 10 negative
link(X,Z)	covers 19 positive, 35 negative
link(Z,Y)	covers 19 positive, 45 negative
link(Z,W) or can-reach(Z,W)	disallowed (no "old" variable)
can-reach(X,Y) or can-reach(Y,X)	disallowed (termination not guaranteed)
can-reach(X,Z) or can-reach(Z,Y)	disallowed (termination not guaranteed)

For each literal L that is allowed, we have listed on the right the number of positive and negative examples of *can-reach* that are extensionally covered by the clause

can-reach(X,Y) :- L.

where extensional covering is defined as in the beginning of this chapter. The other literals are disallowed and are not considered. Some are disallowed because they do not contain at least one "old" variable, i.e., a variable that occurs in previously added literals or in the head of the clause. This is a peculiar choice wired in the FOIL system in order to reduce the hypothesis space. The last four literals are disallowed because of termination problems. In general, FOIL will allow for recursive clauses only of the following type:

p(X_1, ..., X_i, ..., X_n) :- ..., q(X_i,Y), ..., p(X_1, ..., Y, ..., X_n), ...

where q is a relation given in the background knowledge that is found to be a well-order relation. This restriction aims at avoiding nonterminating recursive clauses (see also sections 6.5 and 7.3, and [38]).

We must now choose the literal to be added to the body of the clause. In this case the choice is indeed simple. The first literal, link(X,Y), is the best from all points of view. In fact, the obtained clause will cover ten positive examples and no negative example, and thus represents a consistent and useful description of reachability. Precisely because there are no covered negative examples to get rid of, generation of the first clause stops, and

can-reach(X,Y) :- link(X,Y).

is added to the learned program; it will not be removed or reconsidered. The 10 covered positive examples are removed. FOIL would now proceed to the generation of the second clause. Again, the clause body is initially empty. The literals that may possibly be added are the same as above, but we list them again, because the number of covered positive examples has obviously changed:

link(X,Y)	covers 0 positive, 0 negative
link(Y,X)	covers 0 positive, 10 negative
link(X,Z)	covers 9 positive, 35 negative
link(Z,Y)	covers 9 positive, 45 negative

... (other literals are disallowed just as for the first clause)

The first two literals are useless, as they lead to covering no positive examples. The third literal is better than the fourth, as it covers fewer negative examples. The third literal is then added to the clause antecedent, but the process is not finished; the remaining 35 negative examples that are covered need to be excluded. We now have the situation:

can-reach(X,Y) :- link(X,Z), ?.

where the question mark has to be replaced by a new literal, and possible choices are as follows:

link(X,Y)	covers 0 positive, 0 negative
link(Y,X)	covers 0 positive, 10 negative
link(X,Z)	disallowed (already present)
link(Z,Y)	covers 5 positive, 0 negative
link(W,Y)	covers 9 positive, 24 negative
link(Z,W)	covers 9 positive, 19 negative
link(W,Z), link(X,W)	covers 9 positive, 35 negative
link(W,T), can-reach(W,T)	disallowed (no "old" variable)
can-reach(X,Y), can-reach(Y,X), can-reach(X,Z), can-reach(X,W)	
can-reach(W,Y), can-reach(Z,W), can-reach(W,Z)	
	disallowed (termination)
can-reach(Z,Y)	covers 9 positive, 0 negative

Two of the possible literals — link(Z,Y) and can-reach(Z,Y) — produce a clause that is consistent, but can-reach(Z,Y) is preferable, as it also leads to covering all the remaining positive examples. The generation of this clause is then finished, no positive examples remain to be covered, and no other clauses need be generated. The obtained program is

can-reach(X,Y) :- link(X,Y).
can-reach(X,Y) :- link(X,Z), can-reach(Z,Y).

This program is also correct in the sense that all and only the positive examples can be derived from it. The reason why things work out so well and cases when problems arise will be discussed in full detail in chapter 7.

Here, we would like to analyze the problem of choosing a suitable literal to be added to the body of the clause being generated. Suppose FOIL has to choose between literals $Q(\vec{X},\vec{Y},\vec{Z})$ and $R(\vec{X},\vec{Y},\vec{Z})$, to replace the question mark in the clause

$P(\vec{X})$:- $S(\vec{X},\vec{Y})$, ?.

We have seen informally, in the reachability example, that the general principle is to cover extensionally as many positive examples as possible while excluding negative examples. In order to formalize this intuition, we introduce the following quantities:

$T^+ = |\{<\vec{X},\vec{Y}> \text{ such that } <\vec{X}> \in P^+ \text{ and } <\vec{X},\vec{Y}> \in S^+\}|$

$T^- = |\{<\vec{X},\vec{Y}> \text{ such that } <\vec{X}> \in P^- \text{ and } <\vec{X},\vec{Y}> \in S^+\}|$

$T_Q^+ = |\{<\vec{X},\vec{Y},\vec{X}> \text{ such that } <\vec{X},\vec{Y}> \in T^+ \text{ and } <\vec{X},\vec{Y},\vec{Z}> \in Q^+\}|$

$T_Q^- = |\{<\vec{X},\vec{Y},\vec{Z}> \text{ such that } <\vec{X},\vec{Y}> \in T^- \text{ and } <\vec{X},\vec{Y},\vec{Z}> \in Q^+\}|$

$T_Q^{++} = |\{<\vec{X},\vec{Y}> \text{ such that } <\vec{X},\vec{Y},\vec{Z}> \in T_Q^+\}|$

4.2. FOIL

$$\text{Gain}(Q) = T_Q^{++}(I - I_Q)$$
$$\text{where } I = -\log_2(T^+/(T^+ + T^-))$$
$$I_Q = -\log_2(T_Q^+/(T_Q^+ + T_Q^-))$$

and, for any relation V, V^+ is the set of argument tuples corresponding to the positive examples of V or derived from the background knowledge.

The quantity Gain(R) is computed accordingly. FOIL will choose the literal with the higher gain, and this choice leads, in fact, to covering more positive and fewer negative examples. This is explained by simple inspection of the above formulas for computing the gain: when I_Q grows, the proportion of covered positive examples becomes smaller. Gain may be effective for clause specialization, but it must be understood that it is a *heuristic* measure — in some cases it may give wrong advice. In FOIL, such cases are particularly serious, because backtracking to different literal choices is not possible. As a consequence, FOIL may fail to find a solution even if it exists, i.e., FOIL is not complete. There are also other facts that make FOIL incomplete, and these will be discussed in chapter 7.

The main reason why the gain measure may produce wrong results is that it implements a greedy search with a one-literal look ahead. It may happen that two literals, A and B, have very low or zero gain, while their conjunction $A \wedge B$ has high gain and is necessary to produce a correct result. In this case, FOIL may choose another literal, C, that could prevent further specializations from covering any positive example. This has been called the "plateau problem" [164]: in the body of the correct clause, gain remains low and constant (on a plateau) until one final important literal concludes the computation and brings the gain to a local maximum. To illustrate this phenomenon, consider the problem of learning the recursive clause of *append*. Suppose the following positive and negative examples are given:

E^+ append([0],[1,2],[0,1,2]), append([],[1,2],[1,2]), ...
E^- append([0],[1,2],[0,1]), append([0],[1,2],[1,2]),
         append(0,1,[0,1]), append(a,b,[a,b]), ...

The target clause is:

append(X,Y,Z) :- list(X), head(X,X1), tail(X,X2),
                 append(X2,Y,W), cons(X1,W,Z).

FOIL should add the literals in the body one at a time. The first literal, list(X), could in fact be selected, because it excludes the last two negative examples and thus has a nonzero gain. However, the following three literals would all have low or even negative gain, and they do not affect the output variable Z. In other words, gain remains on a plateau until the last literal is reached and all remaining negative examples are excluded. To avoid these problems, various techniques have been analyzed. For example, the concept of *relational cliché* [179] leads to a greedy search with a look-ahead that is greater than one literal, depending on the available domain knowledge. This and other improvements will be studied in chapter 6.

5
A Unifying Framework

As we have seen in the previous two chapters, the bottom-up approach to ILP is theoretically well formalized in terms of inversion of some deductive rule, namely, subsumption, resolution, or implication. Conversely, the top-down approach is often considered too empirical and heuristic, without a strong formal basis. Moreover, most top-down systems do not search the whole hypothesis space but use statistical information to guide the search.

In this chapter we show that the extensional top-down approach to ILP can be reformulated as a special kind of theorem proving that involves inverse resolution but not inverse substitutions. As a consequence, we get a formalization of top-down methods, and most top-down and bottom-up approaches turn out to fit into a unifying framework based on inverse resolution.[1] We begin by showing how to do theorem proving by means of inverse resolution.[2]

5.1 Theorem Proving with Inverse Resolution

Inverse resolution can be used to do theorem proving by inverting the derivation process based on resolution, in order to go from the empty clause to the given clause set instead of vice versa, as usual. The idea is to base the task on the particular form of the given clauses. In case of ground clauses, a clause is generated by means of inverse resolution only if it is a subset of one of the given clauses. The process ends when all clauses (or at least a minimally unsatisfiable[3]

---

[1] A different unifying temptative, based on the semantics of ILP has been proposed in [13].
[2] The content of this chapter is mainly theoretical. Since the rest of the book does not rely on the given results, it may be skipped.
[3] A set of clauses S is *minimally unsatisfiable* if it is unsatisfiable but every proper subset of S is satisfiable.

subset of them) have been reconstructed. If read in reverse order, this appears just like a usual refutation of the given set. Since here we are primary concerned with Horn clauses, in the following we will limit ourselves to input/unit refutations.[4] See [87, 86, 85] for a thorough treatment of the use of inverse resolution with arbitrary sets of ground clauses. In the following, we assume familiarity with the basic concepts of resolution and theorem proving, as in [126].

We start by defining the notion of a (unit) refutation built in reverse order at the propositional level. From equation 3.3, given C and $C_1 = \{l_1\}$, an *inverse unit resolution* operation in propositional logic can be defined as follows:

$$C_2 = C \cup \{l'_1\} \tag{5.1}$$

where l'_1 represents the complement of l_1. Equation 5.1 grasps the two situations where C_1 contains the positive literal and C_2 contains the negative literal resolved upon, or vice versa. Let us call C_2 the *inverse resolvent* of C and $C_1 = \{l_1\}$. An *inverse unit deduction* is defined as follows:

Definition 25 *Given a set of propositional clauses S and a clause C, a list of clauses $C_0, C_1, ..., C_n$ is an* inverse unit deduction *of C from S if and only if $C = C_0$ and:*

- *C_0 belongs to S and $n = 0$, or*

- *C_0 is a proper subset of a clause in S and there exist in $C_1, ..., C_n$ two clauses C_i and C_j such that:*
    - *at least one of C_i and C_j is a unit clause (let it be $C_j = \{l_j\}$), and*
    - *C_i and C_j are subsets of clauses in S and*
    - *C_i is the inverse resolvent of C_0 and C_j (i.e., $C_i = C_0 \cup \{l'_j\}$) and*
    - *for $k = i$ and $k = j$ there exists in $C_k, C_{k+1}, ..., C_n$ a sublist $C_k, ..., C_m$ that is an inverse unit deduction of C_k from S.*

An inverse unit deduction of the empty clause from S is called an *inverse unit refutation* of S. In the following, unless already stated, by inverse deduction (refutation) we mean an inverse unit deduction (refutation). The above definition grasps the idea of a unit derivation built in reverse order. In fact, if $C_0, ..., C_n$ is read as $C_n, ..., C_0$, it turns out to be a usual unit deduction of C_0 from S, where each C_i ($0 \leq i \leq n$) is either a clause from S or there exist two clauses C_j and C_k

---

[4] We recall that in *unit* deductions at least one of the parent clauses involved in a resolution step is a unit clause, while in *input* deductions at least one of the parent clauses is one of those given initially. It is well known ([39]) that unsatisfiable Horn clause sets have input/unit refutations.

5.1. Theorem Proving with Inverse Resolution

$(j, k < i)$ such that at least one of them is a unit clause and C_i is the resolvent of C_j and C_k.

We clarify the idea with an example. Suppose we are given the following set S:

c1 = ¬A¬C¬H, c2 = ¬A¬D, c3 = A, c4 = ¬BC, c5 = B, c6 = H.

Just as resolution of two complementary unit clauses is the last step in a normal deduction, so it is the first step of an inverse refutation. Initially we have the empty clause; we open two branches and label them with two complementary unit clauses consisting of the first two complementary literals (say A and ¬A) found in the given set[5] (we will build the inverse refutation from bottom to top, so it reads from top to bottom as a classical resolution refutation — see figure 5.1a, first step). Now we focus our attention on the two unit clauses, in order to build an inverse deduction for each of them from S.

Consider $\{\neg A\}$. Since clause c1 contains ¬A, we open from $\{\neg A\}$ a new pair of branches. The first one is labeled $\{\neg A \neg C\}$ (intuitively, $\{\neg A\}$ with ¬C added). The other branch is labeled with $\{C\}$, the unit clause built from the complementary of the literal added (figure 5.1a, second step). In other words, clause $\{\neg A \neg C\}$ is the inverse resolvent of clauses $\{\neg A\}$ and $\{C\}$. A similar reasoning can be done for clause c2, which also contains the literal ¬A, by producing clauses $\{\neg A \neg D\}$ and $\{D\}$ from $\{\neg A\}$. As a consequence, the problem of building an inverse derivation for $\{\neg A\}$ has been split into the problem of building an inverse derivation of the two clauses $\{\neg A \neg C\}$ *and* $\{C\}$, *or* of or building an inverse derivation for $\{\neg A \neg D\}$ *and* $\{D\}$ (figure 5.1a also reports the first step of the alternative solution of building $\{\neg A \neg D\}$ from $\{\neg A\}$ and $\{D\}$).

By proceeding in this way, from clause $\{\neg A \neg C\}$ we open two branches. One of them is labeled $\{\neg A \neg C \neg H\}$, and the other is labeled with $\{H\}$ (figure 5.1a, third step). Since the two generated clauses belong to the given set, we can stop on this side. Via a similar reasoning, we build an inverse deduction for clause $\{C\}$ by using clauses $\{\neg BC\}$ and $\{B\}$ (figure 5.1a, fourth step). The complete inverse deduction of $\{\neg A\}$ from S turns out to be $\{\neg A\}, \{\neg A \neg C\}, \{C\}, \{\neg A \neg C \neg H\}, \{H\}, \{\neg BC\}, \{B\}$. It can be verified that this list of clauses satisfies definition 25. If read in reverse order, we get a classical (unit) deduction of clause $\{\neg A\}$ from S. Moreover, since we trivially also have an inverse deduction for clause $\{A\}$, the inverse refutation is completed. If read from top to bottom, the inverse refutation represents a classical unit derivation of the empty clause from the given set.

In [39] Chang proves that a set of ground clauses S has a unit proof if and only

---

[5]Obviously, we could have chosen different pairs of complementary literals to start the deduction, and in general this is required to make the strategy complete, unless the given set is minimally unsatisfiable.

if it has an input proof (we recall that an input derivation is also a *linear* one, since one of the parent clauses involved in each resolution step is the resolvent obtained at the previous step). In fact, if S has an input refutation, there can be other input refutations for S and, in general, it can also have different unit refutations. These refutations can be obtained by resolving the various clauses in S in different orders. The next theorem points out a particular property of the relationship between an input and a unit refutation in S.

Theorem 10 *For every input refutation of an unsatisfiable set S of propositional clauses there exists a unit refutation of S where complementary literals are resolved in reverse order w.r.t. the input refutation.*

Proof Because inverse resolution builds unit refutations in reverse order, we show that, given an input refutation for S, there exists an inverse unit refutation for S where the same literals are introduced in the same order they are resolved in the input refutation. We prove the theorem by induction on the number N of resolution operations performed in the input refutation.
N = 1.
Obviously S is of the form $\{l, \neg l\}$ for some atom l, and the theorem is trivially true.
N = k+1. And assume the theorem holds for $1 \leq N \leq k$.
Let IR be an input refutation of S. Let A be a clause involved in that refutation, and let l be a literal in A such that $\{l\}$ is the unit clause obtained at step k of IR. There must exist in S a unit clause $\{\neg l\}$ that is resolved against $\{l\}$ at step k+1, completing the refutation of S. Let S_1 be S with A replaced by A-$\{l\}$. Obviously S_1 is unsatisfiable, and the first k steps of IR represent an input refutation for S_1. Call such a refutation IR_1. By the induction hypothesis there exists an inverse unit refutation for S_1 of length k (let it be IUR_1) where all the literals are introduced in exactly the same order as they are resolved in IR_1. Now we reintroduce the literal l in A and, from IUR_1, we can complete the inverse unit refutation of S at the k+1-th step by adding the literal l to A-$\{l\}$ via $\{\neg l\}$, which is in S. □

The above relationship is much easier to understand visually. figure 5.1b reports the input refutation corresponding to the inverse unit refutation of figure 5.1a. Same-numbered operations involve the same occurrences of the same literals (figure 5.1b must be read from top to bottom).

As we have seen in chapter 3, extending inverse resolution to first-order logic requires, in principle, the use of *inverse substitutions*, with an exponential complexity [169]. The next theorem shows that this is not the case if we limit ourselves to input refutations without factoring. In fact, given an input refutation, we rely on the same reordering of resolved literals as shown at the ground level, in order

5.1. Theorem Proving with Inverse Resolution

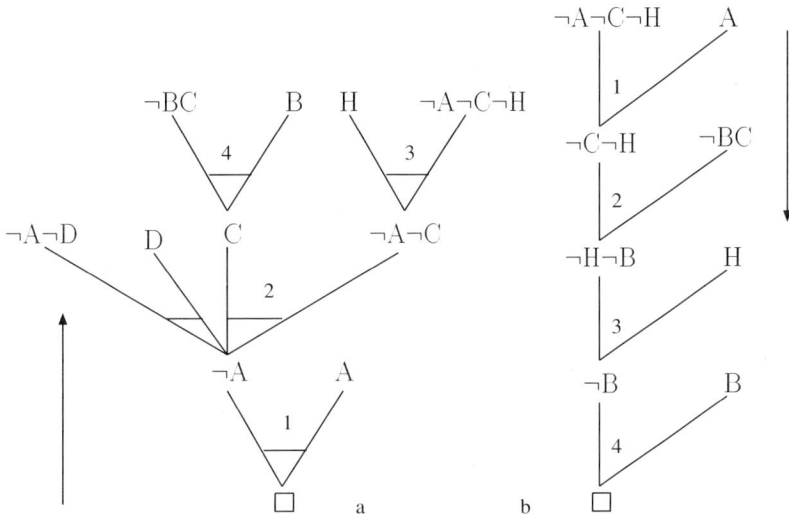

Figure 5.1: (Inverse) unit (a) and input (b) refutation for S.

to build the (corresponding) inverse unit refutation. The difference is that here we have first to check that the two involved literals are unifiable.

First we define the notion of *inverse (unit) refutation* at the first-order level. In the following, given a literal l, l' represents a literal with the same predicative symbol as l, but negative if l is positive and vice versa. We recall that $|l|$ denotes the atom of literal l:

Definition 26 *Given a set of clauses S, a list of clauses $C_0, C_1, ..., C_n$ is an inverse unit refutation of S if and only if $C_0 = \Box$ and, for $0 \leq i \leq n$, $C_i = \{l_1\sigma_{1_1}, l_2\sigma_{1_1}, \sigma_{2_1} \ldots \sigma_{2_j}, \ldots, l_m\sigma_{1_1}, \sigma_{2_1} \ldots \sigma_{2_j}, \ldots, \sigma_{n_1} \ldots \sigma_{n_k}\}$ is such that (note that for $i = 0$, it must be $m = 0$, as C_0 is the empty clause):*

- $\{l_1, l_2, \ldots, l_m\}$ *is a clause belonging to S or*

- $\{l_1, l_2, \ldots, l_m\}$ *is a proper subset of a clause in S and there exist in $C_{i+1}, ..., C_n$ two clauses C_p and C_q such that:*

    - *at least one of C_p and C_q is a unit clause (let it be $C_q = \{l\sigma\}$), and*
    - $C_p = C_i \cup l'\sigma_{1_1}, \sigma_{2_1} \ldots \sigma_{2_j}, \ldots, \sigma_{n_1} \ldots \sigma_{n_k}, \sigma_s, \ldots, \sigma_t, \sigma$, *and*
    - $\sigma_s, \ldots, \sigma_t$ *are the unifiers introduced in steps between clauses C_i and C_{p-1}, and*

– $l\sigma$ and $l'\sigma_{1_1}, \sigma_{2_1} \ldots \sigma_{2_j}, \ldots, \sigma_{n_1} \ldots \sigma_{n_k}, \sigma_s, \ldots, \sigma_t, \sigma$ are complementary literals (i.e., $|l|$ and $|l'\sigma_{1_1}, \sigma_{2_1} \ldots \sigma_{2_j}, \ldots, \sigma_{n_1} \ldots \sigma_{n_k}, \sigma_s, \ldots, \sigma_t|$ are unifiable through σ).

The above definition is much easier to understand operationally, by showing how to build the tree associated with the inverse refutation (for simplicity let us assume literals l and l' below have disjoint variables). Suppose we are given an (unsatisfiable) set S of clauses. We build an inverse refutation for S as follows.

At the first step, if two literals l and l' occur in S and a substitution σ_1 exists such that $|l\sigma_1| = |l'\sigma_1|$, then we can open from the empty clause (that is, C_0) two branches labeled $\{l\sigma_1\}$ and $\{l'\sigma_1\}$ respectively. In general, suppose that the first literal l_1 of a clause $A \in S$ has been introduced at the i-th step in the inverse refutation using substitution σ_i (i.e., we have a branch in the tree labeled with $\{l_1\sigma_i\}$). Then, at the k-th step we may add a literal l_j to the subset of A built up to that point (ignoring the introduced unifiers) by using literal l'_j if and only if l'_j occurs in S and $\exists\ \sigma_k$ such that $|l\sigma_i\sigma_{i+1}...\sigma_k| = |l'\sigma_k|$, where $\sigma_i,...,\sigma_{k-1}$ are the unifiers used between steps i and k-1. The inverse refutation is completed when all branches are labeled with clauses from the given set, ignoring the introduced unifiers. It can be easily verified that such a construction satisfies definition 26.

Figure 5.2 below reports the inverse refutation tree built with the following set of clauses:

S = P(X,Y)Q(X,Z), ¬P(a,W)R(Y,Z), ¬Q(a,b), ¬R(a,b).

by using the following unifiers:

$\sigma_1 = \{X/a,\ Y/W\}$, $\sigma_2 = \{Z/b\}$, $\sigma_3 = \{W/a\}$.

The above definition of inverse refutation in first-order logic is justified by the following theorem:

Theorem 11 *For every input refutation of an unsatisfiable set S of clauses there exists an inverse unit refutation of S where complementary literals are introduced in the same order they are resolved in the input refutation and where the same unifiers are involved.*

Proof Again, we prove the theorem by induction on the number N of resolution operations performed in the input refutation.
N = 1.
Obviously S is of the form $\{l, \neg l'\}$. Then $|l\sigma_1| = |\neg l'\sigma_1|$ for some substitution σ_1 and the theorem is trivially true.

5.1. Theorem Proving with Inverse Resolution

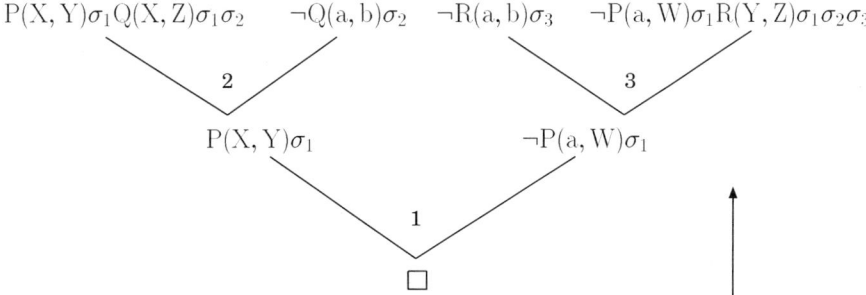

Figure 5.2: Inverse unit refutation for S

N = k+1. And assume the theorem holds for $1 \leq N \leq k$.

Let IR be an input refutation of S. Let A be a nonunit clause in S resolved against the center clause at the j-th step.[6] Let l be a literal in A such that $\{l\sigma_j...\sigma_k\}$ is the unit clause obtained at step k of IR, where $\sigma_j,..., \sigma_k$ are the unifiers used in resolution operations from step j to step k. There must exist in S a unit clause $\{\neg l'\}$ that is resolved against $\{l\sigma_j...\sigma_k\}$ at step k+1 using unifier σ_{k+1} and completing the refutation of S (i.e. $|l\sigma_j,...,\sigma_k\sigma_{k+1}| = |\neg l'\sigma_{k+1}|$). Let S_1 be S with A replaced by A-$\{l\}$. Obviously S_1 is unsatisfiable, and the first k steps of IR represent an input refutation for S_1. Call such a refutation IR_1. By the induction hypothesis there exists an inverse unit refutation for S_1 of length k (let it be IUR_1), where all the literal occurrences are introduced exactly in the same order as they are resolved in IR_1, using the same unifiers. Now, to get an inverse unit refutation of S from IUR_1, we simply apply to l all unifiers $\sigma_j,..., \sigma_k$ used from the introduction of the first literal of A (at step j) to step k, and perform an inverse resolution operation between $l\sigma_j...\sigma_k$ and $\neg l'$ that can be unified via the substitution σ_{k+1}, as previously assumed. □

Observe that whereas in propositional calculus, inverse deductions read from top to bottom appear to be ordinary deductions, in first-order logic this is no longer true. In figure 5.3a an input refutation for an unsatisfiable set of clauses is shown, and figure 5.3b reports the corresponding inverse unit refutation. Note how the inverse refutation, if read from top to bottom, does *not* turn out to be an ordinary refutation. For example, at the fourth step, unifier σ_4 is applied only to literals D and ¬D, and not to C. However, if we consider the clauses at the leaves of the

---

[6]In linear derivations, the center clause is the last clause obtained by resolution. For example, if figure 5.1b the center clauses are $\{\neg A \neg C \neg H\}$, $\{\neg C \neg H\}$, $\{\neg H \neg B\}$, and $\{\neg B\}$.

refutation tree of figure 5.3b and remove unifiers σ_1, ..., σ_4, we obtain the set of clauses given initially. For simplicity, first-order literals are represented with capital letters, without reporting their terms. But literals A and $\neg$A are considered to be complementary only if there is a substitution σ such that $|A\sigma| = |\neg A\sigma|$).

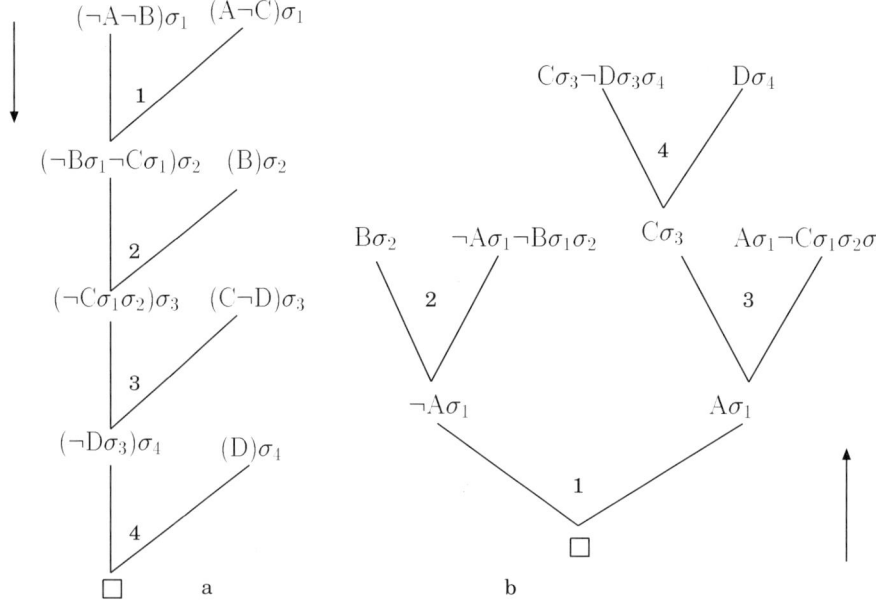

Figure 5.3: An input refutation (a) and the corresponding inverse unit refutation (b)

As an obvious consequence of theorem 11, we have the following:

Theorem 12 *Inverse unit refutation is complete for Horn logic.*

Proof Follows from the fact that input resolution is complete for Horn logic ([126]).
□

Finally, note that there is no need to formally prove that there is an inverse unit refutation for a set S *only if* S is unsatisfiable (i.e., that inverse unit refutation is correct). Suppose S is not unsatisfiable but we are able to build an inverse unit refutation for S. Then, by using the definition of inverse unit refutation and theorem 11, we can immediately build an input refutation for S, a contradiction.

5.2 Extensional Top-Down Methods Revisited

We have shown that "inverse resolution + substitution" can be used as a deductive rule. The refutation tree of figure 5.3b can be seen as made up of a set of connected Vs, each V corresponding to a single inverse resolution operation. Since substitutions, and not inverse substitutions, are used, this operation will be indicated with V_θ, in order to distinguish it from the classical V operator of bottom-up inverse resolution-based methods. figure 5.4 shows the general form of the V_θ operator:

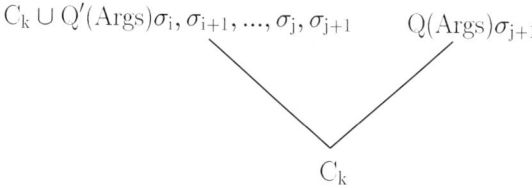

Figure 5.4: The V_θ operation

That is, by applying the V_θ operator, from clause C_k we can build clause C_{k+1} = $C_k \cup Q'(\text{Args})\sigma_i,\sigma_{i+1},...,\sigma_j,\sigma_{j+1}$ if there exists a substitution σ_{j+1} such that $|Q'(\text{Args})\sigma_i,...,\sigma_{j+1}| = |Q(\text{Args})\sigma_{j+1}|$, where C_{k+1} and $\{Q(\text{Args})\}$ are subsets of clauses belonging to the given set S and $\sigma_i, ..., \sigma_j$ are the substitutions used in the previous applications of the V_θ operator from the introduction of the first literal of C_k. Note that the V_θ operator grasps the two situations in which the unit clause can be made up of a positive or of a negative literal. This definition is sufficient for building inverse refutations of sets of Horn clauses, for example, to check if a ground example P(a,b) is derivable from a set of Horn clauses[7] describing a concept P.

Now, suppose we are given a set of positive and negative examples E^+ and E^-, a background theory BK, a positive example P(a,b) and a clause C extensionally covering P(a,b) and not covering negative examples in E^- (as usual, we assume BK being consistent, but BK $\not\vdash$ P(a,b)). Clearly, S = C ∪ ¬P(a,b) ∪ E^+ ∪ BK is a (minimally) unsatisfiable set of Horn clauses. As a consequence, S has an input refutation IR that starts by resolving the head of C with ¬P(a,b). Moreover, this does not hold if we replace P(a,b) with any of the negative examples in E^-. But from the results of the previous section, we know that there must exist a corresponding inverse unit refutation IUR for S that starts by introducing from the empty clause the head of C and ¬P(a,b) and that uses the same unifiers involved

---

[7]In fact, to build a Horn clause we have to require that the unit clause Q(Args) is made up of a negative literal, except in the first step.

in IR. We can build that inverse refutation by repeatedly applying the ∇_θ operator defined above.

Now, suppose we do not have C, but we are given a set of clauses (that is, the hypothesis space HS) containing C. Again, $S' = HS \cup \neg P(a,b) \cup E^+ \cup BK$ is unsatisfiable, and we can identify C by building an inverse refutation for S', where exactly one clause is taken from HS. For each such clause C' we have to check whether, for some $e^- \in E^-$, $C' \cup E^+ \cup BK \vdash e^-$ (i.e., $C' \cup \neg e^- \cup E^+ \cup BK$ is unsatisfiable) or not. In the former, we discard C' and try another clause; in the latter, C' = C.

Intuitively, it is easy to see that we are reformulating the extensional learning process of a clause C in terms of theorem proving with inverse resolution. Clause C is built by means of specialization steps (i.e., by adding literals to the body of C), on the basis of the positive examples and of the allowed specializations. This can be rewritten in terms of the ∇_θ operator (which rebuilds clauses), as it is formalized in the next theorem.

Theorem 13 *Let there be given a positive example e^+, a set of positive and negative examples E^+ and E^-, a background knowledge BK and a hypothesis space HS (a set of Horn clauses). Then there exists in HS a clause C extensionally covering e^+ if and only if there exists an inverse unit refutation IUR for $HS \cup BK \cup E^+ \cup \neg e^+$ such that exactly one clause $C \in HS$ is involved in IUR and is used exactly once. Moreover, C does not extensionally cover any negative example in E^- if and only if there does not exist any inverse unit refutation for $C \cup BK \cup E^+ \cup \neg e^-$ for each $e^- \in E^-$.*

Proof
($\rightarrow$) (By induction on the number k of literals in C)
k = 1.
Let $e^+ = P(a,b)$, and let the guessed clause extensionally covering P(a,b) be the unit clause C = P(X,Y). We build the corresponding inverse refutation by starting from the empty clause and opening one branch labeled ¬P(a,b) and the other labeled $C\sigma_1$ (where $\sigma_1 = \{X/a, Y/b\}$). This corresponds to applying the instance of the ∇_θ operator depicted in figure 5.5.

If no negative example is extensionally covered by C, then E^- is empty, and there is obviously no inverse unit refutation for examples in E^- using C. As a consequence the theorem holds.
k = 2.
Let C = P(X,Y) :- Q_2(Args) be such that its body is extensionally evaluated as true on example P(a,b). This means that there exists a substitution σ_2 such that $Q_2(\text{Args})\sigma_1\sigma_2$ is a given positive example of Q_2 (if it is defined extensionally) or is derivable from its definition (when a logic program for computing Q_2 is given).

5.2. Extensional Top-Down Methods Revisited

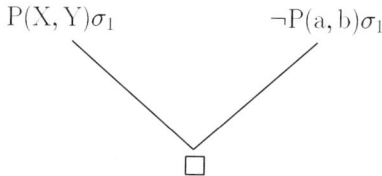

Figure 5.5: First step of the inverse refutation

But, as a consequence, we can apply the V_θ operator to P(a,b) = P(X,Y)σ_1 and $Q_2(Args)\sigma_1\sigma_2$, as in figure 5.6, to build P(X,Y)σ_1 :- $Q_2(Args)\sigma_1\sigma_2$.

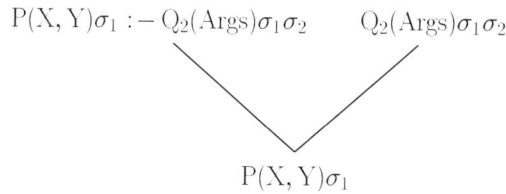

Figure 5.6: Second step of the inverse refutation

By connecting this instance of the V_θ operator to the previous one through P(X,Y)σ_1, we get an inverse unit refutation for C $\cup$ $Q_2(Args)\sigma_1\sigma_2$ $\cup$ ¬P(a,b). If no negative example P(c,d) is extensionally covered by C, this means that there exists no unifier σ such that $Q_2(Args)\{X/c, Y/d\}\sigma$ is a positive example of Q_2. But then there is no input refutation for C $\cup$ BK $\cup$ E^+ $\cup$ ¬P(c,d), and hence no inverse unit refutation, and the theorem holds.

Let the theorem hold for k-1. It is trivial to extend it to k by generalizing the case k=2. Suppose clause C = P(X,Y) :- ..., $Q_{k-1}(Args)$ extensionally covering example P(a,b) has been built. Suppose C covers some negative example in E^-, and hence the body of C is specialized by adding literal $Q_k(Args)$ such that P(a,b) is still covered but no negative examples are. This means that for $2 \leq i \leq$ k, there exists a substitution σ_i such that $Q_i(Args)\{X/a, Y/b\}\sigma_2, \ldots, \sigma_{i-1}\sigma_i$ is a positive example of Q_i (or is derivable from its definition), and for every negative example P(c,d) it is the case that $Q_k(Args)\{X/c, Y/d\}\sigma_2, \ldots, \sigma_k$ is not a positive example of Q_k (nor is it derivable from its definition) for any σ_k. By the induction hypothesis, there is an inverse unit refutation for C $\cup$ BK $\cup$ E^+ $\cup$ ¬ P(a,b) ending with P(X,Y)σ_1 :- ...,$Q_{k-1}(Args)\sigma_1, \ldots, \sigma_{k-1}$, and hence an inverse unit refutation for $\{C \cup Q_k(Args)\} \cup BK \cup E^+ \cup \neg P(a,b)$ by using the V_θ operation of figure 5.7. Moreover, this is not the case for any negative example P(c,d) by hypothesis.

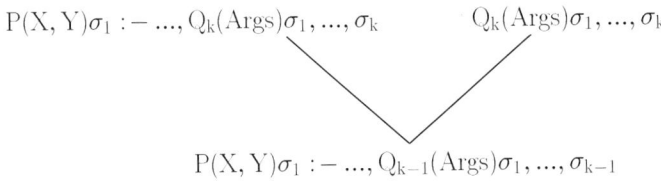

Figure 5.7: K-th step of the inverse refutation

($\leftarrow$) Let e^+ = P(a,b) and let |C| = k.

Since $BK \cup E^+ \cup \neg e^+$ is satisfiable and $S = C \cup BK \cup E^+ \cup \neg e^+$ is not, there exists an input refutation for S with top clause C starts starts by resolving the head of C against $\neg P(a,b)$. As a consequence, by theorem 11 there exists an inverse unit refutation for S that starts by introducing from the empty clause the head of C and $\neg$ P(a,b). Since C must be used exactly once, and this is the only clause we can use from HS, in each step of the inverse unit refutation one of the involved clauses always belongs to $BK \cup E^+ \cup \neg e^+$. As a consequence, for each literal $Q_i(Args)$ $\in$ C introduced by means of the V_θ operator at step i ($2 \leq i \leq$ k), it must be the case that $Q_i(Args)\sigma_1, \ldots, \sigma_i$ is a positive example of Q_i (or is derivable from its definition) for some unifiers $\sigma_1, \ldots, \sigma_i$. In particular, $\sigma_1 = \{X/a, Y/b\}$. But then, C extensionally covers P(a,b), by definition of extensional covering. Moreover, for each negative example P(c,d) suppose there exists no inverse unit refutation for $C \cup BK \cup E^+ \cup \neg$ P(c,d). Then there exists at least one i such that $Q_i\{X/c, Y/d\}, \sigma_2, \ldots, \sigma_i$ is not a positive example of Q_i (nor is it derivable from its definition) for any unifiers $\sigma_2, \ldots, \sigma_i$. But then C does not extensionally cover P(c,d) by definition of extensional covering. □

The intuitive meaning of theorem 13 is that when we are learning a clause by means of an extensional evaluation of predicates and recursion, we are in fact performing a special kind of theorem proving. We are looking for a minimally unsatisfiable subset S of $HS \cup BK \cup E^+ \cup \neg e^+$ such that exactly one clause C is taken from HS and used once in the refutation. If the refutability of S is proved by means of inverse resolution, then the reconstruction of C by means of the V_θ operator turns out to be equivalent to the top-down extensional learning task of C.

As a consequence of the above discussion, the V_θ operator can be seen as an inductive specialization rule, as it can be used to induce clauses by specializing an initial overgeneral description, which entails every positive and negative example of the target concept. Since this operator is based on the inversion of the resolution rule, inverse resolution used as an inductive rule turns out to be a unifying framework for top-down extensional methods and bottom-up methods based on inverse resolution: clauses are learned by adding literals to clause antecedents, that is, by inversion of the resolution rule, which removes literals. In top-down methods, overgeneral descriptions guessed initially are specialized by using the V_θ operator, which plays the role of a specialization rule, by using substitutions. In bottom-up methods, overly specific descriptions guessed initially are generalized by applying the V operator, which plays the role of a generalization rule, by using inverse substitutions.

5.3 Example

We clarify the above relationship by stating a learning task of the recursive clause for *append* (as it would be done in the top-down extensional approach — section 4.2) in terms of the V_θ operator. Suppose we are given the following ground unit clauses, which are positive and negative examples for *append*:

$e_1^+ =$ append([],[b],[b]), $e_2^+ =$ append([a],[b],[a,b]),
$e_1^- = \neg$append([],[b],[]), $e_2^- = \neg$append([a],[b],[b]).

We are also given the following set P of predicates that make it possible to build a definition of *append*: P = {null, head, tail, cons, assign, append}

Let HS be the set of all Horn clauses whose head is "append(X,Y,Z)" and whose body is made up of literals with a predicative symbol in P. Background knowledge BK is as follows:

null([],[]).
head([A|_],A).
tail([_|B],B).
cons(C,D,[C|D]).
assign(E,E).

Now we start the learning task by looking for a clause C ∈ HS that covers e_2^+, i.e., such that C ∪ BK ∪ $\{e_1^+\}$ ∪ $\{\neg e_2^+\}$ is unsatisfiable (for brevity, we do not consider alternative paths; see also figure 5.8).

We start from the empty clause and generate two branches, one labeled ¬append([a],[b],[a,b])σ_1 and the other labeled C = append(X,Y,Z)σ_1, with σ_1 = {X/[a], Y/[b], Z/[a,b]}. Because $(\forall e^-)$ C ∪ BK ∪ $\{e_1^+\}$ ⊢ e^-, we must continue the inverse derivation.

At the next step, a literal needs to be chosen. There are many possibilities, and extensive backtracking would be required. For the sake of exposition, here we consider only the literal choices that are good, i.e., that lead to a clause with the desired properties. Suppose we select from L the literal head(X,H). From C we open two branches, one labeled head([A|_],A)σ_2 and the other one labeled:
C = append(X,Y,Z)σ_1 :- head(X,H)$\sigma_1\sigma_2$
with $\sigma_2 = \{A/a, H/a\}$.

At the third step, tail(X,T) is selected, and from C we open one branch labeled tail([_|B],B)σ_3 and the other labeled:
C = append(X,Y,Z)σ_1 :- head(X,H)$\sigma_1\sigma_2$, tail(X,T)$\sigma_1\sigma_2\sigma_3$
with $\sigma_3 = \{B/[], T/[]\}$.

At the fourth step, append(T,Y,W) is selected, and from C we open a branch labeled append([],[b],[b])σ_4 and the other one labeled:
C = append(X,Y,Z)σ_1 :- head(X,H)$\sigma_1\sigma_2$,tail(X,T)$\sigma_1\sigma_2\sigma_3$,append(T,Y,W)$\sigma_1\sigma_2\sigma_3\sigma_4$
with $\sigma_4 = \{T/[], W/[b]\}$.

Finally, cons(H,W,Z) is selected, and from C we open two branches labeled, respectively, cons(C,D,[C|D])σ_5 and:
C = append(X,Y,Z)σ_1 :- head(X,H)$\sigma_1\sigma_2$, tail(X,T)$\sigma_1\sigma_2\sigma_3$,
              append(T,Y,W)$\sigma_1\sigma_2\sigma_3\sigma_4$, cons(H,W,Z) $\sigma_1\sigma_2\sigma_3\sigma_4\sigma_5$.
with $\sigma_5 = \{C/a, D/[b]\}$.

At this point it is the case that $\forall e^- \ C \cup BK \cup \{e_1^+\} \not\vdash e^-$. It can easily be verified that there exists an input refutation of $C \cup BK \cup \{e_1^+\} \cup \{\neg e_2^+\}$ where at the first step C is resolved against $\neg e_2^+$ and where the substitutions $\sigma_1,..., \sigma_5$ are employed, in that order. By removing substitutions introduced along the inverse refutation,

C= append(X,Y,Z) :- head(X,H), tail(X,T), append(T,Y,W), cons(H,W,Z)

represents the learned recursive clause for *append*. It is an easy exercise to check that the used substitutions would correspond to the assignment of values to variables performed in an extensional evaluation of the body of C, as shown in section 4.2.

Figure 5.8 reports the above construction in terms of V_θ operations. The input refutation for $C \cup BK \cup \{e_1^+\} \cup \{\neg e_2^+\}$ can be obtained simply by executing the resolution operations indicated by the V_θ operators in reverse order.

5.3. Example

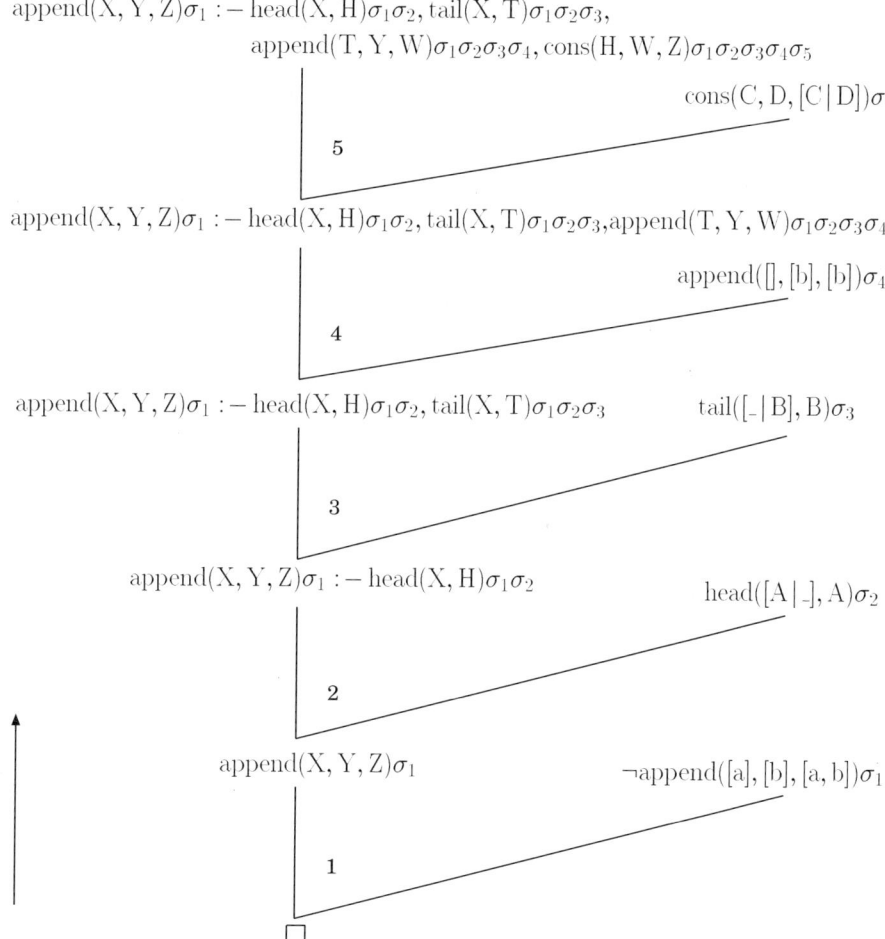

Figure 5.8: Learning the recursive clause for *append*

II

ILP with Strong Bias

6
Inductive Bias

The notion of inductive bias was introduced by Tom Mitchell in [136], and defined as any information that influences inductive learning from examples. As such, bias will include any input besides examples, and any parameter or strategy that may be modified by the user of a learning system. There is now some agreement on dividing this broad notion of inductive bias into three different categories: language bias, search bias, and stopping criterion.

Based on the definition of the ILP problem that was given in chapter 2, language bias is simply some description of the hypothesis space $\mathcal{P}$ containing all logic programs that we could expect the system to learn. Search bias is any information telling the system how the space $\mathcal{P}$ of possible programs should be searched: which programs should be ignored, which should be considered first, which clauses should be considered first, and which predicates should be more often added or removed from clause antecedents. This is a generalization of what had been called a preference criterion [129]. By contrast, a stopping criterion [129, 19] should tell the system when the search for the desired logic program should stop. In chapter 2 we implicitly assumed some bias that brings the system to a halt whenever the learned program is complete and consistent with respect to the given examples. In most Pattern Recognition applications, one would rather stop when some *degree* of completeness and consistency has been reached. Such a choice has also been made in some ILP applications [111, 117].

The importance of bias was experimented with in early Machine Learning and Pattern Recognition research [51]. In particular, it was observed that stronger language bias (i.e., smaller hypothesis spaces $\mathcal{P}$) would lead to better performance of the learned programs on a test set of new examples not available to the system during the learning phase. This fact has been explained in beautiful generality by the works of Vapnik and Chervonenkis [194, 195, 193] and further developed within the Computational Learning Theory community and in the Pattern Recognition literature [64, 171]. The first observation of Vapnik and Chervonenkis is based directly on Bernoulli's Theorem: the difference between the percentage of errors made by the learned program on the given examples and the same figure measured on a separate set of test data grows with the size of the hypothesis space $\mathcal{P}$ of possible programs. The main result of Vapnik and Chervonenkis is that the same holds for infinite hypothesis spaces, where cardinality is replaced by a measure of the expressiveness of the hypothesis space, the so-called Vapnik-Chervonenkis dimension of $\mathcal{P}$. The conclusion of the above is that the size or the expressiveness of the hypothesis language should be constrained as much as possible, for otherwise the behavior of the learned program on new data will be unpredictable, and usually unrelated to completeness and consistency as measured on the given examples. Obviously, the hypothesis space cannot be too small either, because it must contain some program that has an acceptable accuracy on the available data. Bias must, then, be weak enough to allow for complete and consistent programs, and strong enough to prevent total degradation of performance on new data.

Although it took time to understand why bias was important for accuracy, its importance for the efficiency of learning is immediate and rather obvious. If there are more possible programs to consider, it may take longer to find one that is acceptable, based on the available examples. But, to this purpose, it is necessary also to consider the search bias and the stopping criterion. Clever and informed heuristics may lead to efficient searching of even large hypothesis spaces.

We would like, now, to relate the above considerations to ILP proper, and to software development applications of ILP. First, we must note that the hypothesis language used in ILP is often Horn clauses; by far a more expressive language than those used in Pattern Recognition (e.g., linear discriminants or prototypes for nearest neighbor classification) and in propositional Machine Learning (e.g., decision trees or propositional classifiers). For the above concerns on accuracy, Horn clauses are hopeless: even the weakest notions of inductive success, such as identification in the limit (see section 2.4), cannot be met without appropriate restrictions. Some form of language bias is therefore necessary for restricting the hypothesis space, more necessary than it had been in previous Machine Learning research. We need hypothesis spaces of possible logic programs that are extremely restricted, based on specific knowledge about the problem at hand: if not, the learned program would be useless when used on new input values. The same holds for efficiency: the issue is magnified in ILP, as searching a space of logic programs is more difficult and slower than tuning linear discriminants or growing decision trees, as clauses depend on each other through recursion and contain variables that may be chosen or instantiated in many different ways. Only strong bias will make ILP learning practical. Finally, when we deal with Software Engineering applications, strong bias is usually available from a user/programmer who knows a lot about the target program and is able to cooperate with the learning system.

Strong bias only, can make ILP useful and practical for software development. In this part of the book we concentrate on ILP algorithms assuming that strong biases are available, and, in this chapter, on languages and methods for specifying such biases. With the help of the user, the proposed algorithms are efficient and reliable. Lessons should be learned from the work done on program synthesis during the 1970s. The goal of producing programs automatically just from examples or from logical specifications has led to failures or to methods that could not convince the practitioner. A useful tool must be embedded in a larger framework, where the user continuously interacts with the system in many different ways. Inductive Logic Programming can become one of these ways.

6.1 Refinement Operators

We will start our survey with a concept that was introduced in section 4.1, in connection with the MIS system: the concept of a refinement operator. This is actually a method for describing a space $\mathcal{C}$ of possible clauses, where the possible programs are simply sets of possible clauses, i.e., $\mathcal{P} = 2^{\mathcal{C}}$. In other words, a refinement operator defines a language bias.

Shapiro defines a refinement operator as a function ρ mapping clauses to finite sets of clauses (page 119 in [176]). For a given clause C, the set $\rho(C)$ contains the *refinements* of C. Moreover, it is required that, for all $D \in \rho(C)$, if D covers a ground example, then C cover it, too. In other words, a refinement must be a specialization. In MIS, covering is decided extensionally: a clause $P(\vec{X})$:- α covers a fact $P(\vec{a})$ if there is a substitution σ such that $\alpha[\vec{X}/\vec{a}]\sigma$ is true in the target model. We recall that, with the eager strategy, this is checked by querying the user for the truth value of the literals in $\alpha[\vec{X}/\vec{a}]$ (an existential query).

One can define language bias by means of a refinement operator ρ as follows: A clause D belongs to the set $\mathcal{C}$ of possible clauses if it is the empty clause, or if it belongs to $\rho(C)$ for some clause $C \in \mathcal{C}$. This is what we will call a *dynamic* or *generative* language bias: the possible programs, or the possible clauses, are not listed, nor is their syntax captured by some template; by contrast, a method is given for generating the possible clauses step by step, usually by adding literals to the body in top-down systems. A discussion of the advantages of generative and static language biases will be developed later in this chapter.

An example of a refinement operator aimed at illustrating the algorithms in MIS was given in section 4.1. We now give another example showing how particular syntactic restrictions can be coded in a refinement operator. The example is drawn from [176] and is concerned with definite clause grammars. This restricted form of Prolog programs is defined, for instance, in [50], and has an expressive power that is equivalent to the one of context-free grammars. For instance, the following clauses define a binary predicate s, where $s(X, Y)$ is true whenever X is a prefix of the list Y, and X is a simple English sentence:

s(X,Y) :- np(X,U), vp(U,Y).
np(X,Y) :- det(X,U), n(U,Y).
np(X,Y) :- det(X,U), n(U,[that|Z]),vp(Z,Y).
vp([runs|X],X).
vp([is−happy|X],X).
det([every|X],X).
n([boy|X],X).

This recognizes sentences such as [every, boy, is-happy], and [every, boy, that, is-happy, runs]. The syntax of clauses in definite clause grammars is obviously quite restricted: all predicates are binary, arguments are flat lists of terminal symbols, and new variables are introduced as a second argument in some literal, and are used in the next literal as a first argument. Below is a definition of a refinement operator ρ that generates clauses of just this kind. We say that $D \in \rho(X)$ if one of the following holds:

- C is the empty clause, and $D = n(X, Y)$, where n is a predicate corresponding to a nonterminal symbol.

- D is obtained by replacing a variable Y of C with a term $[t|Z]$, where Z is a new variable. Moreover, we require that Y occur once in C as a second argument of some predicate.

- D is obtained by adding to the body of C a literal $n(Y, Z)$, where n corresponds to a nonterminal symbol and Z is a new variable. Again, we require that Y occur once in C as a second argument of some predicate.

- D is obtained by replacing a variable Y of C with the variable that occurs as a second argument in the head. Y must occur once in C as a second argument of some predicate.

When starting from a marked clause with the goal of covering some new positive example, MIS may use this refinement operator to produce clauses that are legal in a definite clause grammar.

As language bias is problem-dependent, it should be important to allow users to easily change refinement operators. The system MARKUS [84] is a modification of MIS that addresses this issue. Instead of being wired inside the system,

MARKUS's refinement operators are obtained from the user via a more friendly specification language. Other elements of language bias that are not strictly domain dependent but, rather, related to the size of the search space, are given to the system via separate clause generation parameters. These include the maximum number of literals in a clause, the maximum number of existential variables in a clause antecedent, and the maximum complexity of terms in the head of a clause.

A problem in all dynamic bias specifications is the repeated generation of clauses. As a very simple example, consider the refinement operator ρ defined as follows:

if C is the empty clause, then $\rho(C) = A$
if C is A:-α, then $\rho(C)$ is A:-α, lit, where lit is B or C.

In this case, we can refine A:-B and obtain A:-B, C, or refine A:-C and obtain A:-C, B, which is equivalent to A:-B, C. Although in a more complicated setting, MIS suffers from the same problem, and may generate some clauses more than once. If we consider that after a clause is generated in the refinement graph, its more specific descendants may also be generated, we realize that this is a serious problem.

In the first version of the ML-SMART system [19] the problem was solved by inserting all generated clauses in a hash table, and checking for previous generations before every potential specialization step. Although more demanding from the point of view of space complexity, this solution proved to be efficient and transparent to the user. By contrast, Michalski's first-order learning system INDUCE [128] avoided an instance of this problem by ordering literals, and disallowing the addition of a literal that precedes the literals that are already present. In the above example, if we consider the alphabetic ordering of literals B and C, the clause A :- C, B would not have been generated. This solution is efficient and does not require extra hash table space, but affects the system's output as it disallows a priori some orderings of the literals. This may cause problems when there are variables, input-output restriction and requirements of determinate literals. The improvement of MIS described in [98] adopts a similar solution by ordering all possible refinement operations. MARKUS also follows this principle, but also defines an ordering between different instantiations of the same refinement operation. Another difference of MARKUS with respect to MIS consists in the fact that all examples are considered during refinement: the first generated clause that covers some new uncovered positive examples and does not cover any negative example is added to the learned program. This brings the method closer to what is done in FOIL and in other more recent top-down systems.

Another descendant of MIS that stresses the importance of well-chosen refinement operators is proposed by Marc Kirschenbaum and Leon Sterling in [113]. The system is called MISST (MIS with skeletons and techniques). Their perspective is appropriate for software development applications. Part of their motivation starts from an adaptation of Wirth's stepwise refinement [201] to logic programming. The development of a Prolog program is divided into two phases: writing a set of program *skeletons* that should capture the control structure, and augmenting skeletons with output producers by means of so-called *techniques*. This is an example of a skeleton for scanning a list and then doing something when some condition holds:

search([X|Y]).
search([X|Y]) :- search(Y).

We may then use techniques to further refine such a skeleton and determine which condition must hold when the search stops and what needs to be done at that moment. For instance, the technique *collect*, developed by the authors within the MISST system, adds one variable to the relevant predicate, to be used for output. The output variable is intended to match a flat list. Based on the other goals in the body of the clause, the collect technique may or may not concatenate the head of the list in the first argument to the output. For instance, the collect technique may use the above given *search* skeleton to produce a program that returns the remainder of a list after the number 1 has been found:

remainder([1|Y],Y).
remainder([X|Y],Z) :- remainder(Y,Z).

MISST basically works like MIS but is strongly biased by a refinement operator that uses skeletons and techniques. The first step in the refinement consists in the generation of all possible skeletons. The idea behind this is that a program without a skeleton will collapse and could hardly be correct. This avoids a phenomenon frequently observed in top-down ILP systems: in the early stages of specialization, literals are added before the appropriate kind of recursive call. After skeleton generation, refinement proceeds more smoothly: output variables are added, variables are instantiated, literals may be added following a number of possible techniques. However, only the *collect* technique was available in the implementation when the article was published. We must comment that although presented as a modified refinement operator, the specialization with skeletons and techniques does not match exactly the philosophy of a generative method. The skeleton gives a quasi-finished schema for the desired program clauses rather than a method for generating the clauses one literal after the other. This brings us closer to the topic of the next section, and also to the bias specification methods proposed later, where language bias is based on clause templates and syntactic approximations of programs.

6.2 Clause Templates

Bias specification via clause templates was used in later versions of the ML-SMART system [18], in MOBAL [107], and in more recent work [190]. Early ideas on schemata are found in [71]. In ML-SMART such templates were called *predicate sets* and have been used successfully in diagnosis applications [78, 20]. Later, the notion of a predicate set was given a clearer formalization and was extended to a Prolog notation with clause, literal, and term sets. This notation will be described in section 6.5 below, for two reasons. First, it describes sets of possible Prolog programs and not just sets of possible clauses. Second, it is the basis of the program induction methods and of the Software Engineering applications described in the rest of the book. Therefore, it needs a more detailed discussion.

In MOBAL the templates are called *rule models*, and they are used in the RDT module of the system [107]. RDT is the module that learns clauses from examples. A rule model is like a Prolog clause, except that predicate symbols are substituted by *predicate variables*. A rule model is, then, a kind of second-order schema that may be instantiated to a normal Prolog clause by turning the predicate variables into appropriate Prolog predicates. For example, the model:

P(X,Y,Z) :- Q(X1,X2,X), R(X1,Y), P(X2,Y,W), S(X1,W,Z).

instantiates to the following two clauses:

append(X,Y,Z) :- cons(X1,X2,X), no_op(X1,Y), append(X2,Y,W), cons(X1,W,Z).
intersection(X,Y,Z) :- cons(X1,X2,X), member(X1,Y),
         intersection(X2,Y,W), cons(X1,W,Z).

where we may think of a given background knowledge including:

cons(X,Y,[X|Y]).
member(X,[X|Y]).
member(X,[_|Y]) :- member(X,Y).
no_op(X,Y).

As we have seen, a rule model may be instantiated to clauses serving quite different purposes, depending on which actual predicates are used. In RDT, the choice of the predicates is also constrained by a so-called topology, which is a kind of dependency graph appropriate for the application domain: the predicate in the consequent of a clause is required to depend on the predicates in the antecedent. The details of this mechanism for limiting the possible instantiations of predicate variables are found in [107]. A similar notion of dependency is found in S. Russell's *determinations* [170].

The notion of rule model has recently been extended to more general *clause templates* by Tausend [190]. A main improvement over rule models consists in the fact that the arguments in a literal may also be abstracted into a variable. This will allow us to provide schemata for defining predicates of different arity. For instance, the following clause:

subset(X,Y) :- cons(X1,X2,X), member(X1,Y), subset(X2,Y), no_op(X1,Y).

will not be a legal instantiation of the above-given rule schema for P(X,Y,Z). In fact, subset(X,Y) does not match P(X,Y,Z) because it has only two arguments, and similarly no_op(X1,Y) does not match S(X1,W,Z). However, the clause for *subset* has a structure that is similar to the one found for *append* and *intersection*, and we would like to cover all three with just one clause template. This is achieved by introducing argument variables that may actually instantiate to a list of separate arguments.

In order to do so, and also for allowing for other, more sophisticated restrictions, the clause template no longer has the Prolog-like form of rule models: it is represented as a record including one field for the head of the clause, one field for the antecedent, and one field for additional conditions. The fields for the head and for the antecedent contain records that describe individual literals. The fields for a literal include the predicate name Pred, the arguments Args, the new variables NVars introduced by the literal, the type and mode of the arguments, the functors that may occur in the literal, and other informations The predicate name may be a variable, as in rule models. Here, however, the arguments field may also contain a variable that may be instantiated to the list of actual arguments. For example, a template that would cover the above given clauses for *append*, *intersection*, and *subset* is:

Head: [Pred: P, Args: A1, NVars:_, ...]
Body: [Pred: Q, Args: A2, NVars:{X1,X2}, ...]
[Pred: R, Args: A3, NVars:{}, ...]
[Pred: P, Args: A4, NVars:_, ...]
[Pred: S, Args: A5, NVars:{}, ...]
Conds: $2 \leq \text{length}(A1)$
$\text{length}(A4) \leq 3$
$2 \leq \text{length}(A5)$

where an underscore (_) means that the value of the field is not relevant, i.e., no

6.2. Clause Templates

additional constraint is specified. For instance, there is no restriction on which or how many new variables are introduced with predicate P in the above clause template. By contrast, predicate R is required to introduce no new variables.

Another constraint that may be useful and is not shown above concerns the fact that a variable introduced by some literal may be known to occur in a literal that follows. This restriction could be specified by complicated formulas in the Conds field of the clause. However, it may be simpler to specify this by a graph representation [203, 190, 33]: every record for a literal is represented by a node of the graph, and edges specify so-called connection paths. If there is a link from the node for literal l1 to the node for literal l2, then a new variable in l1 must also occur in l2. Details are found in [190]. In general, there are a number of conflicting goals when providing such a specification. On the one hand, one would like to exclude all clauses that are not useful, and add as many constraints and conditions as possible. On the other hand, the template should be simple and easy to read for a user or for a programmer. Moreover, it should be sufficiently general to cover the clauses that are needed in the target program.

Rule models and templates surveyed in this section are a form of *static bias*: a clause is possible, and may be part of a program $P \in \mathcal{P}$, if it matches a given schema. Although it applies to Prolog programs, and not just to clauses, the clause set bias language discussed in section 6.5 also falls under this category. By contrast, *generative bias* languages do not provide a template to be matched but, rather, a set of operators that construct clauses incrementally, usually by instantiating some variables or by adding literals to the antecedents. As we have anticipated, refinement operators are a form of generative bias. Domain theories used in some forms of analytic learning and Antecedent Description Grammars, discussed in the next section, also fit into this framework. Although generative languages may be appropriate for describing in a concise way a very large space of possible clauses, we believe that static languages are more appropriate in software development contexts. The reason is that there is a large gap separating a generative language and the Prolog clauses that are produced. It takes time for a programmer to determine whether a clause can be generated or not, and a small modification in the bias specification may cause important changes in the space $\mathcal{P}$ of possible programs. This has been called the *unfolding problem* for generative bias languages: the specification of which clauses are possible has to be "unfolded" several times before these clauses are generated. Therefore, the hierarchical structure of the bias specification and the one of the programs that may be learned is different. When developing Prolog programs, the programmer will soon reach some syntactic approximation of the desired program where the control structure is more or less determined but the precise input-output behavior may need further work. Programs with mutations, sets of possible clauses and literals, and templates of different kinds seem

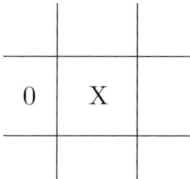

Figure 6.1: An example of the concept "player O loses"

appropriate for describing such syntactic approximations. Asking the programmer to provide a generative mechanism that produces all the clauses in the desired program seems less realistic.

6.3 Domain Theories and Grammars

The key word *Explanation-Based Learning* (EBL) was used for some time to indicate a number of knowledge-intensive learning methods. Usually, Explanation-Based Learning is *deductive*, or *analytic*, in the sense that it uses examples and prior knowledge to deduce a new concept description that may be useful for future classification. Thus, EBL is not really a form of induction: the obtained concept descriptions are implicitly known beforehand, as they are a logical consequence of the given domain theory. However, they may lead to more efficient classification of future examples. For this reason, EBL has been especially applied to learning problems that arise in planning and robotics. A survey of EBL research is found in [70]. Here, we will present an alternative interpretation and view the use of a domain theory in EBL as a form of bias. The same view is adopted for Cohen's Antecedent Description Grammars [47, 48].

As one of our favourite examples of EBL, consider the tic-tac-toe board of figure 6.1, and suppose that the rules of the game are written in a Horn clause program that we shall call a "domain theory".

Now, the fact that the game position in figure 6.1 leads to a loss for player "O" is a logical consequence of the domain theory. Normally, EBL systems would develop a proof of this fact and would then generalize the proof as far as it still holds. The leaves of the generalized proof tree would then be output as a learned concept description. In our example, one could obtain:

loses(O) :- moves(X,5), moves(O,Y), side(Y).

6.3. Domain Theories and Grammars

side(2). side(4). side(6). side(8).

This rule is correct and, in fact, it is a consequence of the rules of the game, i.e., of the domain theory. For this reason, EBL has sometimes been presented as a form of lemma generation. Although the learned rule says nothing new with respect to the domain theory, it may be useful if games frequently produce situations such as the one of figure 6.1. In that case, the learned rule can be applied immediately, without requiring longer inference with the whole domain theory. For this reason, EBL is also referred to as speed-up learning. For the same reason, the learned rules are usually required to be *operational*, i.e., easy or efficient to evaluate. Accordingly, a predicate may be defined as operational or nonoperational depending on the difficulty of its evaluation. An operational rule is required to contain predicates that are all operational. For instance, the rule:

wins(player1,position1) :- possible_move(player1,position1,position2),
                        loses(player2,position2).

would not be considered operational, because its evaluation may require many recursive calls with a high degree of nondeterminism. In other words, this rule requires the expansion of the whole game tree. By contrast, the previous rule saying the "O" loses when moving on the side of a tic-tac-toe board would be operational, as it contains only predicates specifying the position of X and O in the current board situation.

In order to reach our goals, we now need two observations. First, as it was emphasized early on [137], EBL may work with just one example. The discussion above shows this clearly. Second, if the domain theory is correct, the learned rule is also correct. This is obvious, as the learned rule is a logical consequence of the domain theory. However, EBL research soon became interested in using many examples and imperfect domain theories [17, 198, 52, 155]. The use of many examples is also useful when the domain theory is correct in the context of speed-up learning: even though we know that the learned rule is correct, we do not know how useful it will be. It may happen that a new example that satisfies the conditions in the learned rule is never encountered again, and the rule stays in memory without producing any advantage. Minton [134] studies situations where this phenomenon causes a performance loss. A natural way to overcome this problem is to prefer rules that cover many examples and not just one. It will then be more probable, under appropriate assumptions, that the learned rule will be useful in future cases.

The interest in imperfect domain theories arose also in classification applications, and is motivated by the fact that prior knowledge obtained through a domain expert may not be 100 percent correct. In this case, using many examples is even more important. The rule obtained via EBL is a consequence of the domain theory, but it may be incorrect just like the domain theory. If the rule is confirmed by many positive examples, it will then be preferred to other consequences of the domain theory for which there is no factual evidence.

In order to state our view of EBL, we need to put these observations together. The domain theory is a way to specify a bias, to describe in a concise way a space $\mathcal{C}$ of possible clauses: a clause is permitted by the bias, i.e., it belongs to $\mathcal{C}$, if it is a logical consequence of the domain theory. A learning system, be it EBL or inductive, will then explore the space of possible clauses to select a logic program that is complete and consistent with respect to the available examples.

Suppose, for instance, that the following domain theory is given:

p(X) :- s(a,X).
p(X) :- s(X,b).
s(X,Y) :- q(Y), r(X).
s(X,Y) :- r(Y), q(X).
q(a). r(a). r(b).

and that p(a) is a positive example and p(b) is negative. Suppose also that q and r are defined as operational, while s and p are not. The clauses

p(X) :- q(X), r(a).
p(X) :- r(X), q(a).
p(X) :- q(b), r(X).
p(X) :- r(b), q(X).

are all logical operational consequences of the domain theory.

The first clause covers only p(a).
The second clause covers p(a) and p(b).
The third clause covers no examples.
The fourth clause covers only p(a).

Then, the clauses that cover only positive examples (the first and the last) could be output as a learned description for predicate p. The domain theory had the role of describing these four possible clauses while excluding others that might have also been consistent with the examples (e.g., p(X) :- q(X)). In other words, the domain theory has defined a language bias.

The version of ML-SMART described in [17] and FOCL [155] are similar systems that learn relational concepts using a domain theory as a language bias. There are obviously some differences and much algorithmic detail that we cannot go into in this book. However, their basic learning strategy can be summarized as follows. Let us consider a top-down learning framework such as the one of FOIL: clauses are specialized step by step, until only positive examples are covered, and more

6.3. Domain Theories and Grammars

consistent clauses are generated until all positive examples are covered. Testing whether a clause covers some example is done extensionally, i.e., by evaluating the literals in the body on the basis of the background knowledge and of the available examples.

Suppose we want to learn a definition for the unary predicate p, and the available predicates for building such a definition are q and r, also unary. FOIL would start with the clause p(X), with an empty antecedent. Then more literals would be added. In this case, we could add either q(X) or r(X). As before, suppose p(a) is positive and p(b) is negative. Then the literal q(X) has a higher gain as it covers just the positive example and would be chosen. Negative examples are not covered and specialization stops, yielding the clause p(X) :- q(X). More clauses are not needed, as there was only one positive example.

In our simplified description of ML-SMART and FOCL, we have one starting clause for every definition of p in the domain theory. In our example, p(X) :- s(a,X) and p(X) :- s(X,b) would both be possible. If there is no definition of the target predicate in the domain theory, the clause with an empty antecedent is used for starting, as in FOIL. As we see, clause antecedents may then contain predicates that are nonoperational. These predicates cannot be checked directly on the examples, and have no effect on coverage. Specialization may be done in three ways:

(1) adding an operational predicate, as in FOIL,
(2) adding a nonoperational predicate, or
(3) replacing a nonoperational predicate with its definition in the domain theory.

It may then happen, as in case (2), that specialization only adds a nonoperational predicate. The same occurs in case (3) when the antecedent of the clause used from the domain theory contains no operational literals. In this case, coverage would not be affected and gain would be zero. Only later, when operational predicates start to be added, that specialization step might turn out to be useful. We would then need a top-down method that allows for zero-gain specializations (e.g., the version of FOIL described in [161]) or in which some kind of beam search or backtracking is possible.

If pure EBL is used, only steps of type (3) are allowed. The domain theory is unfolded until fully operational and consistent clauses are obtained. For instance, the starting clause p(X) :- s(a,X), could be specialized to p(X) :- q(X), r(a) by using the rule s(X,Y) :- q(Y), r(X) in the domain theory. Such deductive specialization steps are evaluated as usual: the specialization is useful if, after adding both the literals q(X) and r(a), more positive examples or fewer negative examples are covered. This can be done with an information-based heuristic, as in FOCL, or with ad hoc heuristics in the context of a best-first search, as in ML-SMART. In this case, the domain theory will play the role of a strict language bias, as only the clauses that are obtained by unfolding the theory may possibly be learned. Alternatively, the bias may be weakened into a form of preference bias by also allowing specializations of type (1) and (2), while still giving precedence to deductive steps of type (3). This is the philosophy behind the particular choices followed in ML-SMART and FOCL.

Within this framework, it is also easy to describe the notion of *relational clichés* [154, 178]. Suppose only specializations of type (1) and (2) are possible, with a small modification of step (2):

(2') instead of adding a nonoperational predicate, which would then be useless because steps of type (3) are disallowed, add all the literals in the body of a clause that defines that nonoperational predicate.

We also assume that the antecedents of clauses in the domain theory are operational. Such clause antecedents are called clichés and are useful for adding a group of operational literals in just one step, in the context of an extensional top-down learning system. This is useful when adding one literal at a time produces no gain, and only the addition of the last literal in the group finally proves to be useful. This usually happens because the first literals are needed only to compute information to be used later. For example, when learning the concept bird(X), part_of(X,Y) may produce no gain, but part_of(X,Y) $\wedge$ wing(Y) would be useful. One could then define the cliché has_wing(X) :- part_of(X,Y) $\wedge$ wing(Y), where has_wing is nonoperational, to be used in specialization steps of type (2'). Again, a cliché is a form of preference bias, as it favors clauses that contain some conjunctions of literals.

We have shown how to describe the set $\mathcal{C}$ of possible clauses with a domain theory. The rules in the theory unfold until a clause is generated where all literals in the body are operational. A similar idea is the basis of Cohen's *Antecedent Description Grammars* (ADGs) [47, 48]. The antecedents of the possible clauses are seen as strings of literals and are defined by a context-free grammar; the productions in the grammar unfold until a string of terminal symbols is generated. The literals that are written as a terminal string would correspond to the operational literals used with a domain theory. ADGs have been used in the system Grendel, which follows a FOIL-like scheme but unfolds grammar productions where FOIL would perform arbitrary specialization steps.

As an example, consider the above given domain theory that defined the unary predicate p with operational predicates q and r. Here is the corresponding ADG:

body(p(X)) $\rightarrow$ s(a,X)

6.3. Domain Theories and Grammars

body(p(X)) → s(X,b)
s(X,Y) → [q(Y)], [r(X)]
s(X,Y) → [r(Y)], [q(X)]

where brackets are used for delimiting terminal strings, and the notation body(p(X)) identifies the start symbol of the grammar. The facts q(a), r(a), r(b) are not part of the grammar, although they were included in the corresponding domain theory, because they do not help specifying the language bias. By contrast, they will be included in the background knowledge at learning time.

Let use now consider a more complex example, and define a bias appropriate for learning clauses such as the following:

append(X,Y,Z) :- cons(X1,X2,X), no_op(X1,Y), append(X2,Y,W), cons(X1,W,Z).

Suppose, for instance, that we want to allow for clause antecedents where the only predicates that may occur are *cons*, *no_op*, *member*, and *append*, and at most three new variables are used. The following grammar specifies this bias:

body(append(X,Y,Z)) → rels
rels → []
rels → rel2(X,Y,Z,X1,X2,W), rels
rels → rel3(X,Y,Z,X1,X2,W), rels

rel2(X,Y,Z,X1,X2,W) → lit2(X,X)
rel2(X,Y,Z,X1,X2,W) → lit2(X,Y)
...
rel2(X,Y,Z,X1,X2,W) → lit2(W,W)

rel3(X,Y,Z,X1,X2,W) → lit3(X,X,X)
rel3(X,Y,Z,X1,X2,W) → lit3(X,X,Y)
...
rel3(X,Y,Z,X1,X2,W) → lit3(W,W,W)

lit2(X,Y) → [no_op(X,Y)].
lit2(X,Y) → [member(X,Y)].
lit3(X,Y,Z) → [cons(X,Y,Z)].
lit3(X,Y,Z) → [append(X,Y,Z)].

This grammar generates a nonterminal string that is the antecedent of the clause for *append* given above. The grammar can also be used for *intersection* by substituting intersection(X,Y,Z) for append(X,Y,Z) in the first and in the last productions. The bias would then allow for the clause:

intersection(X,Y,Z) :- cons(X1,X2,X), member(X1,Y),
                intersection(X2,Y,W), cons(X1,W,Z).

As grammars such as the above tend to be quite verbose, Grendel uses an ADG specification that includes macros with an escape to Prolog. A macro is a statement of the type:

A ← B where G

where A ← B has the syntax of an ADG production and G is a Prolog goal. A, B, and G may share variables, and the macro will be expanded to all productions obtained by substituting Prolog's computed answers for G in A and B. For instance, the above grammar could be simplified by using the following macros and Prolog clauses:

rel2(X,Y,Z,X1,X2,W) → lit2(A,B) where members([A,B],[X,Y,Z,X1,X2,W])
rel3(X,Y,Z,X1,X2,W) → lit3(A,B,C) where members([A,B,C],[X,Y,Z,X1,X2,W])

members([],_).
members([X|Y],Z) :- member(X,Z), members(Y,Z).

where *member* is defined as usual. The macros would expand to all productions previously needed for *rel2* and *rel3*.

Recently, Grendel has been extended to deal with "lazy" macros, which are expanded as follows:

while there is an undefined nonterminal in the generated ADG **do**
        select one such nonterminal N
        find a macro "A → B where G" such that N=Aσ
        expand the macro N → Bσ where Gσ

In other words, the macros are expanded only for the instantiations of the nonterminals that arise during the generation of the grammar, and when they arise. Such macros can be used to define quite sophisticated restrictions. Suppose, for instance, that we require the possible clauses for *append* and *intersection* to be connected: each literal must contain at least one variable that is in the head of the clause or occurs in a previous literal of the antecedent. If, again, we have at most three new variables, the following ADG defined with lazy macros will do:

body(append(X,Y,Z)) → rels([X,Y,Z],[X,Y,Z,X1,X2,W])
rels(CVars,Vars) → []
rels(CVars,Vars) → [L], rels(CVars1,Vars) where
               lit(L), variables(L,V), members(V,Vars),
               not intersection(V,CVars,[]), union(CVars,V,CVars1)

lit(cons(X,Y,Z)).
lit(append(X,Y,Z)).
lit(no_op(X,Y)).
lit(member(X,Y)).

where variables(L,V) is defined in Prolog to unify V with a list containing the variables of literal L, *members* was defined above, and *intersection* and *union* are defined as usual. The lazy macro in the third line of the grammar specification is expanded only after substituting [X,Y,Z] for CVars and [X,Y,Z,X1,X2,W] for Vars. This produces a sentential form still containing the nonterminal *rels*, asking for a further expansion step, using the same lazy macro. At this point, CVars1 will have been instantiated to [X,Y,Z|T], where T is the list of new variables added by the literal L that was obtained in the first step. The bias defined by this grammar still admits our target clauses for *append* and *intersection*, but excludes a large number of clauses that were possible with the previous bias specification.

6.4 Bias in Bottom-up Systems

The forms of bias discussed in the previous sections are most appropriate for top-down learning systems. This is especially true for refinement operators and for unfolding rules used with domain theories and grammars: the clauses that are permitted by the language bias are obtained with a number of predefined specialization operators that can be used naturally in a top-down learner. For templates, one could also imagine their use in a bottom-up framework. For example, whenever the *lgg* of two clauses is generated, we can check whether the obtained generalization matches some given clause schema. If it does not, the generalization is rejected and alternative clauses are considered. However, both rule models and Clause Sets (described in the next section) have been used in top-down systems (RDT of MOBAL [107], FILP [21], and TRACY [22]).

An analysis of bias in bottom-up systems is found in [1]. The important observation there (also found in [147]) is that bottom-up systems usually work in two phases: first, a so-called *starting clause* is generated by modifying one given positive example, then the starting clause is generalized until an acceptable concept definition is obtained. In [1] both steps depend on inductive bias. A generic bottom-up learning procedure, called NINA, is proposed. It can be simplified as follows:

NINA(E^+, E^-, BK, Bias)   /*BK is the background knowledge*/
P := the empty program
for all e∈E^+ such that P ∪ BK $\not\vdash$ e **do**
    C := *starting_clause*(e, BK, P, Bias)
    if BK ∪ P ∪ {C} ∪ E^- is consistent, **then**
        P := *generalize*(C, P, BK, E^+, E^-, Bias).
return P

starting_clause(e, BK, P, Bias)
C := e with constants replaced by variables
if C satisfies Bias **then**
    while there is a specialization C′ of C such that
        P ∪ {C′} satisfies Bias and BK ∪ P ∪ {C′} $\vdash$ e **do**
        C := C′
    else return fail
return C

generalize(C,P,BK,E^+, E^-,Bias)
if there is C′ ∈ P such that
    (a) BK ∪ P ∪ lgg(C,C′) ∪ E^- is consistent, and
    (b) P ∪ lgg(C,C′) satisfies Bias
    then remove C′ from P and add lgg(C,C′)
    else add C to P
return P

The main algorithm matches most specific-to-general ILP methods, including, e.g., GOLEM [145], CLINT [57], and ITOU[166]. NINA has been used as a generic bottom-up learner to emulate such systems by setting the Bias parameter to appropriate evaluation functions. However, it should be noted that the creation of the starting clause has a top-down flavor. The starting clause is obtained by adding information to the positive example being considered. This may be done by adding literals that are deduced from the background knowledge and the example, as done via saturation in ITOU and IRES [169], or by genuine forms of specialization, as done in APT [146] with the help of the user. As a consequence, forms of language bias such as refinement operators and Antecedent Description Grammars can be

6.4. Bias in Bottom-up Systems

used without problems: the starting clause is made more specific by applying a refinement operator or by rewriting a literal with a production of the ADG. By contrast, when the Bias parameter is used in the generalization procedure, the algorithmic framework is clearly bottom-up. After a generalization of the starting clause C and of a clause $C' \in P$ has been generated, we must check whether it satisfies the given bias. This is done more easily if bias is specified via templates. And, in fact, NINA uses a bias language that is a generalization of rule models of RDT and of the Clause Set formalism described in the next section.

There are actually two distinct forms of bias considered in NINA: syntactic and semantic. Syntactic bias simply specifies a set $\mathcal{C}$ of possible clauses, and may be easily described with templates. Semantic bias tells the system whether a clause is acceptable also on the basis of the background knowledge, the partial program learned at some moment, and the available examples. An example of semantic bias is determinism, as defined in chapter 3: unless we make a priori assumptions, we must check whether a literal is determinate by running the learned program and the background knowledge on the input values provided by the examples. As GOLEM's bias is based on ij-determinism, also defined in chapter 3, NINA must include a semantic bias check before generating a clause.

Another issue of interest in NINA (and necessary for emulating CLINT) is the possibility of modifying the bias when no appropriate clause can be generated: a demand-driven *shift of bias*. This possibility is considered only when generating a starting clause. Suppose that a series B_1, B_2, ..., B_k of weaker and weaker biases is defined. NINA first uses the strongest bias B_1, corresponding to the smallest hypothesis space. If the starting clause produced by the above given procedure is inconsistent with respect to the negative examples, then the next bias B_2 is used, until a consistent starting clause is found or B_k is reached and a failure is detected. More on shift of bias and representation change is found in [140].

The system NINA, which we have just summarized, can be used as a tunable bottom-up ILP learner: by changing its parameters, i.e., the semantic and the syntactic bias, one can simulate existing learning methods or experiment with new forms of bias. The same can be done with Grendel and Antecedent Description Grammars for the case of top-down systems: most biases used in general-to-specific learning can be described with ADGs, and Grendel implements the corresponding specialization operators. One may wonder whether a generic framework can be found that includes both top-down and bottom-up methods. One positive answer is found in DeRaedt's algorithmic scheme called Gencol [57]. A more recent and extensive study with an implementation is found in [147], where the HAIKU system is described. Here is a simplification of the main procedures:

HAIKU(BK, Examples, Language_Bias, Search_Bias,
        Stopping_Criterion, Local_Stopping_Criterion
        Intermediate_Validation, Partial_Learning_Criterion)
P := the empty program
while not Stopping_Criterion **do**
        Bound := Starting_Bound(Examples, BK, Language_Bias)
        P' := Search(Bound, BK, Local_Stopping_Criterion, Language_Bias,
             Search_Bias, Intermediate_Validation, Partial_Learning_Criterion)
        P := P ∪ P'
return P

Search(Bound, BK, Local_Stopping_Criterion, Language_Bias,
        Search_Bias, Intermediate_Validation, Partial_Learning_Criterion)
P' := the empty program
while not Local_Stopping_Criterion **do**
        remove a clause C from Bound using Search_Bias
        Clauses := Operator_Application(C)
        if C'∈Clauses does not satisfy Language_Bias, remove C' from Clauses
        Bound := Bound ∪ select_some(Clauses, Intermediate_Validation)
        Accepted_Clauses := select_some(Bound, Partial_Learning_Criterion)
        Bound := Bound - Accepted_Clauses
        P' := P' ∪ Accepted_Clauses
return P'

In top-down systems, the starting bound is typically the empty clause or a clause of the type $p(X_1, ..., X_n)$, where p is the n-ary target concept. As a consequence, the starting bound does not depend on any given example, and is usually unchanged at every iteration of the main loop. The stopping criterion for the main loop is usually related to completeness: HAIKU stops when all or most positive examples are covered by the learned program P. The internal loop in the Search procedure ends when Local_Stopping_Criterion is true. In a top-down system such as FOIL, MIS, or ML-SMART, the program P' produced by the Search procedure is just one clause, and the Local_Stopping_Criterion is consistency with respect to the negative examples. Similarly, Partial_Learning_Criterion accepts generated clauses that are consistent. The Bound contains a set of clauses that may still be specialized in a useful way, e.g., clauses that cover at least one positive example. With greedy search, as in FOIL, Bound would contain just one clause that is being specialized by appropriate operators. The same holds for depth-first search. With best-first search, as in MIS and FILP, Bound contains the frontier of the specialization graph being searched.

In bottom-up systems, the starting bound is usually based on one positive example, possibly with the addition of some literals, as done in ITOU or APT. It corresponds to the "starting clause" of NINA, discussed early in this section. As a consequence, the Bound typically changes at every iteration of the main loop. The internal loop explores the search subspace determined by the starting bound. A similar scheme is followed in Michalski's *star* methodology. In the internal loop, the clauses in the Bound are modified by generalization operators, and a clause is accepted by Partial_Learning_Criterion when further generalization would produce inconsistencies. If the output partial program P' must contain just one clause, this is also the Partial_Stopping_Criterion. Otherwise, more than one clause may be obtained. For example, with the *star* methodology, all possible maximal generalizations that are still consistent must be produced before Local_Stopping_Criterion is true and the Search procedure returns a partial solution P'.

In the above framework, we may observe a number of different biases. The language bias, as usual, defines the syntax of the clauses that may possibly be learned. Search bias, used when selecting the clause to be specialized or generalized in the Search procedure, affects the order used by the system to consider the possible clauses. Finally, there is a form of bias, which has been called "validation" bias [147], including the Partial_Learning_Criterion for deciding when some clause can be accepted and the stopping criteria. With Software Engineering applications, we are mostly interested in strong language bias. The search space must be small and in some cases all of it must be searched, because the user will require a solution program if one exists. As a consequence, search bias can affect only efficiency, and stopping criteria are simply completeness and consistency. Such a software development scenario is the motivation of our language bias formalism, presented in the next section.

6.5 Clause Sets

The bias language that we have used and that will serve throughout the rest of the book uses standard Prolog notation, with the addition of clause, literal, and term sets. The hypothesis space will be described by a pair <known clauses, possible clauses>. A program P belongs to the hypothesis space if P = known clauses ∪ P1, where P1 is a subset of the possible clauses. The simplest syntactic tool for specifying inductive bias within the present framework is given by *Clause Sets*: known clauses are listed as in a Prolog program, while possible clauses are surrounded by brackets denoting a set. For instance, there follows a possible description of a priori information for learning a logic program for *member*:

member(X,[X|_]).
{member(X,[Y|Z]) :- cons(X,W,Z).}

cons(X,Y,[X|Y]).
{member(X,[Y|Z]) :- X≠Y, member(X,Z).
member(X,[Y|Z]) :- cons(Y,Z,W).
member(X,[Y|Z]) :- member(X,Z).}

This means that the learned program will have to include the first clause, which is known, possibly followed by the second clause "member(X,[Y|Z]) :- cons(X,W,Z)."; the third clause "cons(X,Y,[X|Y])." will have to follow. Finally, some or all of the remaining clauses may be appended to the program. There are sixteen different logic programs satisfying these very strict requirements; among these some represent a correct implementation of *member*. All the user will need to do at this point is provide positive and negative examples, e.g., member(a,[b,a]), member(c,[b,d,c]) and ¬member(a,[b]). The procedures described in the next two chapters will select, from among the 16 possible inductive hypotheses, a program deriving the positive examples and not deriving any negative example. As the bias is so strong, the task is very easy in this case, and the learned program can only be a correct version of *member*.

Unfortunately, a priori information is not always so precise, and the set of possible clauses may be much larger. As a consequence, the user may find it awkward, or even impossible, to type them one after the other. To this purpose we define *literal sets*. If a clause occurs in a clause set, then some conjunctions of literals of its antecedent may be surrounded by brackets, denoting a set. In this case the clause represents an *expansion* given by all the clauses that may be obtained by deleting one or more literals from the set. Formally:

{P :- A, {B, C, ...}, D} =
    {P :- A, {C, ...}, D} ∪ {P :- A, B, {C, ...}, D}

A case with variables is shown in figure 6.2.

In other words, the expansion of a clause is the set of clauses obtained by replacing the literal sets with a conjunction of any of its literals. With this syntactic mechanism, one can define in a concise way a large set of possible clauses. Figure 6.3 gives an example of inductive bias for learning *intersection*.

The clause set contains $2^5 + 2^6 = 96$ clauses, and there are 2^{96} permitted programs. Then, even if the given bias may seem quite informative, it still allows for a very large set of different inductive hypotheses. The learning procedure will select a program that is correct with respect to given examples, e.g.:

int([a],[a],[a]), int([],[a],[]), int([b,a],[a],[a]),
¬int([a],[a],[]), ¬int([],[a],[a]), ¬int([b],[a],[b]),

6.5. Clause Sets

```
q(X) :- b(X).
{p(X) :- {q(X), a(X,Y)}.
q(X) :- c(X,Z), {q(Z)}}.
```
(a)

```
q(X) :- b(X).
{p(X).
p(X) :- a(X,Y).
p(X) :- q(X).
p(X) :- q(X), a(X,Y).
q(X) :- c(X,Z).
q(X) :- c(X,Z), q(Z).}
```
(b)

Figure 6.2: (a) Clauses with literal sets ... (b) and their expansion

member(a,[a]), member(a,[b,a]), ¬member(a,[]).

The possible programs that are consistent with the above examples are all correct versions of *intersection* and *member*.

For defining sets of possible clauses even more concisely, our last tool is given by *term sets*: a term occurring in a literal within a literal set may be replaced by a set of terms listed within brackets. The literal is then duplicated in the set where it occurs with different arguments, as indicated by the term set. For instance:

{..., p({X,Y,Z},W), ...}

is the same as:

{..., p(X,W), p(Y,W), p(Z,W), ...}.

In general, term sets are expanded by means of the following rule:

$$\{p(..., \{t_1, ..., t_n\}, ...)\} = \{p(..., t_1, ...), ..., p(..., t_n, ...)\}. \tag{6.1}$$

One predicate may have more than one argument that is a term set. For example:

{..., p({X,Y},{W,Z}), ...} is the same as

---

int([],_,[]).
{
int([X1|X2],Y,Z) :- {member(X1,Y), notmember(X1,Y)},
      {int(X2,Y,Z), int(X2,Y,W), cons(X1,W,Z)}.
member(X,Y) :- {cons(X,Y,Z), cons(X,Z,Y), cons(W,Y,Z),
      cons(W,Z,Y), member(X,Z), member(W,Z)}.
}
cons(X,Y,[X|Y]).
notmember(X,[]).
notmember(X,[Y|Z]) :- X≠Y, notmember(X,Z).

Figure 6.3: Inductive bias for *intersection*

{..., p({X,Y},W), p({X,Y},Z), ...} and therefore the same as
{..., p(X,W), p(Y,W), p(X,Z), p(Y,Z), ...}.

This syntactic device is useful to avoid the rewriting of a predicate with similar arguments. The a priori information shown in figure 6.4 defines a larger set of $2^{10} + 2^5 + 2^9 = 1568$ possible clauses by using term sets. Inductive bias specified as described above is both flexible and adequate for the inductive synthesis of more complex programs. Flexibility is achieved by allowing the user to provide a priori information of different strength and to adapt it to the particular case study. Stronger and more informative prior knowledge is defined by a large set of known clauses and a limited number of possible clauses, i.e., the literal sets must be small and well constrained within the structure of the rest of the program. This will lead to efficient induction, and few examples are required.

If such strong information is not available, while examples abound, then a larger set of possible clauses may be defined with more frequent literal and term sets. The approach can also be applied to complex, real-size programs, and represents a new perspective on inductive synthesis. Learning very complex programs is probably just a dream, but this does not mean that ILP cannot be a useful tool for building large software systems. Most clauses in these programs must be hand-coded, and the basic structure of the program must be determined with traditional techniques. However, our approach would allow the programmer to leave some parts of the code underdetermined, and to fill the gaps with examples. Inductive bias could be

6.5. Clause Sets

```
{
int(X,Y,Z):-{null({X,Z}), head(X,X1), tail(X,X2),
              assign(W,Z), cons(X1,W,Z),
              member(X1,Y), notmember(X1,Y),
              int(X2,Y,{Z,W})
             }.
member(X,Y):-{head(Y,{X,KW}), tail(Y,Tail),
              member({X,KW},Tail)}.
notmember(X,Y) :- {head({Y,Z},{X,KW}), diff(X,KW),
                   tail({Y,Z},Tail), notmember({X,KW},Tail)}.
}
notmember(X,[]).
null([]).
cons(X,Y,[X|Y]).
head(X,[X|_]).
tail(X,[_|X]).
diff(X,Y) :- X≠Y.
assign(X,X).
```

Figure 6.4: Inductive bias for *intersection*, with term sets

defined in our framework and would look like a normal Prolog program, with small literal sets and optional clauses occurring here and there. For this reason we also believe that the syntax of a language for declarative bias in ILP should not go too far away from Prolog.

In any case, the presented framework can be applied to common ILP problems, and usual forms of bias can be formulated with clause and literal sets. Even very weak forms of bias can be obtained by using large term sets. For instance, the following set allows for any clause defining *member* with *cons* and ≠ with at most six typed variables (three of type "atom" and three of type "list"):

```
{member(X,Y) :- {cons({X,A1,A2},{Y,L1,L2},{Y,L1,L2}),
                 member({X,A1,A2},{Y,L1,L2}),
                 {X,A1,A2}≠{X,A1,A2}. }}.
```

Obviously, such poor information produces very large sets of possible clauses, and it is preferable to constrain the use of term sets. However, in some cases it may be cumbersome to avoid the use of large literal sets and specify the possible clauses on a one-by-one basis. To this purpose we provide general mechanisms for eliminating clauses from a set that is considered too large. In particular, the procedure that we have implemented for translating the above formalism into a set of possible clauses accepts a number of options corresponding to general constraints, some of which have been used before in ILP:

1. Predicate modes may be provided that indicate their desired input/output behavior. Every argument of a predicate is labeled as either input or output. Modes need not be unique, e.g., we may have both append(input, input, output) and append(output, output, input). More sophisticated mode declarations involving determinate and nondeterminate literals are found in the PROGOL system [182]. Clause Sets can be reduced according to predicate modes as follows: a clause is permitted only if any input variable of any predicate in the antecedent either occurs earlier in the antecedent or is an input variable in the head. This is called a requirement of instantiated inputs.

2. The output variables in the head of a possible clause may be required to occur as an output of some predicate in the antecedent. This guarantees that an instantiated output is produced when the clause is called.

3. Once an output is produced, one may require that it is not instantiated again. Syntactically, this means that any variable cannot occur as output in the antecedent more than once.

4. Forcing outputs to be used: any output variable in the antecedent must occur either as input in some literal to the right or as output in the head.

5. Forcing inputs to be used: all input variables in the head must occur in the antecedent.

6. Forbidden clauses: it is sometimes easier to define a large set of clauses, and list a smaller number of clauses to be removed from the set, rather to list one by one the clauses that are possible. The procedure for generating a set of possible clauses from our language with literal and term sets also accepts in input a set of forbidden clauses.

7. Forbidden conjunctions: with the same motivations as above, some conjunctions of literals may be ruled out, meaning that no antecedent of a possible clause may contain them. This can be useful for two reasons: the conjunction is always true, e.g., Y is X+1 $\land$ X=Y-1, or it is contradictory, e.g., head(L,A) $\land$ null(L).

6.5. Clause Sets

As clauses become more structured into sequences of input/output computations, and as programs become more deterministic, it is likely that restrictions 1-5 do not exclude the solution while greatly reducing the space of possible clauses to be searched by the inductive method. Obviously, for efficiency reasons, clauses are not generated and then filtered. Instead, a clause is produced only if it is permitted with respect to the specified constraints. Note that in our approach, constraints 1 through 7 play the role of heuristics: the learning procedure will explore only that part of the original hypothesis space delimited by the employed constraints. Finally, even the position of the clauses in the hypothesis space can affect the efficiency of the learning procedure. Since it can be controlled by means of the described language, it represents another heuristic criterion available to the user.

The last point that we must discuss for Clause Sets is the problem of recursive clauses and termination. The learned program must of course terminate, at least on the given examples. Besides that, the inductive methods presented in the next two chapters may require that even the possible clauses form a terminating program. This requirement can either be left to the user or handled automatically.

If left to the user, the set of possible clauses must be designed so that no infinite chain of recursive calls can take place. For example, the inductive bias of figure 6.3 does not have this property, because it allows for the clause:

member(X,Y) :- cons(X,Y,Z), member(X,Z).

which produces a loop when called on any input.

If handled automatically, all the user has to do is indicate which predicates define a well-order relation. A similar point of view is followed in MIS [176]. For instance, cons(X,Y,Z) determines the well-ordering Y<Z. The procedure transforming our formalism into a set of possible clauses will then remove all the recursive clauses that do not match the following pattern:

P(X1, ..., Xi, ..., Xn) :- ..., rel(Y,Xi), ..., P(X1, ..., Y, ..., Xn), ...

where *rel* is any well-order relation. In words, the recursive call must have the same arguments as the head of the clause, except for one that makes it one step closer to termination. This differs from what is done in FOIL, because it guarantees that clauses will always terminate, and not only on the available examples. Obviously, more information is required, i.e., the indication of the well-order relations.

Some of the biases described in this section may seem too strong or too difficult to specify for the user. However, efficient learning requires that both the examples and the set $\mathcal{P}$ of possible programs be carefully selected. This is certainly not as demanding as writing the very program that we want to learn, because (1) instantiated information such as positive and negative examples is easier to define and check for correctness, and (2) a set $\mathcal{P}$ of possible programs is less informative than a precisely defined computation rule: it is easier to say that *intersection* is linearly recursive, and requires *member*, than it is to provide a correct program. An extended and partly modified Clause Set language is described in [1] and is used in the systems NINA [1] and CLAUDIEN [61].

7
Program Induction with Queries

Only few systems (e.g., [107, 139, 58]) are able to perform multiple predicate learning. In top-down methods, this is due, in part, to the need for learning clauses one at a time and independently of each other. If we want to learn a program for predicates P and Q, and we try to construct a clause antecedent for P where Q occurs, then the truth value of Q must have been defined by the user or determined extensionally, by means of all of its relevant examples. Something similar occurs with recursion, i.e., for the case when Q=P. We will show in this chapter that, as a consequence of the extensional interpretation of recursion and subpredicates, systems may be unable to learn a program, even when an allowed inductive hypothesis that is consistent with the examples exists. Even worse, it may happen that a program is learned that computes wrong outputs even for the *given* examples.

The FILP system, described in this chapter, solves these problems of top-down methods by querying the user for any example that may be missing, depending on the hypothesis space that has been defined. As a result of this, every learned program behaves as required on the given examples, and such a program is always found if it exists. Moreover, we restrict the inductive hypotheses to logic programs that are *functional*, i.e., such that each n-ary predicate can be associated to a total function as follows: m of its arguments are labeled as input, while the remaining n-m are labeled as output, and for every given sequence of input values, there is one and only one sequence of output values that makes the predicate true. Output values must always exist and be unique, and the whole program must correspond to a total function. The space $\mathcal{C}$ of possible clauses is defined with the Clause Set language described in the previous chapter, and the above functionality restrictions are built on top of the input-output modes that are available with Clause Sets. Thus, functionality must be determined by the user and is assumed also for the examples that are not seen. This is necessary because some examples may be missing and will be queried later.

These requirements do not affect expressive power, as any computable function can be represented by a functional logic program and, on the other hand, make the learning task much easier, because many clauses that would otherwise need to be generated and checked against the examples are now disallowed a priori, and the order of the literals within a clause antecedent is somehow constrained by the need for computing an output value before it can be used as input in another literal. The queries that are asked to the user are existential queries of type II, because they contain unbound variables that must be instantiated. However, these variables are labeled as output and, as a consequence, there is always one and only one answer to every such query.

Therefore, functionality is the central idea that allows us to face what we have individuated as two major problems in ILP: (1) restricting further and in an explicit way the set of allowed inductive hypotheses and (2) being able to learn multiple predicates, in our case by means of input/output queries that make the extensional information sufficient. In the following we will call the predicates that we need to learn the *inductive predicates*, while the others will be either built-in or defined by the user.

FILP does not need a complete extensional specification of the predicates to be learned, up to a certain example complexity, as it happens, e.g., with FOIL [160]. Such a specification can be even more time-consuming and error-prone for the user than actually writing the desired program. By contrast, a very limited number of initial examples is required by FILP, and a few additional input values are presented to the user, and the corresponding outputs are requested. However, not all of these input/output examples are necessary, in the sense that it may happen that, even for a subset of them, there is only one allowed program that is consistent (i.e., the solution is determined). We believe that this problem cannot be remedied unless we give up the extensional interpretation of predicates. But, in that case, the order in which the clauses are generated becomes relevant, and backtracking may be required. Sound and complete learning without queries is analyzed in the next chapter in connection with the TRACY system. The FILP system described here is also used for some of the Software Engineering applications described in part III of the book, and most notably for test case generation, where answers to system queries can be generated automatically.

7.1 The FILP System

In this section we present the FILP system and prove some formal properties about it. As in other top-down methods, clauses are learned one at a time, independently of the ones that were learned previously. Since FILP learns functional relations, it really needs only positive examples. Negative examples are implicitly assumed to be all the ones having the same input values as the positive examples but different output values. In the rest of this chapter, by *example* we usually mean a *positive example*.

7.1.1 A functional mode for variables

It is well known that in Logic Programming, variables do not have a fixed role: they can act as input or output variables as desired. For example, the predicate *append*(X,Y,Z) can be used with mode *append*(in,in,out) to append two lists or with mode *append*(out,out,in) to split a list into two sublists.

On the other hand, if we want to learn functional logic programs (logic programs whose input-output behavior is functional), we need to specify a (functional) mode for every variable of every literal used in the learning task, in order to employ and learn only functional relations. For example, *append*(in,in,out) would be a legal way to use append, but *append*(out,out,in) would not, because it does not represent a function. On this ground, in FILP the user is asked to provide a functional mode for all predicates, and this mode is then used to constrain the allowed clauses as follows:

1. Suppose Q and P have mode Q(in,out) and P(in,out); the literal Q(W,Z) can occur in an intermediate clause P(X,Y) :- α, Q(W,Z), γ iff either (a) W=X (i.e., the input is bound because it is passed as input in the head of the clause) or (b) W occurs in α (i.e., it is computed before Q is called);

2. A clause is in an acceptable final form only if the output variables of its head occur in the body, i.e., only if the output is not left unbound.

For example, suppose we have to learn a concept c with a mode for variables c(in,in,out), using predicates a, b, d with a mode for variables a(in,out), b(in,out), d(in,in,in,out). Then the clause "c(X,Y,Z) :- a(X,W),b(Y,K),d(X,W,K,Z)" is a legal one because every input variable is defined before being used, and the output variable of c is at last instantiated.

7.1.2 A basic version of FILP

This subsection contains a basic version of FILP (BFILP), without queries for adding the missing information, and an example of its use, in order to describe the approach and to prepare the discussion of the problems stemming from it and the extension that is needed. This basic algorithmic scheme is similar to the ones of ML-SMART [17] and FOIL, but uses a bias specification with Clause Sets and requires functionality constraints. As a consequence, it does not need any negative example. It also accepts more than one inductive predicate, although the extension presented later is necessary for making this feature work in general. In the following, α and γ represent generic conjunctions of literals.

Basic FILP:
for all inductive predicates P **do**
while examples(P) $\neq \emptyset$ **do**
    Generate one clause "P($\vec{X}$) :- α"
    examples(P) $\leftarrow$ examples(P) $-$ covered(α)

Generate one clause:
$\alpha \leftarrow$ true
while covered(α) $\neq \emptyset$ **do**
    if consistent(α) **then** return(P($\vec{X}$) :- α)
        else 1. choose a predicate Q and its arguments Args
              2. if no such Q is found, then backtrack on 1.
              3. $\alpha \leftarrow \alpha \wedge$ Q(Args)

where every predicate Q can be defined by the user (intensionally) by means of logical rules or (extensionally) simply by giving some examples of its input-output behavior. In particular, clauses can be recursive and, in this case, Q = P, and its truth value can be determined only by the available examples.

Definition 27 *We say that the clause P(X,Y) :- α(X,Y) extensionally covers P(a,b) iff α(a,Y) extensionally computes Y = b, where extensional computation is defined as follows:*

- α = Q(a,Y) with functional mode Q(in,out). Then Q(a,Y) *extensionally computes* Y = b iff Q(a,b) is derivable from the definition of Q or is a given example of Q.

- α = γ(X,T), Q(T,Y) with functional mode γ(in,out) and Q(in,out). Then γ(a,T), Q(T,Y) *extensionally computes* Y = b iff γ(a,T) *extensionally computes* T = e and Q(e,b) is derivable from the definition of Q or is a given example of Q.

7.1. The FILP System

In the algorithm, an example P(a,b) belongs to covered(α) iff α(a,Y) extensionally computes Y=b, and consistent(α) is true iff, for no such example, α(a,Y) extensionally computes Y=c and c$\neq$b. The choice of the literal Q(Args) to add to α is guided by heuristic information and is a backtracking point.

Suppose, for instance, that BFILP has to learn the logic program for *reverse*. Let examples(*reverse*) be:

reverse([],[]), reverse([a],[a]), reverse([c],[c]), reverse([a,b],[b,a]), reverse([b,c],[c,b]), reverse([a,b,c],[c,b,a]).

Suppose we also know that *reverse* depends on the following set of predicates:

null, head, tail, assign, append, reverse.

We also suppose that the usual definitions of *null*, *head*, *tail*, *assign*, and *append*, are given. This is important information, but obviously still very far away from the actual program that we want to learn: we need to associate variables to these predicates and divide the obtained literals among the unknown number of clauses that will be necessary. The order of the literals is partially constrained by their mode:

null(out), null(out), head(in,out), tail(in,out),
assign(in,out), append(in,in,out), reverse(in,out).

BFILP starts to generate the first clause — the antecedent α is initially empty. We need to choose the first literal Q(Args) to be added to α. As we have left the heuristic criterion unspecified, we will choose it so as to make the discussion short. Variables are taken from the clause head or from a finite set of additional typed variables.

Let α=null(Y). A given example is covered, but we cannot accept the clause "reverse(X,Y) :- null(Y)" as it is, because it computes wrong outputs for some given input values, e.g. reverse([a],[]), so more literals need to be added.

Let α=null(Y) $\wedge$ head(X,H); in this case no positive examples are covered. Clause generation fails and we backtrack to the last literal choice.

Let α=null(Y) $\wedge$ null(X); the first example is covered and no wrong outputs can be computed. A clause is generated and the covered example reverse([],[]) is removed from examples(*reverse*).

We proceed to the generation of another clause; α is empty again. Suppose we have already generated α=head(X,H) $\wedge$ tail(X,T); all the remaining examples are covered, but again we have to specialize because α could compute wrong outputs. Let α = head(X,H) $\wedge$ tail(X,T) $\wedge$ reverse(T,W); this clause again extensionally covers all remaining examples. For instance, for the last example we have that head([a,b,c],a) and tail([a,b,c],[b,c]) are true, and reverse([b,c],[c,b]) is a given example. However, the output variable Y is not instantiated and the procedure needs to be continued.

At the next step, suppose we add the literal assign([H],Y). The clause so obtained covers reverse([a],[a]) and reverse([c],[c]), but for reverse([a,b,c],Y) it computes Y=[a], which is not consistent with the data. Further specialization would fail to correct this problem and we need to backtrack, obtaining, e.g.,

$$\alpha = \text{head(X,H)} \wedge \text{tail(X,T)} \wedge \text{reverse(T,W)} \wedge \text{append(W,[H],Y)},$$

which covers all remaining examples and does not compute wrong outputs. The final solution turns out to be:

reverse(X,Y) :- null(Y), null(X).
reverse(X,Y) :- head(X,H), tail(X,T), reverse(T,W), append(W,[H],Y).

7.2 Justification of Extensionality and Problems

In the worst case, all possible literals will be tried every time, and the complexity is exponential in the number of these literals. We view this problem as intrinsic to induction and unavoidable — the only thing we can do is reduce the number of possible clauses by means of strong constraints given a priori by the user. An advantage of extensional methods is that clauses are generated independently of each other. As a consequence, we must search the space of possible clauses (exponential in the number of possible literals), not the space of possible logic programs (= *sets* of possible clauses). This independence of the clauses is made possible by the extensional interpretation of recursion and of the other inductive relations. However, extensionality may also cause problems. In order to analyze these problems, we must adapt the definitions of program completeness and consistency given in chapter 2 to the case of functional logic programs.

Definition 28 *A functional logic program P is complete with respect to the examples E iff* $(\forall\, Q(i,o) \in E)\, P \vdash Q(i,o)$. *A functional logic program P is consistent with respect to the examples E iff* $(\not\exists\, Q(i,o) \in E)\, P \vdash Q(i,o')$ *and* $o \neq o'$.

7.2. Justification of Extensionality and Problems

In other words, a complete program computes all desired outputs, and a consistent program does not compute wrong outputs. Even though the single clauses of P satisfy the functionality constraints, it may happen that P is complete and not consistent, because different values may be computed by different clauses.

Lemma 1 *Suppose BFILP successfully exits its main loop and outputs a logic program P that always terminates for the given examples. Let $Q(X,Y) \;\text{:-}\; \alpha(X,Y)$ be any clause of P; then $(\forall Q(a,b) \in Examples(Q))$ $\alpha(a,Y)$ extensionally computes $Y=b \rightarrow P \vdash Q(a,b)$.*

Proof (by contradiction)
Suppose that (1) $(\forall Q(a,b) \in Examples(Q))$ $\alpha(a,Y)$ extensionally computes $Y=b$ but (2) $P \not\vdash Q(a,b)$. Let $\alpha = \beta(X,Z) \wedge R(Z,W) \wedge \gamma(W,Y)$, where $R(Z,W)$ is the first literal such that:

– R is an inductive predicate (in particular, R could be Q),
– there is an example $R(r,s)$ such that $\beta(a,r) \wedge R(r,s) \wedge \gamma(s,b)$ is extensionally true,
– for any such r and s, $P \not\vdash R(r,s)$.

There must be a literal $R(Z,W)$ in α with these properties because of assumptions (1) and (2). But the example $R(r,s)$ must be extensionally covered, since BFILP has successfully terminated. Therefore, the same argument can be repeated for $R(r,s)$, with a never-ending chain of valid deductions. This contradicts the assumption that the program output by the system terminates on all given examples. □

Theorem 14 *If BFILP terminates successfully, then it outputs a complete program P.*

Proof $(\forall e \in examples)$ P extensionally covers e, since BFILP terminated successfully. By Lemma 1, then, $P \vdash e$, i.e., P is complete. □

The above proof is also valid for systems such as FOIL, and is a partial justification of the extensional evaluation of the generated clauses. However, extensionality forces us to include many examples that would otherwise be unnecessary. In fact, the converse of theorem 14 is not true, with two main negative consequences for top-down methods based on an extensional evaluation of clauses:

1) For a complete and consistent logic program P, it may happen that $P \vdash Q(a,b)$ but none of its clauses extensionally covers $Q(a,b)$. As a consequence BFILP would be unable to generate P, and would not terminate successfully.
Consider this program P:

reverse(X,Y) :- null(Y), null(X).
reverse(X,Y) :- head(X,H), tail(X,T), reverse(T,W), append(W,[H],Y).

Let reverse([a,b],[b,a]) be the only given example. This example follows from P (P ⊢ reverse([a,b],[b,a])) but is not extensionally covered: the first clause does not cover it because null([a,b]) is false, and the second clause does not cover it extensionally because head([a,b],a) and tail([a,b],[b]) are true, but reverse([b],[b]) is not in examples(*reverse*).

2) Let P be a program to compute a function Q and Q(i,o) ∈ examples(Q). Even if, for all clauses Q :- α in P, consistent(α) is true, it may still happen that P ⊢ Q(i,o′) with o ≠ o′. In other words BFILP might generate a program that is not consistent even for the given examples. Consider the following program P:

reverse(X,Y) :- head(X,H), tail(X,T1), head(Y,H), tail(Y,T2), reverse(T1,T2).
reverse(X,Y) :- null(X), null(Y).
reverse([X,Y,Z],[Z,Y,X]).

that can be learned by BFILP with this set of examples:

reverse([],[]), reverse([1],[1]), reverse([3,2,1],[1,2,3]).

Then P ⊢ reverse([3,2,1],[3,2,1]). Nevertheless, reverse([3,2,1],[3,2,1]) is not extensionally covered by the first clause. In fact, reverse([2,1],[2,1]) is not given as an example. In order to prevent BFILP from generating that inconsistent program, in this case we must tell the system that reverse([2,1],[2,1]) is wrong. This is done by adding a positive example, namely reverse([2,1],[1,2]).

7.3 Completing Examples before Learning

There is no reason why particular examples should have to be given by the user. After all, the whole motivation of induction is that some information is missing. The important points are that (1) if a program P consistent with the given examples exists, then it must be found, and (2) the induced program P must not compute wrong outputs on the inputs of given examples. Extensional top-down methods guarantee neither, unless some specially determined examples are given in the inductive relations.

To overcome this problem, FILP queries the user for some of the missing examples, as done with Shapiro's "eager" strategy in MIS. Every possible clause in $\mathcal{C}$ of the type:

7.3. Completing Examples before Learning

P(X,Y) :- A(X,W), Q(X,W,Z), α.

where Q is an inductive predicate with mode Q(in,in,out), is processed with the following procedure:

for every example P(a,b) **do**
    extensionally compute A(a,W), obtaining a value W = c
    ask the user for the value Z computed by Q(a,c,Z)
    add this example to examples(Q)

Adding one example may cause the request for others. Suppose, for instance, that an example A(a,d) is added for A. Then the above procedure might add an example for Q, e.g., the one matching Q(a,d,Z). As a consequence, the procedure must be repeated for every clause, again and again, until no more examples are added for the inductive predicates.

Both for making the above procedure terminate and for guaranteeing the termination of learned programs, we adopt the termination constraint defined in chapter 6. In the context of FILP, however, the well-order relation must be a function. To summarize, any recursive call must be of the type

P(X_1, ... , X_i, ..., X_n) :- ..., Q(X_i,Y), ..., P(X_1, ..., Y, ..., X_n), ...

where Q(X,Y) is a well order function. It is possible to show that if every recursive clause in P satisfies the above constraint, then the example completion procedure terminates.

For instance, suppose again that we want to learn *reverse*. Consider the following clause:

reverse(X,Y) :- tail(X,T), reverse(T,W).

It satisfies the constraint on recursive calls because when tail(X,T) is true, then T is a shorter list than X and this is a well-order relation. Consider the example reverse([a,b,c],[c,b,a]). By using the clause, the user is queried for the value of reverse([b,c],W), and this is added to examples(*reverse*). This new example causes the repetition of the procedure, and the user is queried for reverse([c],W), and at the next step for reverse([],W).

Not all possible examples have been added, only the ones that were useful for that clause, given the initial example in examples(*reverse*). If this is done for all the clauses that are possible a priori, i.e., that satisfy the given constraints, then the problems described in the previous subsection are solved. When speaking of FILP, we will assume in the following that the above completion procedure has been executed as a first step.

Lemma 2 *Suppose the examples given to an extensional learning system are completed with the above given procedure. Suppose also that some program P belongs to the hypothesis space and $Q(a,b) \in examples(Q)$ after the completion. If $P \vdash Q(a,b)$, then the first clause in P resolved against Q(a,b) extensionally covers Q(a,b).*

Proof (by contradiction)
Suppose that (1) $P \vdash Q(a,b)$, where Q(X,Y) :- $\alpha(X,Y)$ is the first clause used in the proof, but (2) Q(a,b) is not extensionally covered by this clause.
Let $\alpha(X,Y) = \beta(X,Z) \wedge R(Z,W) \wedge \gamma(W,Y)$. Suppose that $P \vdash \beta(a,r) \wedge \gamma(s,b)$ and $P \vdash R(r,s)$, but $R(r,s) \notin examples(R)$. There must be one literal R(Z,W) having this property, because of assumptions (1) and (2); let R(Z,W) be the first such literal. The user must have been queried for R(r,W), because $\beta(a,r)$ is extensionally covered. Since $R(r,s) \notin examples(R)$, the answer must have been W=w≠s. But then no clause could extensionally cover R(r,s), or it would be inconsistent, while $P \vdash R(r,s)$. We could now repeat the same argument for R. This would produce a nonterminating chain of resolution steps, and a finished proof of Q(a,b) would never be obtained, contradicting the hypothesis that $P \vdash Q(a,b)$. □

Theorem 15 *If a complete and consistent program P exists, then FILP will terminate successfully.*

Proof (by contradiction)
If FILP does not terminate with a solution, there must be an example Q(a,b) that it cannot cover. Since P is complete, $P \vdash Q(a,b)$. Take the first clause Q(X,Y) :- α resolved against Q(a,b). By lemma 2, $\alpha(a,Y)$ extensionally computes Y=b. But this clause would have been expanded by FILP and found to cover the example. Moreover, consistent(α) is true, because P is consistent and by the contrapositive of lemma 1, and therefore the clause would have been generated and the example would have been covered. □

Theorem 16 *If FILP terminates successfully, then it outputs a consistent program P.*

Proof If P is not consistent, then there must be some example Q(a,b), such that $P \vdash Q(a,c)$ and b≠c. But, by lemma 2, some clause Q :- α of P will extensionally cover Q(a,c). But, in that case, consistent(α) would have been false and FILP would not have generated that clause. □

By virtue of theorem 14, this program will also be complete. As a consequence, FILP is a sound and complete induction method.

7.4 Discussion

FILP is able to learn in a few seconds all the classical logic programs used as test cases in ILP, such as *reverse, intersection, partition* and *quicksort*, and so on. A report on the performances of FILP can be found in [21]. An extensive learning session using FILP will be thoroughly described in chapter 11. Here, we discuss some major characteristics of FILP.

First of all, since FILP *knows* it is learning a function, it needs only positive examples of the program to be learned. This makes the task of the user easier, because s/he has to think only in terms of "what the program must compute" and not in terms of "what the program must not compute." Nonetheless, for every given positive example Q(a,b), all the corresponding negative examples $\{Q(a,k)|k \neq b\}$ are implicitly known and can be used by FILP. Moreover, strong functionality constraints limit the number of legal clauses and consequently increase the efficiency of the system.

Second, FILP requires a very limited number of examples, partially due to the knowledge of FILP about functions. Only ILP systems based on inverse implication would be, in principle, able to work with a more limited number of examples. However, these systems are able to learn only restricted classes of logic programs, such as LOPSTER and CRUSTACEAN, or still remain to be devised.

Third, FILP queries the user for the missing examples. This means that the user need not provide all the required examples to learn a program at the beginning. He or she can forget some examples, and FILP will ask for them. Observe that FILP queries the user only for the examples it really needs, so it will not waste time trying to cover useless examples. A similar technique is used in Shapiro's MIS. However, MIS is an incremental system, and newly added examples may require some previously generated clause to be retracted. This happens both with the contradiction backtracing algorithm and when refining clauses with the eager strategy [176]. In other systems [145, 160] the user must provide all the examples at one time, and usually a superset of the examples needed is given, resulting in a lot of time wasted in covering useless examples. Experience with FILP has shown that the best way to use it is to start with just a few significant examples (most of the time one is enough); the system will query for the missing ones needed to perform the learning task.

Fourth, FILP does not learn concepts *separately*, as would be done by other systems such as FOIL and GOLEM. If we want to learn *quicksort* together with *partition*, we can tell the system that *quicksort* could depend on *partition*. FILP will query the user for the missing examples of *partition*, on the basis of those clauses for *quicksort* containing a *partition* literal in the body. Then these examples will be used to learn *partition* itself. FILP can also work with the extensional definition of a concept. Thus, it is possible to learn *quicksort* without learning *partition*, relying only on its extensional definition (the given or queried examples). On the other hand, it can learn more than two concepts together. We also could give no intensional definition for *append*, but only some examples, and have FILP learn *append* together with *quicksort* and *partition*.

Finally, FILP learns complete and consistent programs, which means, first of all, that programs learned by FILP do not have an unexpected behavior (that is, they do not cover negative examples) as is the case for other extensional methods (such as FOIL). This is especially important for Software Engineering applications, where we want a learned program to always behave as expected, not just sometimes, or even often.

8

Program Induction without Queries

We have seen that the extensionality principle, followed by most ILP systems, brings one important advantage and one important problem. The advantage is that possible clauses may be considered one at a time, without backtracking, on the basis of the examples that they cover extensionally. The problem lies in the possibility of producing inconsistent programs and in the fact that extensional systems such as FOIL may not be complete. In the previous chapter, we developed a technique for solving this problem by means of existential queries in the framework of the FILP system. Here we will take the opposite direction, and avoid both the problem and the queries by giving up extensionality. However, we will then have to accept some backtracking, in the sense that a clause generated at some stage may have to be removed later, as a consequence of the addition of some other clause.

In the system presented in this chapter, clauses are checked against positive and negative examples by running them with a Prolog interpreter. In this way the problems of extensionality are automatically overcome, since a logic program is learned in the same way it will be used. Since searching a space of possible programs would be unfeasible, we consider only partial programs made up of clauses successfully used to prove at least one positive example (we will also call such partial programs *traces*). Partial programs are put together and checked against the negative examples. If some negative example is derived, backtracking occurs. The induction procedure is called TRACY because it finds a solution by tracing derivations of positive examples. The learning algorithm is automatically suitable for multiple predicate learning, and it can work with any number of positive and negative examples. In particular, in no sense does it require an extensionally complete set of positive examples.

The complexity of the method is not as good as for extensional approaches, which only need to enumerate allowed clauses and evaluate them independently. However, it is not as bad as enumerating all allowed programs (sets of clauses), because only the sets of clauses that are derivation traces for some positive example need to be examined. If the examples are sufficiently simple and well chosen, this means a dramatic improvement.

Experiments with TRACY (which can be found in [22]) demonstrate that meaningful programs with multiple predicates can be learned with acceptable complexity. The approach can scale up well with respect to the size of the programs to be learned, and less easily with respect to the set of possible inductive hypotheses $\mathcal{P}$. Therefore, it is a viable inductive tool for the synthesis of real-size programs but requires considerable collaboration from the user. However, when compared with the FILP system described in the previous chapter, it does not require the user to answer queries of any kind.

In the spirit of the seminal work of Shapiro's MIS [176], TRACY is not the first intensional approach to the ILP problem (see, e.g., [144, 58, 61]). However, two distinct features of our approach are that (a) the induction procedure does not require any interaction with the user and does not rely on any special provided example in order to be sound and complete, and (b) it can learn sets of clauses instead of just one clause at a time.

8.1 The Induction Procedure

To describe TRACY, we need the following definition:

Definition 29 *Given a set of clauses S and an example e such that $S \vdash_{SLD} e$, a clause of S is successful (with respect to e) if it used in the proof of e.*

The basic algorithm is quite simple, and in some way it resembles the approach of extensional learning methods. The difference is that here we learn sets of clauses instead of single clauses. TRACY works as follows. Candidate clauses (CC) are produced from a description of the hypothesis space (HS) until a set of successful clauses (a partial program) deriving some positive example e^+ is found. The partial program p is added to the partial programs discovered previously, and the covered examples are removed until no more positive examples remain. At every step, the whole set of clauses learned up to that point is checked against the negative examples, and if some of them are derived, the learning task backtracks to a different derivation for e^+. If no consistent set of clauses can be found in CC, a new clause from the hypothesis space is generated and added to CC, and a different possible

8.1. The Induction Procedure

solution is sought. Here is an informal description of TRACY:

TRACY: Algorithm 1

input: a set of positive examples E+
a set of negative examples E-
a description of the hypothesis space HS
a background knowledge BK
CC ← ∅
P ← ∅
while E+ ≠ ∅ **do**
    c ← generate_one_clause(HS)
    CC ← CC ∪ c
    for each e^+ such that CC ∪ BK $\vdash_{SLD} e^+$ **do**
        let $p \subseteq$ CC be the set of clauses successfully used in the derivation of e^+
        P ← P ∪ p
        if $\exists\ e^-$ such that P ∪ BK $\vdash_{SLD} e^-$ **then** backtrack
        E+ ← E+ - e^+
return P

We note that each p is learned by running CC ∪ BK as a normal logic program on a Prolog interpreter on one of the positive examples, and maintaining a trace of the clauses effectively used in the derivation of that example.

We immediately notice a drawback in the above algorithm. If a set of partial programs consistent with the given examples cannot be found in the current CC, a new clause is added to CC from the hypothesis space, and the search starts again. However, time can be wasted by learning the same partial programs again (i.e., those not involving the new clause) and that were found inconsistent. A partial solution to this problem is to add the new clause at the top of CC, instead of adding it at the bottom. Because of the way the Prolog interpreter works, the first tentative derivations will all involve the new clause, and different partial programs could be found. However, the new clause may initially fail but be found useful later.[1] Until then, we cannot avoid partial programs, discovered before, being rediscovered.

An alternative solution is to search the entire hypothesis space from the very beginning, as is shown in algorithm 2:

---

[1] For example, this can happen if the added clause is the nonrecursive clause of a recursive program we want to learn, and we are using an example involving recursion.

TRACY: Algorithm 2

input: a set of positive examples E+
a set of negative examples E-
a description of the hypothesis space HS
a background knowledge BK

CC ← generate_all_clauses(HS)
P ← ∅
while E+ ≠ ∅ **do**
    for each e^+ such that CC ∪ BK $\vdash_{SLD}$ e^+ **do**
        let $p \subseteq$ CC be the set of clauses successfully used in the derivation of e^+
        P ← P ∪ p
        if ∃ e^- such that P ∪ BK $\vdash_{SLD}$ e^- **then** backtrack
        E+ ← E+ - e^+
return P

Since all clauses of the hypothesis space are always in CC, algorithm 2 does not derive the same partial program more than once. Clearly, a drawback of this version of TRACY is that the hypothesis space must be finite, and it must be completely generated before the beginning of the learning task. If the first clauses of the hypothesis space contain the correct program, time can be wasted producing many clauses that will never be used. Observe that the backtracking feature of TRACY could also be used to discover different programs that are equivalent with respect to the given examples. These programs could then be confronted for efficiency or any other required characteristic.

Finally, a consideration about recursive clauses. In extensional methods, candidate recursive clauses must satisfy some well-order relation, in order to guarantee the termination of learned programs. Here we also need such a condition for making the learning procedure terminate. That is, we require the set of clauses in CC form a terminating program, since otherwise the test CC ∪ BK $\vdash_{SLD}$ e^+ could not terminate. As a consequence, all candidate recursive clauses must satisfy the following pattern:

R(Y1, ..., Yi, ..., Yn) :- ..., wor(Z,Yi), ..., R(Y1, ..., Z, ..., Yn), ...

where wor is any well-order relation, that makes every recursive call of the clause one step closer to the termination. As an example, cons(A,B,C) determines the well-ordering $|B| < |C|$, while tail(A,B) determines the well-ordering $|B| < |A|$. Obviously even more sophisticated techniques can be adopted that apply to sets of clauses and not just to a single clause. A thorough discussion of such techniques can be found in [15] and [38].

8.2 Example

We show in detail the behavior of TRACY (algorithm 1) on a very simple example: learning *member*. Suppose the hypothesis space HS is defined as the set of all clauses whose head is "member(X,Y)" and whose body is composed of a conjunction of any of the following literals (we associate the correct variables to predicates to make the discussion short):

member(X,T), head(Y,H), head(Y,X), tail(Y,T), tail(Y,Z), null(Y), null(Z).

Actually, not all possible clauses can be generated from the above definition of the hypothesis space if some constraints are in force, like the one on recursive clauses of the previous section (for example, "member(X,Y) :- member(X,T)" is not a legal clause and would not be generated). The background knowledge BK will contain the usual definitions for all the predicates above, except obviously for *member*. The examples used are the following:

e_1^+ = member(a,[a]), e_2^+ = member(a,[c,b,a]),
e_1^- = member(a,[]), e_2^- = member(a,[b,c]).

1) The learning task starts by setting CC = P = $\emptyset$. Suppose clause c_1 = "member(X,Y) :- tail(Y,Z), null(Z)." is generated. Let CC = $\{c_1\}$. Now, CC $\vdash e_1^+$ (we omit the background knowledge for brevity, and we use $\vdash$ for $\vdash_{SLD}$) by using c_1, so we set P = $\{c_1\}$; and since P does not derive any of the negative examples, we can continue. Since CC $\nvdash e_2^+$, a new clause is generated from HS and added to CC.

2) Suppose c_2 = "member(X,Y) :- head(Y,H), tail(Y,T), member(X,T)." is generated. We have CC = $\{c_2, c_1\}$. Now, CC $\vdash e_2^+$ using clauses c_1 and c_2. As a consequence we set P = $\{c_1, c_2\}$. However, now P $\vdash e_2^-$, and since backtracking to a different partial program for e_2^+ fails (since there is not such a program in CC), a new clause must be generated. P is reset to $\{c_1\}$.

3) let c_3 = "member(X,Y) :- head(Y,X)." and CC = $\{c_3, c_2, c_1\}$. Now, CC $\vdash e_2^+$ and the first successful clauses used to derive e_2^+ are c_3 and c_2, so we set P = $\{c_1, c_3, c_2\}$. However, again P $\vdash e_2^-$. Now if we backtrack to a different partial program for e_2^+, we find $\{c_1, c_2\}$, which was already discovered at step 2) and found inconsistent, so we must backtrack to the first positive example. P is empty again.

4) At this point CC = $\{c_3, c_2, c_1\}$, and we discover that e_1^+ can be derived from c_3, and we set P = $\{c_3\}$, which is consistent with the examples. Then, e_2^+ is derived from c_2 and c_3, and we set P = $\{c_2, c_3\}$. Now P derives all the positive examples and no negative examples, and represents a legal program for *member*.

We observe from the above example that an extensional system would have been unable to learn *member* with the examples provided, since member(a,[c,b,a]) is not extensionally covered by the recursive clause of *member*. In fact, the positive example member(a,[b,a]) would be required. Note also that *member* could have been learned by using only the second positive example (i.e., the one involving recursion).

Clearly, we could also define a hypothesis space containing clauses with different consequents. As a consequence, multiple predicate learning is automatically achieved.

8.3 Properties of the Induction Procedure

A thorough discussion of the implementation of TRACY (algorithm 2) is reported in section 8.4. Here we address some major issues about the properties of the induction procedure.

8.3.1 Soundness and completeness of TRACY

If we suppose, as stated in section 6.5, that the set of generated clauses CC forms a terminating program, then the following property holds:

Theorem 17 *TRACY is sound and complete.*

Proof Suppose TRACY(E,CC)=P. Then P=$\cup_i P_i$ and $(\forall e_i^+ \in E)$ $P_i \vdash e_i^+$. If derivation is monotone, as it is for Prolog clauses without negation, then we must also have $(\forall e_i^+ \in E)$ P $\vdash e_i^+$, i.e., P is complete. Moreover, TRACY would have backtracked to a different solution or failed if there was some $e^- \in E$ such that P $\vdash e^-$ i.e., P is consistent. Therefore TRACY is sound.

Suppose there is a complete and consistent program P in CC. Then $\forall e_i^+ \in E$ P $\vdash e_i^+$. Let P_i be the subset of clauses of P used in the derivation of e_i^+, and P' = $\cup_i P_i$. Again, since derivation is monotone, P'$\subseteq$P also is complete and consistent. In fact, if P contained Prolog's negation, it might happen that P$\not\vdash e^-$, but P'$\vdash e^-$, although P'$\subseteq$P. As we do not allow for negation here, P' will be consistent.

Finally, TRACY cannot fail, because, for every e_i^+, it would backtrack to P_i, and find it to be consistent. Then it would not backtrack any further and output P' as a solution. □

8.3. Properties of the Induction Procedure

In the case of a very large or *true* infinite hypothesis space, we can take into account the possibility of substituting clauses in CC instead of adding them. However, in this case the system could not be complete any longer.

8.3.2 Complexity of TRACY

A second major point is the computational complexity of the learning task. Extensional methods explore a hypothesis space HS of independent clauses, and hence they have a complexity that is linear in |HS|. On the contrary, an exhaustive search in the space of possible programs (i.e., pick a subset of HS and check it against the given examples) would be exponential in |HS|, and practically unfeasible. Our approach stands between these two, as it takes into consideration only (partial) programs that derive at least one positive example and where each clause is successful.

To estimate the computational complexity of TRACY, let us limit our analysis to clauses in the hypothesis space with the same predicative symbol in the consequent. Moreover, let us suppose all recursive clauses satisfying some well-ordering condition, as discussed at the end of section 8.1. We also need the following:

Definition 30 *Let $C = $ "$P(\vec{X})$:- α, $P(\vec{Y})$, β." where α and β are arbitrary conjunctions of literals. We define the evaluation of clause C with an example $P(\vec{a})$ as the process of (1) matching $P(\vec{a})$ with $P(\vec{X})$ and (2) evaluating $\alpha\{\vec{a}/\vec{X}\}$ in BK (with the Prolog interpreter).*

Definition 31 *Given a positive example e^+ such that $HS \cup BK \vdash_{SLD} e^+$, we define the depth of e^+ be the maximum number of clauses used in its derivation.*

For example, if we are working with sets or lists, the well-ordering condition guarantees that all recursive calls in HS ∪ BK are on a smaller set or on a shorter list. Then, the depth of an example is proportional to the size of the sets or lists that it contains. As a consequence of the above conditions, it often happens that the depth of an example is not related to the clauses in HS but to its syntactic complexity.

Then, for algorithm 2, we have the following:

Proposition: If we have n positive examples and d is the maximum depth on all the examples, then the number of clause evaluations of TRACY — algorithm 2 — is of the order of $|HS|^{nd}$.

Proof For each example e, in the worst case all clauses in HS are evaluated, since all clauses have the same predicative symbol in the head. If a recursive clause is activated, at the next step again all clauses in HS are evaluated by the Prolog interpreter, and so on. Since all clauses satisfy some well-order condition, each recursive call is on a smaller example (i.e., one involving subsets or sublists of those contained in e), and the number of recursive activations of HS cannot be larger then the depth of e. The proposition follows from the number of examples and the maximum depth on all examples. □

A similar result also holds for algorithm 1, but only if we can assure that each partial program is discovered no more than once, as it happens for algorithm 2. In general, algorithm 2 turns out to be more efficient than algorithm 1, if a restricted hypothesis space can be defined. Consider again the example of the previous section. If clauses c_3, c_2, and c_1 are put in CC in that order from the beginning of the learning task, and algorithm 2 is used, a legal program for *member* can be discovered without any backtracking. If clause c_1 comes before the others (that is, CC = $\{c_1, c_3, c_2\}$), backtracking is required, but the wrong partial program $\{c_1, c_2\}$ is discovered only once, and not twice, as in steps 2) and 3) of algorithm 1.

Explicit generation of a hypothesis space is normally considered to be inconvenient. However, we believe that meaningful and relatively complex logic programs cannot be learned without a lot of prior information, i.e., without a careful design of the search space, which must be not only finite but also quite limited. As a consequence, considerable collaboration from the user is required. However, this is certainly not as demanding as writing the very program that we want to learn, because defining a finite set of possible clauses is clearly less informative than a precisely defined computation rule: it is easier to say that *member* is linearly recursive and requires *head* than it is to provide a correct program. Clearly, a small hypothesis space would also help to limit the backtracking required on candidate partial programs. Moreover, if clauses are not learned independently, a dramatic improvement of the learning task can be obtained by generating the clauses in the hypothesis space so that recursive clauses, and in general more complex clauses, are taken into consideration after the simpler and nonrecursive ones. Since simpler and nonrecursive clauses require less time to be evaluated, they will have a weak impact on the learning time, even if useless.

8.3.3 Number and kind of given examples

Unlike in extensional systems, in TRACY there is not *any* relationship between the given examples and the possibility to learn a program complete and consistent with respect to those examples. Simply, if such a program exists in the hypothesis space, it is found. More precisely, if T $\subseteq$ S is a set of clauses successfully used to derive a positive example e^+ (that is, T $\cup$ BK $\vdash_{SLD} e^+$), then sooner or later T will be found by the induction procedure and added to the previously learned clauses. This means that with an intensional evaluation of clauses, a positive example is sufficient to learn all the clauses necessary to derive it. As a consequence, it turns out that TRACY is able to learn *sets* of clauses at a time, instead of just one clause at time, as in most ILP systems. For this reason, most of the time a complete program can be learned using only one well-chosen example[2] (for instance, logic programs typically used as ILP test cases can be learned by TRACY by using just one well-chosen example). In other words, this means that with an intensional learning system we have more chances to avoid redundant information, i.e., to keep small parameter n of the previous subsection. For example, to learn the *reverse* program it is sufficient to use only one of the two examples reverse([a,b,c],[c,b,a]) and reverse([1,2,3],[3,2,1]) (in the example of section 8.2, it is easy to verify that example e_2^+ would be sufficient to learn the entire program for *member*). Moreover, as one example is responsible for the learnability of all the clauses required to derive it, it is better to choose it as simple as possible, in order to limit its depth (i.e., parameter d of the previous subsection). In this way, fewer recursive calls will be required, increasing the speed of the learning task. For example, to learn *append* it can be sufficient to use as an example append([a],[b],[a,b]) instead of append([a,b,c,d],[e],[a,b,c,d,e]). By limiting the number and the depth of the positive examples, it is possible to improve the performance of the system without affecting its ability to learn.

The above arguments should be contrasted with the situation in extensional systems, where normally very many examples are required by the induction procedure, and where two important issues are the problem of learning from *good* examples and *sparse* examples [123]. In general, extensional systems succeed when the positive examples include a *Basic Representative Set* [123] of the target program. But providing a Basic Representative Set often requires knowing the program to be learned.

8.4 A Simplified Implementation

A simplified (but running) version of TRACY (algorithm 2) is reported in figure 8.1. The actual implementation of TRACY is slightly different, to achieve greater efficiency.

Since TRACY works by tracing derivations of positive examples, let us call a (partial) program deriving at least one positive example a *trace*. To record a trace of the clauses deriving a positive example e^+, in the implementation of the

---

[2]Obviously, this happens only if a program complete and consistent with respect to the given examples exists in the hypothesis space. Moreover, such a program can also be different from the one the user has in mind.

consult(file_containing_the_set_of_clauses_HS).

allowed(X).

marker(X) :- assert((trace(X))).
marker(X) :- retract((trace(X))),!, fail.

tracy :- listpositive(Posexamplelist), tracer(Posexamplelist,Trace).

tracer([Example|Cdr],Trace) :- Example, setof(L,trace(L),Trace1),
                               notneg(Trace1), tracer(Cdr,Trace).
tracer([],Trace) :- setof(L,trace(L),Trace).

assertem([]) :- !.
assertem([T1|T]) :- assert(allowed(T1)), assertem(T).

prep(T) :- retract(allowed(X)), assertem(T),!.

resetallowed(T) :- abolish(allowed,1), assert(allowed(X)), !.

notneg(T) :- listnegative([]).
notneg(T) :- prep(T), asserta((marker(X) :- true,!)),
            listnegative(Negexamplelist), trynegs(Negexamplelist),
            resetallowed(T), retract((marker(X) :- true,!)), !.

notneg(_) :- resetallowed(T), retract((marker(X) :- true,!)),!,fail.

trynegs([A|B]) :- A,!,fail.
trynegs([A|B]) :- trynegs(B).
trynegs([]) :- !.

Figure 8.1: The TRACY algorithm

8.4. A Simplified Implementation

algorithm, every clause in the hypothesis space HS is numbered and modified by adding to its body two literals. The first one, *allowed*(n) is used to activate only the clauses that must be checked against the negative examples. The second one, *marker*(n), is used to remember that clause number n has been successfully used while deriving e^+. Hence, in general, a clause in HS takes the following form:

$P(X_1,\ldots,X_m)$:- $allowed(\text{n}),\gamma,marker(\text{n}).$

where γ is the actual body of the clause and n is the number of the clause in the set. Below, we assume that each clause in HS is augmented with the two predicates described above. By contrast, the background clauses BK are not numbered or changed in any way. In the algorithm, the output, if any, is the variable Trace containing the list of the (numbers of the) clauses representing the learned program P. Due to the backtracking mechanism of Prolog, more than one program (trace) can be found in the learning task. We assume the two literals *listpositive(T)* and *listnegative(T)* build a list T of the given positive and negative examples, respectively.

The behavior of the learning task is quite simple:

- Initially, the set HS of candidate clauses is read into the Prolog interpreter, together with the learning algorithm. Then the learning task can be started by calling the predicate *tracy*. A list of the positive examples is formed and the *tracer* procedure is called on that list.

- For every positive example, *tracer* calls the example itself, firing all the clauses in HS whose heads match that example. Observe that, initially, an *allowed*(X) predicate is asserted in the database: in this way all clauses in HS are *allowed* to be used in the definition of the example.

- Then, a trace, if any, of (the numbers associated to) the clauses successfully used in the derivation of that example is built. In fact, for every such clause, the *marker* procedure asserts a *trace* fact whose argument is the number of the clause itself, and then *setof* is used to record all those numbers, that correspond to the clauses successfully used in the derivation. The trace is added to the traces found for the previous examples.

- The resulting trace is checked against the set of the negative examples calling the *notneg* procedure. If *notneg* does not fail (i.e., no negative examples are covered by this trace), then a new positive example is taken into consideration; otherwise, backtracking occurs and a new trace for the current example (and possibly for the previous ones) is searched. The *notneg* procedure has quite an intuitive behavior. First, only the clauses in the trace are *allowed* to be checked against the negative examples, by retracting the *allowed*(X) clause and asserting an *allowed*(n) if the n-th clause is in the trace. This is done with the *prep* and *assertem* predicates. Then a list of the negative examples is formed and we check if they can be derived from the clauses in the trace. If at least one negative example is covered, then *trynegs* fails and backtracking occurs. Otherwise, all the clauses in HS are reactivated by again asserting *allowed*(X), and the next positive example is considered.

We conclude this section with an example.

8.4.1 Learning "Intersection(X,Y,Z)"

Learning the complete program to build the *intersection* of two input lists is not a trivial task for an ILP system. The program is composed of seven clauses, three for *intersection*, two for *member*, and two for *notmember*. We have to learn *notmember* separately because cut and negation are not handled by TRACY. We start by defining a source file as indicated in figure 6.4, augmented with the information about forbidden conjunctions of predicates, mode declarations, and examples of the concept to be learned as reported in figure 8.2.

Observe that we forbid any clause containing literals that cannot be true at the same time, such as null(A) and head(A,_). Note also that we do not give any example of *member* or *notmember*. According to the discussions of chapter 2, we then have some form of predicate invention and multiple predicate learning. The source file is turned into an actual set of clauses by applying three of the constraints described in section 6.5: "intermediate output variables must be used," "output variables in the head must be instantiated," and "intermediate output variables must not be overwritten." This produces a hypothesis space of only twenty-four possible clauses, (which are listed in figure 8.3) containing a correct program for *intersection*, *member*, and *notmember* (note that in figures 6.4 and 8.3 the *intersection* predicate is indicated as *int*).

We give TRACY the set of possible clauses of figure 8.3, the set of known clauses outside the brackets of figure 6.4, and the sets of positive and negative examples, and TRACY comes out with the following programs for *intersection*, *member*, and *notmember*:

int(X,Y,Z) :- null(X),null(Z).
int(X,Y,Z) :- head(X,X1),tail(X,X2),member(X1,Y), int(X2,Y,W),cons(X1,W,Z).
int(X,Y,Z) :- head(X,X1),tail(X,X2),notmember(X1,Y),int(X2,Y,Z).

8.4. A Simplified Implementation

/⋆ forbidden conjunctions of predicates ⋆/

!(null(A),head(A,_)).
!(null(A),tail(A,_)).
!(member(A,B),notmember(A,B)).
!(head(_,_),head(_,_)).
!(member(_,_),member(_,_),member(_,_)).
!(notmember(_,_),notmember(_,_),notmember(_,_)).

/⋆ mode declaration ⋆/

intersection_inout(in,in,out).
null_inout(out).
head_inout(in,out).
tail_inout(in,out).
assign_inout(in,out).
cons_inout(in,in,out).
diff_inout(in,in).
member_inout(in,in).
notmember_inout(in,in).

/⋆ positive examples ⋆/

intersection+([a],[b,a],[a]).
intersection+([b,a],[a],[a]).

/⋆ negative examples ⋆/

intersection-([a],[a],[]).
intersection-([],[a],[a]).
intersection-([a],[b,a],[]).
intersection-([b],[a],[b]).

Figure 8.2: Completion of the source file for learning *intersection*

```
int(X,Y,Z):-allowed(1),null(X),null(Z),marker(1).
int(X,Y,Z):-allowed(2),null(Z),marker(2).
int(X,Y,Z):-allowed(3),null(Z),head(X,X1),member(X1,Y),marker(3).
int(X,Y,Z):-allowed(4),null(Z),head(X,X1),notmember(X1,Y),marker(4).
int(X,Y,Z):-allowed(5),head(X,X1),tail(X,X2),
           member(X1,Y),int(X2,Y,Z),marker(5).
int(X,Y,Z):-allowed(6),head(X,X1),tail(X,X2),member(X1,Y),
           int(X2,Y,W),assign(W,Z),marker(6).
int(X,Y,Z):-allowed(7),head(X,X1),tail(X,X2),member(X1,Y),
           int(X2,Y,W),cons(X1,W,Z),marker(7).
int(X,Y,Z):-allowed(8),head(X,X1),tail(X,X2),notmember(X1,Y),
           int(X2,Y,Z),marker(8).
int(X,Y,Z):-allowed(9),head(X,X1),tail(X,X2),notmember(X1,Y),
           int(X2,Y,W),assign(W,Z),marker(9).
int(X,Y,Z):-allowed(10),head(X,X1),tail(X,X2),notmember(X1,Y),
           int(X2,Y,W),cons(X1,W,Z),marker(10).
int(X,Y,Z):-allowed(11),head(X,X1),tail(X,X2),
           int(X2,Y,W),cons(X1,W,Z),marker(11).
int(X,Y,Z):-allowed(12),tail(X,X2),int(X2,Y,Z),marker(12).
int(X,Y,Z):-allowed(13),tail(X,X2),int(X2,Y,W),assign(W,Z),marker(13).
member(X,Y):-allowed(14),head(Y,X),marker(14).
member(X,Y):-allowed(15),head(Y,X),tail(Y,Tail),member(X,Tail),marker(15).
member(X,Y):-allowed(16),head(Y,KW),tail(Y,Tail),
            member(KW,Tail),marker(16).
member(X,Y):-allowed(17),tail(Y,Tail),member(X,Tail),marker(17).
notmember(X,Y):-allowed(18),head(Y,X),marker(18).
notmember(X,Y):-allowed(19),head(Y,X),tail(Y,Tail),
               notmember(X,Tail),marker(19).
notmember(X,Y):-allowed(20),head(Y,KW),diff(X,KW),marker(20).
notmember(X,Y):-allowed(21),head(Y,KW),diff(X,KW),
               tail(Y,Tail),notmember(X,Tail),marker(21).
notmember(X,Y):-allowed(22),head(Y,KW),diff(X,KW),
               tail(Y,Tail),notmember(KW,Tail),marker(22).
notmember(X,Y):-allowed(23),head(Y,KW),tail(Y,Tail),
               notmember(KW,Tail),marker(23).
notmember(X,Y):-allowed(24),tail(Y,Tail),notmember(X,Tail),marker(24).
```

Figure 8.3: Set of possible clauses for learning *intersection*

member(X,Y) :- head(Y,X).
member(X,Y) :- tail(Y,Tail),member(X,Tail).

notmember(X,[]).
notmember(X,Y):-head(Y,KW),diff(X,KW),tail(Y,Tail),notmember(X,Tail).

(i.e., clauses 1, 7, 8, 14, 17, 21, plus the nonrecursive clause of *notmember*, which was known and given directly in figure 6.4). Learning time is 1.13 seconds in the actual implementation of TRACY.

8.5 Discussion

TRACY represents a novel approach to clause learning and ILP that is sound and complete with respect to the given examples. Unlike classical top-down and bottom-up methods, generated clauses are not evaluated extensionally, examples are not required to be complete in any sense, queries are not necessary, and sets of clauses are learned at a time. The user is responsible for defining a finite hypothesis space (for example, via the Clause Set language of section 6.5) that is then searched by the inductive procedure. General constraints can be applied to further limit the dimension of the hypothesis space. Moreover, the user can modify the ordering of the possible clauses in order to improve the efficiency of the induction procedure. The backtracking feature of TRACY can also be used to discover different programs equivalent with respect to the given examples. These programs can then be confronted for efficiency or any other required characteristic. These features make the method appropriate for fully automatic program induction when strong bias is available. Such conditions are natural in software development applications.

The first system that was able to evaluate the current hypothesis on the basis of criteria that are, in part, intensional is Shapiro's MIS. However, this is true only for the contradiction backtracing algorithm, while refinement is based on an extensional notion of coverage. In other words, MIS works intensionally when trying to repair inconsistencies, in order to find a clause that is responsible for the derivation of a negative example. For repairing incompleteness, the refinement method, equipped with the *eager* or the *lazy* strategy, makes clauses more specific in a manner that is similar to what is done in most other top-down extensional systems, such as FOIL. If the *adaptive* strategy is used, then the evaluation of the refined clause is partly intensional but depends on the current hypothesis, while TRACY's evaluation depends only on the hypothesis space. Another difference is that MIS reads negative examples incrementally, while TRACY requires them to be given at the beginning.

An intensional technique that is related to TRACY is the "unfolding" algorithm of Bostrom and Idestam-Almquist [28]. A clause P :- A, γ that is responsible for deriving a negative example is replaced with all the clauses of the form P :- β, γ, where A :- β is a clause in the current hypothesis. A more general scheme involving substitutions is possible. This unfolding process continues, and any obtained clause that covers only negative examples is removed. With respect to TRACY, this concerns only the negative examples; inconsistencies are resolved by unfolding the responsible clause and removing some of the obtained clauses, while TRACY resolves inconsistencies by forcing backtracking in the top-level procedure. However, the unfolding algorithm could be integrated in TRACY as an additional method for dealing with negative examples.

Experiments with TRACY have shown us that learning logic programs by adopting a pure intensional evaluation of clauses is feasible if (1) we avoid searching a space of possible programs and limit ourselves to set of successful clauses and (2) we limit the size of the hypothesis space by some form of prior information and strong constraints. Even if the intensional approach is, in general, less efficient if compared with the extensional approach, it seems particularly suitable for Software Engineering applications, where the requirements for complete and consistent programs, and the ability to find them whenever they exist in the hypothesis space, are a primary demand. In extensional systems many examples are required to assure soundness and completeness, and a lot of knowledge can be necessary to guess the right ones. Many of these examples can be useless; nevertheless, they must be covered by the system. With an intensional approach, soundness and completeness come for free, since they do not depend on the number and kind of given examples. Actually, this is paid with an increase of the computational complexity, which is intrinsic in the intensional evaluation of clauses. However, an intensional system can work with very few and simple examples of the target concept(s). This is important to limiting the computational cost of the system, and it is fundamental if no more examples are available. We believe that a careful choice of the examples, together with a judicious design of the hypothesis space, can make the efficiency of intensional systems comparable with that of extensional systems. An example of the possibilities of TRACY will be presented in chapter 11. There, we will show how to use TRACY to synthesize a logic program much more complex than logic programs normally learned by ILP systems.

III

Software Engineering Applications

9
Development, Maintenance, and Reuse

The *Software Process* [104] is at the same time a very creative and a very tedious task. In the earlier stages, a proposed problem is analyzed and understood. A possible algorithmic solution is outlined and alternative choices are taken into consideration. The general structure of the software package is designed by locating and putting together the parts of the system under development. Much ingenuity is required to carry on all of these tasks until a good solution seems to be found. But then a longer, less creative, and error-prone activity must start: an actual program must be produced. Taking care of all of the implementation details, when turning an abstract computation rule into an actual program, is a well-known problem of the imperative programming paradigm. Temporary variables, initialization values, starting and ending conditions in loops, call by value or by reference, pointers, allocation and deallocation of chunks of memory, and much more are part of the daily work of a C or Pascal programmer.

In principle, implementation problems should disappear in the higher-level and more mathematical notation of the logic programming paradigm. A first-order logic language is available for the specification of a computation rule and for executing the computation at the same time. Nonetheless, every logic programmer knows that many implementation choices have to be made, when writing a logic program, even if the algorithm to implement seems to be clear. First, the basic components of the program must be identified. Basic functors on lists probably will be needed, such as *head*, *tail*, *cons*, and *null*; so will more complex tests and operations, such as *member*, *append*, and *reverse*. Often, classical Boolean and arithmetic operators are also required. Then the actual structure of the program must be determined.

For example, we have to decide whether the program must be recursive or not, simply recursive or double recursive, how many different cases must be handled (e.g., how many clauses), termination conditions (e.g., nonrecursive clauses), and so on. Also, a choice of the structures to use must be made, and this is not always clear from the problem: do we need simple variables, lists, trees, sets, graphs? Deciding all of the above may require, in fact, a great deal of knowledge, but it still does not make a program. All the pieces must be put together in a certain way, in order to get a precise computation rule, that is, an actual program.

This concerns only one part of the life of a program, be it imperative or logic based. Software must be maintained. Software maintenance is probably even more costly and delicate than the implementation phase. Users tend to think that the first version of a program they get is acceptable, whereas in [177] it is estimated that 55 percent of all the software errors have to be corrected during the maintenance period, after the software is released. Also, maintenance can be needed because of changes in the specification of the program, new requirements from the user, changes in the data structures, moves to different hardware systems, and so on. Maintenance requires taking into consideration, examining, and carefully analyzing programs that may have been written much earlier, perhaps by other programmers. Structure and documentation may be insufficient. For these reasons, maintenance is a very delicate phase of the software process, and is time-consuming and expensive. According to [74], it represents about 70 percent of the software budget.

A task that is close to maintenance is software reuse. We want to reuse software as much as possible because, on the one hand, developing software is expensive and time consuming. On the other hand, software development is a highly repetitive process: similar data structures (e.g., lists or trees) and similar operations (e.g., sorting or searching) are normally used, possibly in slightly different ways. That is, programs are often variations on similar themes that recur again and again. Reusing the software poses problems similar to maintaining the software, because the software must be analyzed, understood, and possibly modified for the new requirements. But achieving a certain degree of software reuse is important, for it is considered to be one of the few techniques that are really able to improve software productivity [34].

Before a program is released, we want it to be as bugfree as possible. That is, we have to test it against the presence of errors. This is the *testing* phase of the software process; when we try to make sure the program does what it is supposed to do. This is done by running the program on well-chosen inputs (the *test cases*) that should be able to show the presence of errors, i.e., wrong outputs. Testing is very important in the software process. Since removing errors in the maintenance stage of the software life is so costly, we must try to locate them as soon as possible, before the program is released and marked "reliable." Fortunately, testing is one part of the software process that can be automated to a high degree, and software tools for testing are available [93]. We will say more on testing in chapter 10, where an alternative approach to testing, based on ILP techniques, will be presented.

Finally, when an error is found (in the testing phase or later, during the maintenance phase), we must remove it. This is the debugging phase of the software process. In fact, debugging is difficult because knowing the presence of an error does not always tell us where the error is located, and which specific piece of software is responsible for it. Many strategies have been worked out to improve the debugging phase, including backtracking and cause postulation, and automatic tools are available. Debugging is also a delicate phase because correcting an error requires changing the software, and we must be careful, in order to avoid generating further errors.

The above are probably the main parts of the software process. Together, they contribute to the same goal: producing usable software. The efforts of thousands of researchers, during more than thirty years, have contributed to highlighting, understanding and working out strategies for solving the problems and improving the various phases of the software life. But, in the previous chapters, we have presented several techniques that can be regarded as a truly alternative method for producing software, within the declarative paradigm. In fact, the core of ILP is (or should be) the synthesis of logic programs. An ILP system can be seen as putting together a given set of basic software components in different ways, in order to find a program consistent with the computation rule observed in the examples. As a consequence, in these last three chapters we want to propose ILP as an alternative approach to Software Engineering, especially (but not limited to) in the logic programming paradigm.[1] In an inductive setting, development, maintenance, reuse, and the debugging phases of logic programs become different aspects of the same inductive process, and will be discussed in this chapter. In chapter 10 we will discuss the problem of logic program testing. In chapter 11, the development and testing of a complex program will be analyzed in detail.

9.1 Introduction

As we noted previously, it is now commonly believed that the examples provided to an ILP system are, by themselves, insufficient for the generation of a logic program: one needs strong constraints on the clauses that could possibly be gener-

---

[1] Another use of ILP related to Software Engineering can be found in [49]. Here, an unknown executable program is run in order to get examples of its input-output behavior. These examples are then used to learn a logic program that will represent a possible specification of the executable in a first-order language. This technique is a form of *reverse engineering*.

ated. In chapter 6 we saw different proposals for describing such constraints. The constraints must be sufficiently strong to make the induction process feasible and reliable, but are normally much less informative than the actual program that we want to learn.

This can suggest a different understanding of the ILP problem: constraints and examples are seen as a real programming language, and we move from Program Induction to *Inductive Programming*. In other words, we do not want to "learn" a computation rule from the available information; we actually "program" this computation rule by means of syntactic requirements and examples of the desired input-output behavior. As a first consequence, examples should be few and well chosen, and not taken as coming from random experiments, as is usually done in Machine Learning. The goodness of chosen examples is a well-known problem in Machine Learning, but is not so important in ILP, if the goal is the synthesis of true logic programs. If one has in mind a certain computation rule that must be translated into an actual program, typical examples of that computation rule are normally also "available" in his/her mind. Often, the computation rule is precisely the one defined by the available examples. That is, the examples one has in mind define the computation rule, and not vice versa.

An *inductive program*, then, represents a set of possible object programs: the ones that are defined as possible by the constraints and are consistent with the examples. It is obviously easier to define a space of possible programs than to choose precisely which of these programs is the correct one. Inductive inference will play the role of a compilation into one of the possible object Prolog codes that will compute correct outputs for the given examples. This approach is related to the idea of programming by examples [11, 187], but it builds on the ILP techniques we have seen so far, and it focuses on a new programming style rather than on the general goal of automatic programming. Logic Programming is a good object language for inductive programming, because the intermediate computations correspond to intermediate predicates or to recursive calls, and can be instantiated with separate examples. Moreover, it allows us to specify constraints as sets of possible clauses in a natural way.

Software development in an inductive logic programming language is a truly incremental process unifying traditionally separate phases, such as programming, debugging, maintenance, and re-engineering. Detecting a wrong output or realizing that we now want a different output often results only in the addition or in the modification of some examples, while the constraints, which require most of our programming work, can normally remain unchanged. Another form of program refinement is the process of making the constraints stronger, and is required from the programmer when the compilation is too slow. In fact, this is not exactly a compilation in the sense of a straightforward translation, but a search within a space of possible object programs. This space needs to be kept small by providing meaningful constraints, if we want the generation of the object code to be reasonably efficient. Programming time is traded off against compilation time and, in a sense, the user can choose how "inductive" a certain program should be.

It must be stressed that a number of constraints were present in classical Machine Learning research and in the earlier approaches to ILP that were not always known to the user. We move from Program Induction to Inductive Programming if we make these constraints explicit and "programmable." For instance, from this point of view, the source files of figure 6.4 and figure 8.2 — which describe a hypothesis space, some constraints, and a set of positive and negative examples for learning *intersection* — actually represent an inductive program for *intersection*. figure 6.4 (together with figure 8.2) is a program because it describes a computation rule: the one defined to be consistent with the examples while still lying within the space of possible clauses defined by the constraints. In this perspective, what is shown in figure 6.4 and figure 8.2 is the user program, while the usual logic program for *intersection*, which could be learned by an ILP system, plays the role of an object code. In Inductive Programming the inductive inference of the object code corresponds to a form of compilation.

9.2 Inductive Logic Programming Languages

An inductive program is made from examples and constraints. The constraints specify the set of possible object codes and the inductive compilation procedure will select one of these object codes, so that it is consistent with the given examples. An *inductive programming language* is mainly a language for specifying constraints of this kind, i.e., for specifying a set of allowed object programs. As we consider the case of logic object programs, what we are actually considering are *inductive logic programming languages*.

All the formalisms we saw in chapter 6 for defining a language bias can be regarded as inductive logic programming languages: each of them can be used to write an inductive program. An inductive program represents, in fact, a set of clauses. We will also call this hypothesis space an *expansion*, since the description given in the ILP language could be expanded to build that explicit set of possible clauses. Normally, ILP systems do not require an expansion to be produced, with the exception of TRACY. Next, an object Prolog code is defined as possible if its clauses belong to the expansion of the inductive program. This represents an inductive constraint in the sense that the object program output by the compilation procedure will have to be among those possible and to be consistent with the examples (i.e., covering the positive examples and not covering the negative examples).

The notion of expansion of an inductive program is naturally associated with the possibility of having constraints of different strengths for a particular object program: the larger the expansion, the weaker the constraint, as the number of possible programs will be larger in this case. This defines a partial order between inductive programs — an example using the Clause Sets formalism is given in figure 9.1. The program at the top of the graph is the weakest, defining an expansion of eight possible clauses. As we move down the figure, additional constraints are added; for instance, the inductive program at level 1 on the right requires the object program to be tail recursive. More knowledge and more programming time should result in stronger constraints, while weaker inductive programs are easier to write but require more examples and more time for compiling into an object Prolog code.

An inductive logic programming language should allow the user to express easily his/her approximate intuitions of the final shape of the object program. Even if the actual compilation into a Prolog code is done one predicate at a time, this should be transparent to the user, who will simply think in terms of possible global object programs and will work on the inductive program by refining the constraints and by adding examples, as will be illustrated in the next section.

Just as there is, in practice, only one logic programming language, it would also be nice to have basically one inductive logic programming language. Moreover, if we want to make ILP useful for Software Engineering, the potential user should not be compelled to learn a description language really different from the language of the target programs. Mainly for this reason, of the many different approaches that have been proposed for describing spaces of clauses and representing biases in ILP (see chapter 6 and [190, 189]) we feel the most suitable one the Clause Sets notation, because it is the simplest. In fact, it differs from the Logic Programming language only in the use of brackets, whereas the other tools have a syntax usually quite complex and different from the simple, classical formalism of logic programs.

In fact, the typical situation when using Clause Sets is when the target program is not learned from scratch and much information is available to the user, who could be, in fact, a logic programmer. Consider, for example, the case of a logic program that must be revised, since it does not cover some positive example and/or some negative example is covered. Then the program is wrong, but it is plausible to assume it is not "completely" wrong. As a consequence, it can be used as a starting point, a template to define a possible hypothesis space, by surrounding clauses and literals with brackets. The programmer, who is supposed to have some knowledge about the desired program, may know some clause that is correct and may put it in the background knowledge. Other clauses may be perceived as wrong, or at least not completely correct, and a set of mutants of each of them can be defined by using brackets. The actual number of allowed clauses defined in this way depends on the particular problem and on the programmer's knowledge, and it can be very

9.2. Inductive Logic Programming Languages

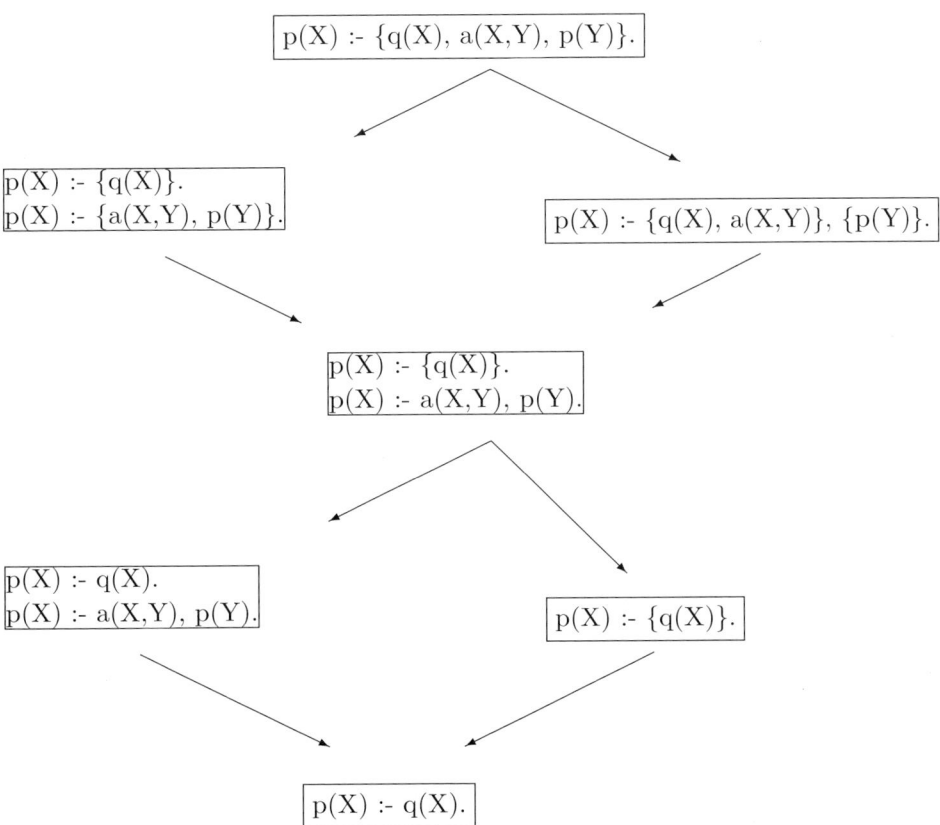

Figure 9.1: Weaker and stronger constraints

easily controlled by means of brackets and available constraints. The resulting space of clauses turns out to be designed on the basis of the initial program as a set of possible mutations. The set of positive and negative examples not properly classified by the initial program is added, and the learning system can search for a revised version of the program.

Even if not for theory revision, similar situations are quite common in program development. Normally, a programmer has in mind a basic idea of the program, but some points can be (at least initially) unclear. As we already noted, these include deciding whether a clause should be recursive or doubly recursive, if a particular operation should be made on the input list or on its tail, if a test for *less* or *less_or_equal* should be made, and so forth. With Clause Sets, the user can easily define the basic structure of the target program and a set of alternative choices for (some) clauses of the program. Testing for the correct alternative is then left to the induction procedure, on the basis of the provided examples.

9.3 The Inductive Software Process

An inductive program does not describe a unique computation rule; it defines a *set* of such computations. Inductive inference will play the role of a compilation phase and will select an object (Prolog) program that is (1) defined *as possible* by the constraints and (2) consistent with the examples. The complexity of this compilation phase depends on the strength of the constraints, i.e., on the number of possible programs, not on the size of the object programs, which may be much more complicated than the examples given in this section. There may be more than one object program satisfying conditions (1) and (2), and this is the set of computation rules that is described with the inductive program. The programmer does not need to know which actual objet program will be selected from among this set of possibilities, any more than a C programmer knows how the translation and optimization phases work in the C compiler in use. As the constraints are refined and as more examples are added, the possible computation rules will reduce to a few, and may be equivalent on most inputs.

Software development is, in general, a process that is never completely finished. Inductive programming acknowledges this fact to a greater degree than traditional programming. An inductive program starts with approximate constraints that may need improving for two reasons: they may be too weak (they define too large a set of object programs) and/or they may exclude the "correct" object program. Initially, a few negative and positive examples are given: the examples the programmer feels to be representative of the computational rule s/he has in mind. This initial program is not expected to be close to the solution, but it may be compiled and executed. As mistakes are found in specific cases, they are simply added to the

9.3. The Inductive Software Process

examples of the inductive program. When we reach the moment when the compilation fails to find an object code that covers all the positive examples, the constraints need to be relaxed in order to allow for more possible object programs. When the compilation becomes unacceptably slow, the constraints need to be made stronger in order to reduce the space of object programs to be searched. This continues until the run-time performance of the program is found to be acceptable. Programming, debugging, and maintenance merge into the same development process.

We show an example of inductive software development leading to a correct program for *intersection*. An initial version of the inductive program is given in figure 9.2, by means of the Clause Sets language.

{
int(X,Y,Z) :- {null({X,Z}), head(X,X1), tail(X,X2),
           member(X1,Y), head(Y,Y1), member(Y1,X),
           int(X2,Y,{Z,W}), cons(X1,W,Z)}.
}
head([X|_],X).
tail([_|X],X).
cons(X,Y,[X|Y]).
null([]).
member(X,[X|_]).
member(X,[_|Y]) :- member(X,Y).
int+([],[a],[]), int+([a],[a],[a]), int-([],[a],[a]).

Figure 9.2: An initial version of the inductive program for *intersection*

As will be discovered later, the program is faulty because several examples are missing, and the constraints rule out the correct object program because one predicate is missing from the clause set. Some predicates, by contrast, are useless, but this only slows down the compilation process.

The compiler we use, the FILP system, translates the inductive program of figure 9.2 into the following Prolog program:

int(X,Y,Z) :- tail(X,X2).
int(X,Y,Z) :- null(Z).

Using a different inductive compiler could, in principle, lead to another object program that is consistent with the three examples that were given, but this would not affect the user very much or change the basic development of this discussion. By using the above program, it will not take long before bugs are found, e.g.:

?- int([a],[],[a]).
yes
?- int([a],[a],[]).
yes

In both cases, we would have expected to get a "no" answer. The inductive program is debugged simply by adding the above cases as negative examples. After recompiling, we obtain the following object program:

int(X,Y,Z) :- null(X), null(Z).
int(X,Y,Z) :- head(X,X1), tail(X,X2), int(X2,Y,W), cons(X1,W,Z).

This code, although still quite incorrect, can already be used and often produces the desired answers, not only on the given examples but also on new data:

?- int([],[a,b],[]).
yes
?- int([a],[a,b],[a]).
yes
?- int([],[a,b],[a]).
no
?- int([b,a],[a,b],[a]).
no

But when we ask for "int([b],[a],[])," we get a "no" answer, which is wrong. Again we debug the program by adding the faulty case to the data, this time as a positive example, since it should produce a "yes" answer. Unfortunately, the compilation now fails to find a program that is consistent with the requirements: this means that the constraints are too strong and exclude the correct object program. This is a more serious form of debugging, as it requires the addition of a predicate to the set defining *intersection*. The compiler signals that the positive example that cannot be covered is "int([b],[a],[])", and since "b" is not member of "[a]," it may be a good idea to add "notmember(X1,Y)" (defined as "not member(X1,Y)"). The semi-automatic generation of the predicate to be added on the basis of the uncovered example and of a given set of possible choices seems to be a problem

9.3. The Inductive Software Process

worth investigating. Here, we may suppose that this is done by the programmer. After adding the new predicate, the following object program is obtained:

int(X,Y,Z) :- null(X), null(Z).
int(X,Y,Z) :- head(X,X1), null(Z), notmember(X1,Y).
int(X,Y,Z) :- head(X,X1), tail(X,X2), int(X2,Y,W), cons(X1,W,Z).

This program may not show its errors well for some time. It may be used together with other subprograms until new bugs are found:

?- int([b,a],[a],[a]).
no
?- int([b],[a],[b]).
yes
?- int([b,a],[a],[]).
yes

If the first is added to the positive examples and the second and third are added to the negative examples, we obtain a correct inductive program for intersection, leading to the usual Prolog implementation.

After some time, when the program is accepted as more or less final, it may be worthwhile to simplify it: the literals that do not occur in the object program ("head(Y,Y1)" and "member(Y1,X)") may be removed. Moreover, some examples may be removed as long as the object code does not change. This leads to a version closer the one of figure 6.4, that is easier to read and explain to others, as well as faster to compile.

Another possible problem in an inductive program consists in an unacceptably slow compilation. This is not the case for the above version of *intersection*, but is to be expected on programs with more predicate sets of a larger cardinality. If the inductive program produces these translation problems, we need to modify it by making its constraints stronger and closer to the desired object program. Figures 9.3a and 9.3b show two versions of *intersection* that are more structured in this sense, with respect to the one of figure 9.2. Figure 9.3b is the one with the stronger constraints. This corresponds to smaller and smaller expansions of the inductive programs, as explained in figure 9.1.

For software maintenance and reusability, inductive programming is quite appropriate. If the application does not change completely, one can often revise a program for a new goal problem by modifying only the examples. This is easier to do, since one has to deal with concrete data rather than with general computation rules, and less error prone. For instance, if we wanted a set difference operation,

```
{
int([],Y,[]).
int([X1|X2],Y,Z) :- {member(X1,Y), notmember(X1,Y),
                    int(X2,Y,{Z,W}), cons(X1,W,Z)}.
}
```

(a)

```
{
int([],Y,[]).
int([X1|X2],Y,Z) :- {member(X1,Y), notmember(X1,Y), int(X1,Y,Z)}.
int([X1|X2],Y,Z) :- {member(X1,Y), notmember(X1,Y),
                    int(X1,Y,W)}, cons(X1,W,Z).
}
```

(b)

Figure 9.3: Stronger (a) and stronger (b) constraints for *intersection*

instead of an intersection, we could reuse the constraints in the programs of figures 6.4 and 9.3, and just change the data. If the predicate for the set difference X-Y is now called "sd(X,Y,Z)," we can keep the same predicate set and subprograms used for *intersection*, and replace the examples with the following:

sd+([b],[a],[b]), sd+([],[a],[]), sd+([a,b],[a],[b]),
sd-([a],[a],[a]), sd-([],[a],[a]), sd-([b],[a],[]).

As a final example, figure 9.4 shows an inductive program for visiting a binary tree in symmetric order (left branch first, then root, then right branch) and copying its nodes into a list. If we wanted to reuse this software for a different goal, namely, for a preorder visit (root first, then left and right branches), we can simply change the first example into "visit+([1,[2],[3]],[1,2,3])" and the last into "visit-([1,[2],[]],[2,1])."

Even if one knows the exact shape of the object code, it may be worthwhile to write an inductive program instead, with some predicate sets, in order to improve

9.3. The Inductive Software Process

```
{
visit([],[]).
visit([X],[X]).
visit([R,STL,STR],L) :- visit(STL,LL), visit(STR,LR),
                       {new_append(3{[R],LL,LR},L)}.
new_append(L1,L2,L3,L) :- append(L1,L2,LT), append(LT,L3,L).
}
visit+([1,[2],[3]],[2,1,3]).
visit+([2],[2]).
visit+([3],[3]).
visit+([],[]).
visit-([],[1]).
visit-([1,[2],[]],[1,2]).
```

Figure 9.4: Inductive program for the in-order visiting of a tree

the reusability of that software. In fact, the program may be used and modified in the future by a less experienced programmer, who will need to change only the relevant examples.

A last remark is useful. Throughout this chapter we are using the terms "logic programs" and "Prolog programs" as equivalent, but in fact they are not. A logic program is a collection of Horn clauses, whereas a Prolog program often contains extralogical predicates that can strongly affect the flow and result of the computation. Experienced Prolog programmers tend to use extralogical predicates — such as *cut* and *fail* — because shorter and more efficient programs can be written through the use of these predicates. Unfortunately, we have observed and argued in [23] that learning logic programs with *cut* is practically unfeasible. Similar results are likely to be expected for other nonlogical predicates. However, this does not really limit the set of relations we can learn, since it is well known [4, 188] that Logic Programming has the computational power of Turing machines. Nonetheless, object logic programs (i.e., the result of the inductive process) can be used as a basis for further changes and improvement by an experienced Prolog programmer. For example, extralogical predicates can be used to simplify the code, "green" cuts can be used to improve the efficiency of the program execution, and "red" cuts can be used to avoid the computation of wrong results. This last change is an alternative to restarting the learning phase with the wrong computations added as new negative examples.

9.4 From Inductive Learning to Inductive Programming

The idea of an inductive logic programming language can be seen both as the end point of a line of research in Machine Learning and as the start of a promising new programming style and discipline. As the natural consequence of earlier work in Machine Learning, the proposal in this chapter stresses a point of view that became more and more common during the 1980s: learning needs explicit prior knowledge (see, e.g., [14] and the references therein) that must be easily expressed. As a new programming discipline, this proposal can be appealing, but it may also generate skepticism. Nevertheless, the result needs not be a total failure or a total success: we try to express this with the picture of "the continuum of inductive logic programs" (figure 9.5).

	Inductive Logic	Automatic	Science
Prolog	Progr. Languages	Program Induction	Fiction

←——————————————————————————————→

Figure 9.5: The continuum of inductive logic programs

At the left end of the line, we have standard Prolog programs. Here examples are not necessary. They may nevertheless play the role of comments, documentation, and recorded test cases. Just a little to the right of this, one uses Prolog programs that may contain some incorrect clauses together with examples that rule them out. More to the right, a cautious inductive programmer using, e.g., Clause Sets, might use only a few predicate sets, perhaps only with the intention of making it easier to reuse the software for similar goals (e.g., figures 9.3b and 9.4). The kind of inductive programming that we feel is more typical is shown in figure 6.4 for *intersection*, *member*, and *notmember*. This is still on the left part of the continuum of inductive programs; the basic skeleton of the object program is given, and the compiler will fill in the missing details on the basis of the given examples. More ambitious approaches would allow for a larger hypothesis space, and would require much longer compilation times and less control on the object program that is generated.

It is obvious that the more we move to the right — i.e., the larger the set of allowed programs — the easier it is to write an inductive program; it may be relatively difficult to write a bugfree *quicksort* program, it is easier to say that

9.4. From Inductive Learning to Inductive Programming

quicksort may be defined with quadratic recursion; and, with the aid of *partition* and *append*, still easier to say that *quicksort* may be written with fewer than ten Prolog clauses. On the other hand, inductive programs that are very easy to write may be quite hard to compile, i.e., it may be difficult for the inductive inference system to select an allowed program that is consistent with the examples. An important consideration is that the number of possible programs is critical, not the complexity of the program that we want to learn. Many induction methods scale up well if the program to be learned becomes longer or more complicated, they may get slower only if the constraints are too weak.

Moving to the right of our imaginary line of programs, the constraints get weaker and weaker, often becoming implicit or hard-wired in the compiler. We stop worrying about inductive languages, and we try to induce programs from reduced information — at some point, from no information at all. While automatic programming of this kind has failed to enter the software production process, and deceived the expectations of early program synthesis, we believe an inductive programming discipline that is situated on the left of our continuum has good chances of being useful. How far to the left will depend on the efficiency of the compiler, on the hardware system, and on the preferences of the programmer.

A final consideration is needed to conclude. In this chapter we have introduced the notions of Inductive Logic Programming Language and of Inductive Programming, with the learning system in use playing the role of a compiler. However, even for classical programming languages, compilers are not equivalent. They can be more or less efficient, and more or less "safe" in producing an object code semantically equivalent to the source program. These issues are even more important when the compiler is, in fact, an ILP learning system. There are three main points to consider.

First, the system must be efficient. We have argued that learning real-size logic programs requires much information from the user that must be expressed through meaningful examples and a restricted hypothesis space. Even in this case, the user must be ready to accept learning times (or compiling times, using the terminology of this chapter) of hours or days. Unlike the classical test cases used in the ILP literature, logic programs made up of tens of clauses, possibly recursive, cannot be learned in a few seconds. Nonetheless, developing those programs by hand could require much more time then synthesizing them automatically.

Second, the system must be sound and complete. The user wants to learn a precise computational rule and will not accept any proposed solution if s/he is not sure that the solution is correct with respect to the provided examples. These examples play a role similar to the test data within classical software development. After a program has been written, it is normally tested using appropriate input values. Only if the corresponding output values are "correct," with respect to some criteria, is there some evidence of the correctness of the developed program. In an inductive setting, input/output pairs are given, together with the inductive program, to the inductive compiler. We expect the synthesized program to be correct *at least* on the provided examples, in order to have some evidence of its correctness.

Third, the learning phase must be autonomous. Obviously, an initial contribution from the user must be put in account. The inductive program must be written; constraints and examples, provided. But the user must not be compelled to assist the system throughout the learning process, because it can take hours or days.

For all the above reasons, we believe top-down methods to be more suitable for Software Engineering applications than bottom-up methods. Although theoretically well grounded, bottom-up methods are, in general, inefficient if compared with top-down methods. GOLEM and CRUSTACEAN are efficient, but the former is neither sound nor complete, and the latter is a restricted learning system. Moreover, many bottom-up systems are interactive, since the user is required to judge each clause guessed during the learning task.

In the light of chapter 5, top-down methods too, turn out to be theoretically well founded. Moreover, they are efficient and can work without any interaction with the user. Also, top-down methods can, more easily than bottom-up methods, be integrated with various forms of declarative bias and clause templates. This makes them particularly appropriate for Software Engineering applications, where clause schemata are often known and available. Top-down methods suffer form the drawbacks of extensionality (section 7.2). To overcome these drawbacks, we saw that we must either provide an extensionally complete set of examples or be willing to answer questions from the system. The first solution can undermine the inherent efficiency of the approach, if achievable at all. The second solution seems to call for interactivity. However, there is a strong difference with respect to the interactivity required in many bottom-up systems. First, the time spent to generate the queries represents only a small part of the whole learning time and, in top-down methods, the queries can be "grouped" at the beginning of the learning task, as a preprocessing step, as in the FILP system. That is, interaction between the user and the system is required only at the beginning of the compilation phase. Second, in top-down methods the queries are about positive and negative examples (i.e., existential queries), and not about learned clauses (i.e., clause and program equivalence queries). If a database of examples of the target concept is available, the system can be modified to look into the database for examples matching the queries instead of interacting with the user. Obviously such a solution is not possible if the queries are about the validity of guessed clauses, as in bottom-up systems.

The above are the main reasons that made us use a top-down method to produce most of the examples of this and the next chapters. In particular, FILP has been used because it is efficient, sound, and complete. It queries the user for missing examples but does not compel the programmer to follow and assist the whole learning process. Some of the experiments of chapter 11 have been made with TRACY. This system cannot be easily classified as top-down or bottom-up. However, it is sound and complete; it does not make queries to the user; and it can be easily integrated with many kinds of declarative bias. Although not as efficient as top-down methods, its ability to work without any extensionally complete set of examples makes it particularly suitable for Software Engineering applications.

10
Testing

Testing is the field of Software Engineering concerned with the problem of detecting the presence of errors in programs by executing them on specific and well-chosen input data. An error is known to be present in a program P when the output is not consistent with the specifications or is perceived as mistaken by the tester. Informally, a program is tested to check whether it does what it is intended to do.

In principle, a set of test data for a program should allow us to discover all the errors in the program. Such a set could be called *adequate*. If no error is detected in a program tested with an adequate test set (for that program), then it is safe to conclude that the program is correct, or error free.

Unfortunately, it can be formally proved that no algorithm exists to generate an adequate set of test data for an arbitrary program. This is a consequence of the first recursion theorem [80], of the undecidability of equivalence between programs, and of the halting problem [97, 88]. In fact, without further assumption, testing can show only the behavior of a program for the chosen test set. It cannot show anything about the behavior of the program for other input data.

Nonetheless, testing is necessary and widely used in software development. It is practical and (relatively) easy to apply, and can give some information about the correctness of a program. After having written a program, the first thing one usually does is run the program on some typical input, in order to check the result of the computation. In fact, this is a simple form of testing, but not always very reliable.

Testing can be seen as a way of distinguishing a program from all the possible (syntactically correct) alternatives to that program. This is very similar to ILP, where a program in the hypothesis space must be identified from among all the other possible programs on the basis of the given examples. More precisely, testing and ILP are, in some way, symmetric. The latter goes from examples to programs, whereas the former goes from programs to examples (input values). In this chapter we show how this relationship and the ILP techniques presented so far can be fruitfully used for program testing.

10.1 Introduction to Testing

The first thing that comes out when testing a program is that both for checking the output and for generating meaningful test cases, we need some information about the "correct" program P_c.

For example, one might have available a correct version of the program or an executable specification. In this case program testing reduces to checking whether the two programs are equivalent, at least on a chosen set of test cases, a set of input/output examples. This also will account for probabilistic equivalence of the two programs on the input values not taken into consideration [35]. This intuitive notion of correctness leads to various forms of syntax-directed [12, 81], specification-based [90, 42] and algebraic testing [191], and allows us to define the notion of *reliability* for test sets [94, 35, 56]:

Definition 32 *Let there be given a test set T for the program P. Let P_c be a correct program. We say that T is* reliable *with respect to P_c if and only if $[\forall x \in T \; P(x) = P_c(x)]$ implies the equivalence of P and P_c.*

As a consequence of the above definition, if P contains errors, this will be shown by the test cases in T. However, this notion of reliability is impractical, since it requires testing for the equivalence of the programs P and P_c on some inputs, and is based on the existence of an executable specification P_c.

Even if such an executable specification is not available, one usually has some a priori knowledge about the correct functionality of the desired program, such as domain and co-domain of the needed subprograms, boundary or otherwise critical values within these domains, and possible interactions among different input and output variables. This leads to techniques based on functional and domain testing [92, 186, 43, 95], and may also be combined with executable specifications [191].

However, what most often happens in practice is that the error detection is done through a direct inspection of the outputs during the normal execution of the program. That is, the user tests the program on the basis of the "correct program she or he has in mind", not a very informative concept. It is common in this case to assume that although the correct program is unknown, there is a known *set of programs* that can be seen as alternative implementations and should contain at least one correct solution. This is the second concept of program correctness analyzed in [35], and leads to a more practical definition of meaningful test data (see also [55, 89]):

Definition 33 *Let there be given a test set T for a program P and a set $\mathcal{P}$ of alternative programs. We say that T is* adequate *with respect to $\mathcal{P}$ if and only if it is reliable with respect to every program in $\mathcal{P}$.*

As a consequence, if $\mathcal{P}$ contains at least one correct program P_c, then the test set will also be reliable for P. Many different testing techniques are based on a relation between the program P to be tested and a set of possible alternatives P_c. In particular, fault-based methods [54, 96, 138, 55, 109] use a set of typical programming errors defined a priori, and alternative programs are obtained by inserting some of these errors in P. In most cases, a simple syntactic change is applied, and hence only one fault at a time is introduced; the set of alternative programs differs from P by exactly one mutation. If at least one correct implementation is obtained from P by a sequence of allowed mutations, and if we can assume that complex errors are detected by an analysis of simpler ones,[1] then all the errors in P can be found.

However, it is not always correct to assume that a complex error can be found by analyzing the simpler ones, and hence it is not always easy to generate test data that are adequate with respect to a large set of mutants. A different proposal is provided by *weak mutation testing* [96]. Let $P_1, ..., P_n$ be the relevant components of program P. Given a test T, let $T_1, ..., T_n$ be the data that are passed to $P_1, ..., P_n$, respectively, when P is called on the inputs of T. Weak mutation testing assumes that if, for all i, T_i is adequate for P_i with respect to its mutations, then T is adequate for P with respect to any combination of these mutations.

Yet another assumption is made in [55], suggesting that it may be enough to make the mutated program's state differ from P's state only after the statement where the mutation occurs (this is shown to be a necessary condition for test data adequacy). In general these kinds of assumptions make the testing system ignore the global effect of errors [138] or the interaction between mutations at the global program level.

Testing based on the inductive learning of logic programs also relies on definition 33 of adequateness of a test set. However, it goes far beyond the testing methods mentioned above, as no locality assumption is made and the set of alternative programs $\mathcal{P}$ may contain *any* program, not just simple mutations of P.

10.2 Induction and Testing Compared

An intuitive symmetry between induction and testing can almost immediately be noticed [197, 41] (see also [89, 35, 108]): induction is the inference from examples

---
[1]This is known as the *coupling effect assumption* [54, 150, 53]. By this assumption, if a test set T is adequate with respect to single mutations of P, then T is also adequate with respect to any mutant of P.

to programs; testing is the inference from programs to input values. Given a test set T of input values for a program P, the examples of P for T are defined as E(P,T)={<i,o> | i ∈ T and P(i)=o}. This notion is formalized by Weyuker as follows [197]:

Definition 34 *A test set T is* inference adequate *for a program P intended to satisfy a specification S if and only if P_I is inductively inferred from E(P,T) and $P_I \equiv P \equiv S$. If only $P_I \equiv P$ is true, then T is said to be* program adequate, *and if only $P_I \equiv S$ is true, then T is said to be* specification adequate.

Here, we are interested in the case where a specification S is not given and, therefore, we will use only the notion of a program-adequate test set. The intuitive meaning of the above definition is as follows: If, given a set E(P,T) of input/output examples, we inductively infer a program $P_I \equiv P$, then T is likely to be useful for testing the program P.

However, definition 34 must refer to some form of induction. EX-identification (section 2.4) and PAC-learning ([192]) have been shown to be too general notions for the learnability of "real" programs. In particular, EX-identification is shown to be easier than testability in [41]: many simple classes of programs are easily EX-identified from examples, whereas a finite test set for those programs, adequate in the sense of definition 33, may not be found. Also, an oracle for the halting problem makes all the partial recursive functions EX-identifiable, but it does not make the previously analyzed testing problems any easier. As a consequence, we must refer to the alternative notion of sound and complete ILP that is closer to testing, because in both cases we have to deal with a finite set of input/output pairs. By contrast, in EX-identification the induction procedure is never aware of having reached a correct guess.

In the previous chapters, several techniques and implemented systems were presented to learn logic programs. Many of these systems could be fruitfully applied to definition 34 for testing a given program P. In particular, we will rely on the learning methods proposed in part II, which are terminating and explicitly make use of a finite set of legal programs $\mathcal{P}$ (i.e., a hypothesis space described by means of Clause Sets). The learned program P_I must belong to $\mathcal{P}$. This is consistent with our discussion on testing given in the introduction, where it was noted that all test case generation procedures that are not specification based refer (sometimes implicitly) to a set $\mathcal{P}$ of alternative programs. As a consequence, definition 34 can then be rephrased in terms of "sound and complete ILP" instead of "inductive inference." Moreover, test data adequacy (definition 33) turns out to be strongly related to finite identification: T is adequate for P if and only if P is the only program that can be learned from E(T,P) with a sound and complete ILP method. The restriction to a finite set of alternative programs $\mathcal{P}$ seems to be acceptable for testing; for instance, all approaches to fault-based testing, such as mutation analysis, are based on this assumption.

The intuitive symmetry between induction and testing can now be made clear: induction is an inference from the pair <E(T,P), $\mathcal{P}$> to a program P in $\mathcal{P}$, whereas testing is an inference from <P, $\mathcal{P}$> to the test set T. Theoretical comparisons of induction and testing can be found in [89, 35, 41], while the problem of *checking* test set adequacy is faced in [197]. In the next section we show how ILP techniques can be used in actually *generating* the adequate test cases for a logic program.[2] In particular, the FILP system will be used in our test case generation procedure.

10.3 Inductive Test Case Generation

A sequence of inductions of programs from examples is used to generate test cases. Initially, there are no examples and, in the end, the generated set of examples will be adequate in the sense of definition 33.

Let P be the program to be tested. At any given moment, the examples generated so far are used to induce a program P'. New examples that distinguish P from P' are added, and the process is repeated until no program P' that is not equivalent to P can be generated. This procedure is described in more detail below.

Test case generation procedure:

Input: a program P to be tested,
   a finite set $\mathcal{P}$ of alternative programs
Output: an adequate test set T

T ← ∅;
loop:
<P',T> ← FILP(E(T,P),$\mathcal{P}$)
if P' = "fail" **then return** T
if ($\exists$ i) P'(i) ≠ P(i)
   then T ← T ∪ {i}
   else $\mathcal{P}$ ← $\mathcal{P}$ - P'
goto loop

In order for the above procedure to work, the learning algorithm FILP must be sound and complete, as in fact it is (see chapter 7). In the test case generation procedure, the test set T is initially empty. The main step in the loop consists of using FILP to learn a program P' that is consistent with the examples generated

---
[2]Some related work for the problem of knowledge base validation can be found in [63].

so far. P′ is then ruled out either by (1) adding an input value to T or by (2) removing it from $\mathcal{P}$. As a consequence, P′ will not be learned again. When FILP cannot find a program P′$\in \mathcal{P}$ that is consistent with the examples, then the only programs with this property are P and those equivalent to it, i.e., the test set T is adequate. This is proved by the following:

Theorem 18 *Let equivalence be decidable for programs in $\mathcal{P}$. Then the above test case generation procedure outputs an adequate test set T for P.*

Proof: Since equivalence is decidable for programs in $\mathcal{P}$, the procedure terminates, as the condition ($\exists$ i) P′(i) $\neq$ P(i) always produces an answer. Suppose, by contradiction, that the obtained test set T is not adequate. This means that there is P′ $\in \mathcal{P}$ and an input i $\notin$ T such that P′(i) $\neq$ P(i), but ($\forall$ v) $\in$ T, P′(v) = P(v). However, just before termination, FILP failed to induce a program P_I. Moreover, P′ is complete and consistent with respect to E(T,P), because ($\forall$ v) $\in$ T, P′(v) = P(v). Then, just before termination, and because FILP is sound and complete, it must be the case that P′ $\notin \mathcal{P}$. As a consequence, P′ must have been removed from $\mathcal{P}$ at some previous iteration. But, in that case, there must have been an input value i such that P′(i) $\neq$ P(i), and this value would have been added to T. This contradicts the assumption that i $\notin$ T and T is not adequate. $\square$

If a decision procedure is available for finding an input i such that P(i) $\neq$ P′(i), this is used directly in the above test generation method. As this is not true in general, examples are found by enumerating (in some random or ad hoc order) the possible inputs i, and stopping when an i is found such that P(i)=o$\neq$P′(i)=o′. This enumeration could also be guided by other test case generation techniques, such as path or functional testing. The requirement of decidable equivalence is not easily verified or accepted. Program equivalence was found to be a major theoretical [35] and practical [55, 109, 53] issue in program testing. In the implementation of our test case generation method, we approximate it by means of its time-bounded semi-decision procedure. Except for this approximation, the system produces adequate test sets with respect to any finite class of programs $\mathcal{P}$.

We conclude with some remarks. We have seen that the test case generation procedure outputs an adequate test set, in the sense that it distinguishes the program to be tested from all alternatives. It is worth noting that if $\mathcal{P}$ contains at least one correct implementation, then the obtained test set will also be reliable, i.e., it will demonstrate any errors that may be present.

The efficiency of the method depends mainly on the size of the space $\mathcal{P}$ of alternative programs, since the most critical step in the test generation process is the induction of a program P′$\in \mathcal{P}$ consistent with E(T,P), for the partial test set T. The size of $\mathcal{P}$ can be controlled by defining it on the basis of the program P to be tested, as a set of possible mutations of P. This is easily achieved by means of the Clause Sets notation, as will be shown in the next section and in chapter 11. On the other hand, the size of the program P can indirectly influence the complexity of the method. This may happen because a more complex program may contain more errors, and may lead the tester to define a larger set $\mathcal{P}$ of alternatives. However, it is reasonable to assume that more complex programs need more testing effort, and more time devoted to defining a restricted, but still meaningful, set of alternative programs. As a consequence, the proposed method stops being practical only when the number of alternatives or possible errors becomes too large. By contrast, usual approaches to fault-based testing may cause problems when the size of the program to be tested is too large. This happens because a larger program may require a higher number of syntactical mutations to be applied systematically to every part of the code.

In [197], Weyuker noted that if program induction techniques were sufficiently developed, there would be no need for testing, as one would generate correct programs automatically from input-output examples, and there would be no need to write a program by hand and test it afterward. However, our program induction procedure is practical just because it can rely upon the program to be tested. Moreover, as we noted in chapter 9, inductive program learning can be useful in the debugging phase of a program. Software is often verified and validated through testing and debugging. Testing is used to expose the presence of errors. Debugging is then used to locate and remove the known errors. In our setting, examples showing the errors of the tested program P are found during the execution of the test case generation procedure. These examples can then be used to learn a program correct with respect to the discovered errors. In other words, by means of program learning, P can be automatically debugged with respect to the errors located in the testing phase.

10.4 Examples

Some examples of test case generation for logic programs with errors of increasing complexity are presented in this section. A more complex case study will be discussed in chapter 11. Here, we consider the problem of merging two lists. In all the examples, the learning system FILP, described in chapter 7, has been used as the induction procedure. Let the following program P for merging two ordered lists, to be tested:

P:
1) merge(X,Y,Z) :- null(X), Y=Z.
2) merge(X,Y,Z) :- null(Y), X=Z.

3) merge(X,Y,Z) :- head(X,X1), head(Y,Y1), tail(X,X2), X1≤Y1,
        merge(X2,Y,W), cons(X1,W,Z).
4) merge(X,Y,Z) :- head(X,X1), head(Y,Y1), tail(Y,Y2), X1>Y1,
        merge(X,Y2,W), cons(Y1,W,Z).

This program is wrong: in clause 3) the comparison X1≤Y1 must be replaced by X1<Y1. Another clause must be inserted for the case X1=Y1. As a consequence of the error, elements occurring in both input lists X and Y are repeated in the output Z. We define the set of alternatives $\mathcal{P}$ on the basis of P by means of Clause Sets as follows:

{
merge(X,Y,Z) :- {null(X), null(Y), X=Z, Y=Z,
        head(X,X1), tail(X,X2), head(Y,Y1), tail(Y,Y2),
        X1<Y1, X1=Y1, X1>Y1, X1≤Y1, X1≥Y1,
        merge(X2,Y,W), merge(X,Y2,W), W=Z,
        cons(X1,W,Z), cons(Y1,W,Z)}
}

The usual definitions for all the predicates in the above Clause Set (except for *merge*) are given. It is easy to check that the hypothesis space HS is defined simply by putting in the literal set all the literals of P, plus some other literals for comparing some of the variables. Hence, HS can be seen as a space of mutations of (clauses of) P. HS contains 2^{18} possible clauses and, as a consequence, $\mathcal{P}$ contains $2^{2^{18}}$ alternative programs, i.e., all possible subsets of the space of clauses. Among the subsets there are versions of the correct implementation of *merge* (in the following, we will use $\mathcal{P}$ as an input of FILP, instead of HS, to conform to the notation used in the previous sections).

The test case generation procedure starts with an empty test set T_0 of input values, and calls FILP. As $E(T_0,P)$ contains no examples, the empty program P_0 is an acceptable output of FILP$(E(T_0,P),\mathcal{P})$.

Pairs of lists X and Y are then enumerated, so that
$P_0 \vdash$ merge(X, Y, Z′), P $\vdash$ merge(X, Y, Z) and Z ≠ Z′
The first such pair that is found is <X,Y>=<[],[]>; for this input, P_0 produces no output and P outputs Z=[]. The new test set is then $T_1 = \{<[],[]>\}$.

FILP$(E(T_1,P),\mathcal{P})$ is called again, yielding P_1:
merge(X,Y,Z) :- X=Z.
This program is an acceptable output of FILP because merge([],[],[]) is derived from

10.4. Examples

it, and the output is the same as that of P.

Pairs of lists X and Y are enumerated, so that
$P_1 \vdash merge(X, Y, Z')$, $P \vdash merge(X, Y, Z)$ and $Z \neq Z'$. The first such pair that is found is:
<X,Y>=<[],[1]>; for this input, P_1 outputs Z=[] while P outputs Z=[1]. The new test set is then $T_2 = T_1 \cup \{<[],[1]>\}$.
FILP(E(T_2,P),$\mathcal{P}$) is called again, yielding P_2:
merge(X,Y,Z) :- Y=Z.
This program is an acceptable output of FILP because merge([],[],[]) and merge([],[1],[1]) are derived from it.

$T_3 = T_2 \cup \{<[1],[]>\}$
P_3:
merge(X,Y,Z) :- null(X), Y=Z.
merge(X,Y,Z) :- head(X,X1), X=Z.
merge(X,Y,Z) :- head(Y,Y1), Y=Z.

$T_4 = T_3 \cup \{<[1],[2]>\}$
P_4:
merge(X,Y,Z) :- null(Y), X=Z.
merge(X,Y,Z) :- null(X), Y=Z.
merge(X,Y,Z) :- head(X,X1), tail(X,X2), merge(X2,Y,W), cons(X1,W,Z).
In this case, FILP queries the user for a missing example, yielding:
$T'_4 = T_4 \cup \{<[],[2]>\}$.

$T_5 = T'_4 \cup \{<[2],[1]>\}$
P_5:
merge(X,Y,Z) :- null(Y), X=Z.
merge(X,Y,Z) :- null(X), Y=Z.
merge(X,Y,Z) :- head(X,X1), head(Y,Y1), tail(X,X2), X1<Y1,
           merge(X2,Y,W), cons(X1,W,Z).
merge(X,Y,Z) :- head(X,X1), head(Y,Y1), tail(Y,Y2), X1>Y1,
           merge(X,Y2,W), cons(Y1,W,Z).

$T_6 = T_5 \cup \{<[1],[1]>\}$
P_6:
merge(X,Y,Z) :- null(Y), X=Z.
merge(X,Y,Z) :- null(X), Y=Z.
merge(X,Y,Z) :- head(X,X1), head(Y,Y1), tail(X,X2), X1<Y1,

$$\text{merge}(X2,Y,W), \text{cons}(X1,W,Z).$$
$$\text{merge}(X,Y,Z) :\!\!- \text{head}(X,X1), \text{head}(Y,Y1), \text{tail}(Y,Y2), X1{>}Y1,$$
$$\text{merge}(X,Y2,W), \text{cons}(Y1,W,Z).$$
$$\text{merge}(X,Y,Z) :\!\!- \text{head}(X,X1), \text{head}(Y,Y1), \text{tail}(X,X2), X1{=}Y1,$$
$$\text{merge}(X2,Y,W), \text{cons}(X1,W,Z).$$

As $P_6 \equiv P$, it is removed from $\mathcal{P}$ and no test case is generated. With FILP, removing P_6 from $\mathcal{P}$ can be done in practice by means of the "forbidden clauses" option in the Clause Sets language, as described in section 6.5. A few more programs equivalent to P are then generated, and, finally, no other program consistent with T_6 can be found and FILP fails, ending the test generation process. T_6 is adequate, and it contains an input, namely X=[1] and Y=[1], that demonstrates the error of P, giving Z=[1,1] as output. The correct output would be Z=[1].

Only seven examples have been required to locate the error, whereas many more would have been necessary in random testing, if there are many possible element values with respect to the average list length. Functional testing would succeed easily if the rather usual criterion of having equal elements in input lists and vectors is adopted [95]. Nevertheless, we view this not as a general criterion but as a specific hypothesis about typical programming errors that is made explicit in the set $\mathcal{P}$ of alternative programs. We share this philosophy with other fault-based testing methodologies, but methods presented in the literature and cited in our references would have problems with the above program. The reason is that the correct program is not a simple mutation of the program P to be tested: it requires one simple modification and the addition of one entire clause. Most approaches to fault-based testing, instead, are only able to generate minor and syntactically simple modifications.

As a slightly more complex case, consider again the problem of merging two ordered lists, but we allow them to contain repeated elements. As before, the output list must be ordered and should contain every element of the input lists only once. This problem requires a procedure for removing the elements that are repeated. Suppose we are given the following:

remove(X,[X|Y],Z) :- !, remove(X,Y,Z).
remove(_,Y,Y).

This does just as much as necessary: it removes the initial occurrences of an element in a list, e.g., remove(a,[a,a,b],[b]), but remove(a,[b,a],[b,a]). Let the program to be tested be the following:

10.4. Examples

P1:
1) merge(X,Y,Z) :- null(X), Y=Z.
2) merge(X,Y,Z) :- null(Y), X=Z.
3) merge(X,Y,Z) :- head(X,X1), tail(X,X2), head(Y,X1), tail(Y,Y2),
       merge(X2,Y2,W), remove(X1,W,T), cons(X1,T,Z).
4) merge(X,Y,Z) :- head(X,X1), tail(X,X2), head(Y,Y1), tail(Y,Y2),
       X1<Y1, merge(X2,Y,W), remove(X1,W,T), cons(X1,T,Z).
5) merge(X,Y,Z) :- head(X,X1), tail(X,X2), head(Y,Y1), tail(Y,Y2),
       X1>Y1, merge(Y2,X,W), remove(Y1,W,T), cons(Y1,T,Z).

In this program the first two clauses are wrong. In fact, any repeated element in the nonempty list will be present in the output. Let $\mathcal{P}$ be defined with the same technique as in the previous example, i.e., by writing a literal set with all the literals occurring in the program to be tested. The generated test cases and corresponding outputs are the following:

merge([],[],[])
merge([1],[],[1])
merge([2],[1],[1,2])
merge([2],[],[2]) – queried by FILP
merge([],[1],[1]) – queried by FILP
merge([1],[1],[1])
merge([1,1,2],[1],[1,2])
merge([1,1,2],[],[1,1,2]) – queried by FILP, it shows the error
merge([1],[2],[1,2])

In this case, we can see that the examples that show the error may be added as a consequence of the queries of FILP. It should also be noted that P1 does not belong to the hypothesis space $\mathcal{P}$; actually, this is not required by the test case generation system. In fact, the program to be tested could be used as a black box and could, in principle, be written in another programming language.

Another buggy program for the same problem as before is the following:

P2:
1) merge(X,Y,Z) :- null(X), null(Y), null(Z).
2) merge(X,Y,Z) :- null(X), head(Y,Y1), remove(Y1,Y,W), cons(Y1,W,Z).
3) merge(X,Y,Z) :- null(Y), head(X,X1), remove(X1,X,W), cons(X1,W,Z).
4) merge(X,Y,Z) :- head(X,X1), tail(X,X2), head(Y,X1), tail(Y,Y2),
       remove(X1,X2,X2r), remove(Y1,Y2,Y2r),

merge(X2r,Y2r,T), cons(X1,T,Z).
5) merge(X,Y,Z) :- head(X,X1), tail(X,X2), head(Y,Y1), tail(Y,Y2), X1<Y1,
          remove(X1,X2,X2r), merge(X2r,Y,T), cons(X1,T,Z).
6) merge(X,Y,Z) :- head(X,X1), tail(X,X2), head(Y,Y1), tail(Y,Y2), X1>Y1,
          remove(Y1,Y2,Y2r), merge(X,Y2r,T), cons(Y1,T,Z).

This program is close to the correct solution, but clauses 2) and 3) still produce problems. In clause 2), any repetitions of the first element of Y are removed but repeated elements that occur later are not: a recursive call of *merge* is missing. A similar problem occurs in clause 3). The error in this program is not easily detected, since a repeated element must be present in the list portion that remains after merging is over, and this element must not be the first. Lists of this kind are not common, and random testing performs poorly. Simple covering techniques are not effective, either, because a few inputs such as X=[1,3,3,5,5], Y=[1,2,4] make all clauses executed many times, but a correct output is obtained. Even sophisticated forms of functional testing would fail. Critical choices of list pairs <X,Y> such as the following do not guarantee error detection: (1) X and Y null, (2) X or Y null, (3) one list is null and the other contains repeated elements, (4) X and Y contain the same element, (5) X and Y contain the same repeated element, (6) X contains a repeated element larger than all elements of Y. The generated test cases and corresponding outputs are the following:

merge([],[],[])
merge([1],[],[1])
merge([1,1],[],[1])
merge([1,2,2],[],[1,2,2]) – shows the error
merge([2,2],[],[2]) – queried by FILP

As a final example of a wrong solution for *merge*, consider the following program:

P3:
1) merge(X,Y,Z) :- null(X), null(Y), null(Z).
2) merge(X,Y,Z) :- null(X), head(Y,Y1), tail(Y,Y2),
          remove(Y1,Y2,Y2r), merge(X,Y2r,W), cons(Y1,W,Z).
3) merge(X,Y,Z) :- null(Y), head(X,X1), tail(X,X2),
          remove(X1,X2,X2r), merge(X2r,Y,W), cons(X1,W,Z).
4) merge(X,Y,Z) :- head(X,X1), tail(X,X2), head(Y,X1), tail(Y,Y2),
          remove(X1,Y2,Y2r), merge(X2,Y2r,T), cons(X1,T,Z).
5) merge(X,Y,Z) :- head(X,X1), tail(X,X2), head(Y,Y1), tail(Y,Y2),
          X1<Y1, merge(X2,Y,W), remove(X1,W,T), cons(X1,T,Z).

10.4. Examples

6) merge(X,Y,Z) :- head(X,X1), tail(X,X2), head(Y,Y1), tail(Y,Y2),
                  X1>Y1, merge(Y2,X,W), remove(Y1,W,T), cons(Y1,T,Z).

Here, in clause 4) X1 must also be removed from X2, not only from Y2. This error can be detected only when the input lists contain the same element, and this element is repeated in one of the two lists. In the set of generated test cases below, it can be noted that more than one generated test case may show the error. Any such input value will of course exclude the correct program, but other (incorrect) programs belonging to $\mathcal{P}$ may still be consistent with the generated examples, and may cause the generation of a new input value where P is again found to produce a wrong output. The generated test cases are the following:

merge([],[],[])
merge([1],[],[1])
merge([1],[1],[1])
merge([1,1],[],[1])
merge([2],[1],[1,2])
merge([2],[],[2]) – queried by FILP
merge([2,2],[1],[1,2])
merge([2,2],[],[2]) – queried by FILP
merge([1,1],[1],[1,1]) – shows the error
merge([1,1,1],[1],[1,1]) – shows the error
merge([1,1,1],[],[1]) – queried by FILP

To conclude, we would like to note that although the program to be tested could be used as a black box and could even be written in a language other than Prolog, its use as a white box still has some advantages. The main issue here is that the program to be tested can help the tester to determine the set $\mathcal{P}$ of mutations, as we have done in the examples of this section. Another minor point is that if the program to be tested is written in Prolog, the method described in this chapter can also be useful for automated debugging, where a debugged program can be based on the logic program learned from the final adequate test set and the corresponding corrected outputs.

11
A Case Study

There are many and diverse application areas where Inductive Logic Programming has been proved successful: ILP techniques have been used for learning classification rules for early diagnosis of rheumatic diseases [118]; for learning rules for predicting the secondary structure of proteins from their amino acid sequence [112, 111]; for automatically discovering rules for relating the activity of drugs to their chemical structure and to the chemical properties of their subcomponents [110]; for the analysis of stresses in physical structures [66]; for learning qualitative and quantitative models of dynamic systems [32, 68]; for learning diagnostic rules from qualitative models and discovering rules for qualitative reasoning [31]; for learning temporal diagnostic rules for physical systems [75]. These and other applications are also described in [30] and [117].

However, it is worth noting that among the above, one important application area is missing: Logic Programming. This may seem strange, since ILP means the *induction of logic programs*. Actually, the goal of an ILP system is to learn a set of Horn clauses. In principle, this set can be regarded as a logic program, but in fact, not every such set is perceived as a logic program by a programmer. Logic programs are considered to be those usually found in textbooks such as [44] and [45]. *Real* logic programs are normally expected to be recursive and to carry on a computation, more than to perform some classification or to draw some logical conclusion.

Many ILP systems are not mainly devoted to learning logic programs just because learning *real* logic programs is very hard. The first reason is the necessity to learn self-recursive or mutually recursive clauses. Top-down methods use an extensional interpretation of recursion. As a consequence, they are liable to failure or to output a wrong solution. Bottom-up methods based on inverse resolution have theoretical problems when learning recursive clauses. Methods based on inverse implication can work only on a limited class of recursive clauses, or their feasibility remain to be proved. A second reason is that even simple logic programs are made up of clauses defining different predicates, but multiple predicate learning has been shown to be difficult.

As a consequence, the kind of *real* programs that ILP systems are able to learn are limited to basic numerical functions or list and set manipulators. These include *multiply, factorial, member, append, reverse, intersection, union, subset,* and so on. The "top" of the performances is normally reached by learning *quicksort*, sometimes together with its main subprogram *partition*.

As we noted in Chapter 9, learning more complex programs may be just a dream for the available ILP systems, if a restricted hypothesis space and strong constraints cannot be devised. If ILP has to be useful for Software Engineering applications, we must be able to synthesize logic programs that are more complex than *quicksort*. To do so, we must exploit all the possible knowledge we may have about the target programs. But Software Engineering is precisely the field where such information is available, through the user of the ILP system, who is supposed to be a Prolog programmer.

In the next two sections we will carry on a learning and testing session for a logic program that is rather more complex than classical logic programs (not just a set of Horn clauses) normally learned by the existing ILP systems. The methodology we will follow should be representative of the use of an ILP system as a tool for Software Engineering applications, in the spirit of the considerations of chapter 9.

11.1 Synthesizing *Insert*

We consider the problem of synthesizing an *insert* program for inserting a new element into a balanced binary search tree, calling a rebalancing procedure if necessary. Let us refer to the well-known algorithm described by Knuth ([114]) and yielding an $\mathcal{O}(nlogn)$ sorting procedure. In this section, we show how to solve the problem by using the TRACY system. In the next section, the problem of testing (a wrong solution for) *insert* will be faced by using the FILP system. In both cases, the formalism of Clause Sets will be used to define the hypothesis space. All the experiments reported below have been done on a Sun Sparcstation 5. TRACY and FILP are written in C-prolog (interpreted). The expansion generator used to turn a Clause Set into an actual set of clauses, used in conjunction with TRACY, is written in C.

First, we state the problem. A binary tree is *balanced* if the depth of the left subtree of every node never differs by more than $\pm$ 1 from the depth of its right subtree. The *balance factor* within each node is +1, 0 or -1, computed as the depth of the right subtree minus the depth of the left subtree. The sought

11.1. Synthesizing *Insert*

program must take in input an element and a balanced tree, insert the element at the right place, and rebalance the tree if necessary. For the sake of simplicity, let us assume that the inserted element is never present in the input tree. To decide whether rebalancing is needed, a second output variable, the *increase factor*, must be used. The increase factor must be set to 1 if the depth of the tree has increased after the insertion, to 0 otherwise. A tree is represented as a list of four elements: [key, left_subtree, right_subtree, balance_factor]. We assume two rebalancing tree procedures (as reported in figure 11.2) are given as background knowledge, for rebalancing a tree that is unbalanced on the left or right subtree, respectively. Each rebalancing procedure has four arguments: the three components of the input tree (root_key, left_subtree, right_subtree) as input and the rebalanced tree as output.

Having defined the problem, a suitable hypothesis space for learning *insert* must be designed. The general structure of the clauses must be decided. To this end, we try to exploit the basic knowledge about the problem, and about logic programming techniques in general, that we might have. First, we note that determining the nonrecursive clause of the wanted program is quite easy, as it often happens in Logic Programming. An empty tree is represented by the empty list "nil," whereas a tree containing only the root is represented by the list [A,nil,nil,0], where A indicates a generic value for the root and 0 that the tree is balanced. Finally, inserting a node into an empty tree encreases its depth. As a consequence, the nonrecursive clause for *insert* is the following:

insert(A,nil,[A,nil,nil,0],1).

If we are pretty sure of the correctness of this clause, we can put it among the known clauses, i.e., in the background knowledge.

To design the set of other possible clauses, we must first decide the form of their head. The consequent of each clause must have two input arguments (the key to be inserted and the input tree) and two output variables (the resulting tree and the increase factor), and thus we could use a head literal like "insert(A,T,Y,Inc)." However, we know that the input tree is a list of four elements that will have to be tested and manipulated in some way, and hence it seems plausible to use the clause consequent "insert(A,[H,L,R,B],Y,Inc)."

Then we have to decide which literals to use for building the clauses in the hypothesis space. Suppose initially we do not have any idea of the structure of the desired program. Then we can design a very simple set of clauses by defining one big literal set with all the literals we suppose could be useful. In terms of the Clause Sets language, the hypothesis space will have the following form:

```
{
insert(A,[H,L,R,B],Y,Inc) :- {
                literals
                }.
}
```

What do we have to put in the *literals* set? First, we will probably need some literal for testing the value of the balance factor and the value of the node to be added with respect to the root. Thus, we put the literals: A<H, A>H, B<0, B=<0, B=0, B>=0, B>0.

Second, clauses of *insert* could be recursive. The added element (represented by the variable A) can be inserted in the left or right subtree, producing a new left (or right) subtree with its own increase factor. We can take care of that by adding the following two literals: insert(A,L,NewL,IncL), insert(A,R,NewR,IncL). As the increase factor can be set to 0 or 1, we need some literals for doing that. Since there are two variables used to hold the increase factor, we also add to *literals* the following: Inc=0, Inc=1, IncL=0, IncL=1.

After the insertion has been done in the left or right subtree, an output tree must be produced. If rebalancing is necessary, we must use the rebalancing procedures. By looking at the literals used for the recursive calls and for the consequent, we define the following two literals: rebalr(H,L,NewR,[NH,NL,NR]), reball(H,NewL,R,[NH,NL,NR]). Since the rebalancing procedures do not produce the balance factor, the actual output of *insert* must be generated by adding this factor, which is equal to zero for rebalanced trees. We use the literal tree(NH,NL,NR,0,Y), where *tree* is defined as in figure 11.2. If rebalancing is not required, we have only to produce the output tree and set its balance factor. If the insertion has been made in the left subtree, the balance factor of the output tree can (a) remain unchanged, if the depth of the left subtree has not increased, or (b) get the value 0 or -1, respectively, if the depth of the input tree was 1 or 0, respectively, and the depth of the left subtree has increased as a consequence of the insertion. However, the balance factor cannot change its value to 1, since this would mean that the input tree was not balanced. Similarly, if the insertion has been made in the right subtree, the balance factor of the output tree cannot be set to -1, but it can get the value 0, 1, or remain unchanged. As a consequence, we add the following two literals: tree(H,NewL,R,{0,-1,B},Y), tree(H,L,NewR,{0,1,B},Y).

Clearly, in the above discussion much knowledge about the program we want to learn is expressed. However, the resulting Clause Set is still far less informing and structured than the precise computational rule we are looking for. In fact, a space of 2^{22} clauses has been defined, hopefully containing a correct *insert* program. We

11.1. Synthesizing *Insert*

can reduce the number of allowed clauses by using the "forbidden conjunction of literals" option of the Clause Sets language. For example, we can rule out double recursive clauses by telling the system that three (or more) *insert* literals cannot occur in the same clause. In the same way, we can rule out any clause where the balance factor is equal to zero and a rebalancing procedure is called. In fact, a perfectly balanced tree never requires rebalancing after an insertion has occurred. The complete list of forbidden conjunctions is reported is figure 11.2. It is worth noting that in a very intuitive and concise way, many clauses can be ruled out, reducing the size of the hypothesis space. A further restriction can be obtained by defining an input-output mode for all the used predicates and then applying some of the constraints available in the Clause Sets language.

Finally, we must provide some positive and negative examples of the target concept. Initially, we probably do not have any idea of which examples will be really useful in the learning task. Thus, we input some examples that we may feel representative of the *insert* program. figure 11.1 below reports the set of positive examples used in our first experiment.[1] The examples, in their list form, are also reported in figure 11.2.

We should also provide some negative examples of *insert*. However, this can be avoided because TRACY, in its actual implementation, can handle the examples in a functional mode, like the FILP system. If we are learning a functional relation, we can tell the system that the negative examples are all the examples with the same input values as the positive examples but with different output values. Since *insert* is, in fact, a function, we can use this feature of TRACY here. As a consequence, when a (partial) trace is discovered, TRACY runs it by using the same input values as in the positive examples. If output values different from those of the positive examples can be computed by the trace, the trace is rejected as inconsistent.

All of the above information is expressed in the source file reported in figure 11.2. The source file is given in input to the expansion generator. By enabling the constraint that "intermediate output variables must be used," an output set of 1368 clauses is produced in about fifteen seconds.[2] This set of clauses is given in input to TRACY. After 1851 seconds of cpu time, TRACY outputs the first solution P_1 (we recall that the backtracking facility of Prolog can be used in TRACY to find alternative solutions):

---

[1] Throughout the chapter, trees will be represented graphically for clarity. In each tree, node keys are positive integers. A positive or a negative sign is used to indicate that the balance factor of that node is +1 or -1. No sign means a 0 balance factor. The increase factor is reported next to the corresponding output tree.

[2] We note that in the actual implementation of TRACY, the constraint "output variables in the head must be instantiated" is always in force.

```
-------------------------------------------------------------------------------
                examples     input pair        output pair

                  e1:          25 -> 50          -50   1
                                                 /
                                                25

                  e2:          75 -> 50          +50   1
                                                   \
                                                    75

                  e3:          75 -> -50          50   0
                                      /          / \
                                     25         25  75

                  e4:          25 -> +50          50   0
                                        \        / \
                                        75      25  75

                  e5:          15 -> -50          25   0
                                      /          / \
                                     25         15  50

                  e6:          90 -> +50          75   0
                                        \        / \
                                        75      50  90
-------------------------------------------------------------------------------
```

Figure 11.1: Initial examples for learning *insert*

P_1 :

```
insert(A,nil,[A,nil,nil,0],1).
insert(A,[H,L,R,B],Y,Inc) :- A<H,B<0,insert(A,L,NewL,IncL),Inc=0,IncL=1,
                             reball(H,NewL,R,[NH,NL,NR]),tree(NH,NL,NR,0,Y).
insert(A,[H,L,R,B],Y,Inc) :- A<H,B>0,insert(A,L,NewL,IncL),
                             Inc=0,IncL=1,tree(H,NewL,R,0,Y).
insert(A,[H,L,R,B],Y,Inc) :- A<H,B=0,insert(A,L,NewL,IncL),
                             Inc=1,IncL=1,tree(H,NewL,R,-1,Y).
insert(A,[H,L,R,B],Y,Inc) :- A>H,B<0,insert(A,R,NewR,IncL),
                             Inc=0,IncL=1,tree(H,L,NewR,0,Y).
insert(A,[H,L,R,B],Y,Inc) :- A>H,B>0,insert(A,R,NewR,IncL),Inc=0,IncL=1,
                             rebalr(H,L,NewR,[NH,NL,NR]),tree(NH,NL,NR,0,Y).
insert(A,[H,L,R,B],Y,Inc) :- A>H,B=0,insert(A,R,NewR,IncL),
                             Inc=1,IncL=1,tree(H,L,NewR,1,Y).
```

11.1. Synthesizing *Insert*

```
insert(A,nil,[A,nil,nil,0],1).
{
insert(A,[H,L,R,B],Y,Inc) :- {A<H, A>H, B<0, B=<0, B>0, B>=0, B=0,
                              insert(A,L,NewL,IncL), insert(A,R,NewR,IncL),
                              Inc=0, Inc=1, IncL=0, IncL=1,
                              rebalr(H,L,NewR,[NH,NL,NR]),
                              reball(H,NewL,R,[NH,NL,NR]),
                              tree(NH,NL,NR,0,Y),
                              tree(H,NewL,R,{0,-1,B},Y),tree(H,L,NewR,{0,1,B},Y)}.
}

/* Forbidden conjunctions of literals */

!(tree(_,_,_,_,_),tree(_,_,_,_,_)).
!(insert(_,_,_,_),insert(_,_,_,_),insert(_,_,_,_)).
!(rebalr(_,_,_,_),reball(_,_,_,_)).
!(Inc=1,Inc=0).  !(IncL=1,IncL=0).  !(A<H,A>H).  !(B<0),B=<0).
!(B<0),B>0).  !(B<0,B>=0).  !(B<0,B=0).  !(B=<0,B>0).  !(B=<0,B>=0).
!(B=<0,B=0).  !(B>0,B>=0).  !(B>0,B=0).  !(B>=0,B=0).
!(reball(_,_,_,_),B=0).  !(rebalr(_,_,_,_),B=0).

/* Definitions of predicates */

tree(H,L,R,B,[H,L,R,B]).
reball(H,[LH,LL,LR,-1],R,[LH,LL,[H,LR,R,0]]).
reball(H,[LH,LL,[LRH,LRL,LRR,1],1],R, [LRH,[LH,LL,LRL,-1],[H,LRR,R,0]]).
reball(H,[LH,LL,[LRH,LRL,LRR,0],1],R, [LRH,[LH,LL,LRL,0],[H,LRR,R,0]]).
reball(H,[LH,LL,[LRH,LRL,LRR,-1],1],R, [LRH,[LH,LL,LRL,0],[H,LRR,R,1]]).
rebalr(H,L,[RH,RL,RR,1],[RH,[H,L,RL,0],RR]).
rebalr(H,L,[RH,[RLH,RLL,RLR,-1],RR,-1], [RLH,[H,L,RLL,0],[RH,RLR,RR,1]]).
rebalr(H,L,[RH,[RLH,RLL,RLR,0],RR,-1], [RLH,[H,L,RLL,0],[RH,RLR,RR,0]]).
rebalr(H,L,[RH,[RLH,RLL,RLR,1],RR,-1], [RLH,[H,L,RLL,-1],[RH,RLR,RR,0]]).

/* input-output mode of predicates */

insert_inout(in,in,out,out).  tree_inout(in,in,in,in,out).
reball_inout(in,in,in,out).  rebalr_inout(in,in,in,out).

/* positive examples */

+insert(25,[50,nil,nil,0],[50,[25,nil,nil,0],nil,-1],1).
+insert(75,[50,nil,nil,0],[50,nil,[75,nil,nil,0],1],1).
+insert(75,[50,[25,nil,nil,0],nil,-1],[50,[25,nil,nil,0],[75,nil,nil,0],0],0).
+insert(25,[50,nil,[75,nil,nil,0],1],[50,[25,nil,nil,0],[75,nil,nil,0],0],0).
+insert(15,[50,[25,nil,nil,0],nil,-1],[25,[15,nil,nil,0],[50,nil,nil,0],0],0).
+insert(90,[50,nil,[75,nil,nil,0],1],[75,[50,nil,nil,0],[90,nil,nil,0],0],0).
```

Figure 11.2: Source file for learning *insert*

P_1 is only partially correct, but it can be used for some time. However, when it is run with the two examples reported in figure 11.3, it fails. Hence, we can just add

```
---------------------------------------------------------------------------
             examples      input pair        output pair

             e7:           10 -> -74           -74   0
                              /  \             /  \
                            -44   92          32   75
                            /                 /  \
                           32                10   44

             e8:           10 -> -58           -58   0
                              /  \             /  \
                            +21   74          21   74
                              \               /  \
                              43             10   43
---------------------------------------------------------------------------
```

Figure 11.3: Positive examples not derived by P_1

these two examples to the source file and start a new learning session. However, some useful information can still be drawn from P_1. By inspecting its clauses, we see that the literal "A < H" always comes together with literals involving the variable "NewL," and never with literals involving "NewR." The opposite is true for the literal "A > H." Intuitively, this suggests that when the element to be inserted is smaller than the root key, we only have to deal with the left subtree, and when the element is larger than the root key, we only have to deal with the right subtree. We can express this knowledge by splitting the Clause Set of figure 11.2 into two separate Clause Sets, one for the clauses dealing with the left subtrees and one for the clauses dealing with the right subtree. Also, since the literal "A < H" ("A > H") always occurs in the clauses dealing with the left (right) subtree, we can put it outside the literal set, meaning that it must always be present. The Clause Set of figure 11.2 is thus replaced by the one of figure 11.4. The information we may have on the desired program has been used here to design a more structured hypothesis space. In other words, a more restricted hypothesis space that is likely to be closer to the final solution.

In fact, under the same conditions as before, the expansion generator outputs only 456 allowed clauses, still in a few seconds. By using these clauses and only

11.1. Synthesizing *Insert*

```
--------------------------------------------------------------------------------
{
insert(A,[H,L,R,B],Y,Inc) :- A<H,
                             {
                             B<0, B=<0, B>0, B>=0, B=0,
                             insert(A,L,NewL,IncL),
                             Inc=0, Inc=1, IncL=0, IncL=1,
                             reball(H,NewL,R,[NH,NL,NR]),
                             tree(NH,NL,NR,0,Y),
                             tree(H,NewL,R,{0,-1,B},Y)
                             }.
insert(A,[H,L,R,B],Y,Inc) :- A>H,
                             {
                             B<0, B=<0, B>0, B>=0, B=0,
                             insert(A,R,NewR,IncL),
                             Inc=0, Inc=1, IncL=0, IncL=1,
                             rebalr(H,L,NewR,[NH,NL,NR]),
                             tree(NH,NL,NR,0,Y),
                             tree(H,L,NewR,{0,1,B},Y)
                             }.
}
--------------------------------------------------------------------------------
```

Figure 11.4: A more structured hypothesis space for learning *insert*

examples e_1, ..., e_6, TRACY discovers program P_1 in 56 seconds. By adding examples e_7 and e_8, the first solution program, P_2, is found after 1870 seconds:

P_2 :

```
insert(A,nil,[A,nil,nil,0],1).
insert(A,[H,L,R,B],Y,Inc) :- A<H,B<0,insert(A,L,NewL,IncL),
                             Inc=0,IncL=0,tree(H,NewL,R,-1,Y).
insert(A,[H,L,R,B],Y,Inc) :- A<H,B<0,insert(A,L,NewL,IncL),Inc=0,IncL=1,
                             reball(H,NewL,R,[NH,NL,NR]),tree(NH,NL,NR,0,Y).
insert(A,[H,L,R,B],Y,Inc) :- A<H,B>0,insert(A,L,NewL,IncL),
                             Inc=0,IncL=1,tree(H,NewL,R,0,Y).
insert(A,[H,L,R,B],Y,Inc) :- A<H,B=0,insert(A,L,NewL,IncL),
                             Inc=1,IncL=1,tree(H,NewL,R,-1,Y).
insert(A,[H,L,R,B],Y,Inc) :- A>H,B<0,insert(A,R,NewR,IncL),
                             Inc=0,IncL=1,tree(H,L,NewR,0,Y).
insert(A,[H,L,R,B],Y,Inc) :- A>H,B>0,insert(A,R,NewR,IncL),Inc=0,IncL=1,
                             rebalr(H,L,NewR,[NH,NL,NR]),tree(NH,NL,NR,0,Y).
insert(A,[H,L,R,B],Y,Inc) :- A>H,B=0,insert(A,R,NewR,IncL),
                             Inc=1,IncL=1,tree(H,L,NewR,1,Y).
```

This program is still only partially correct. After some time we can discover that it fails to derive the positive examples of *insert* of figure 11.5.

```
     examples      input pair          output pair

        e9:         60 -> +50           +50   0
                       /  \             /  \
                      25  -75          25   65
                      /                    /  \
                     65                   60  70

       e10:         70 -> +50           +50   0
                       /  \             /  \
                      25  -75          25   70
                      /                    /  \
                     65                   65  75

       e11:         90 -> +50           +50   0
                       /  \             /  \
                      25  -75          25   75
                      /                    /  \
                     65                   65  90
```

Figure 11.5: Positive examples not derived by P_2

As before, we add these examples to the set of positive examples and start the learning task again. After 3658 seconds TRACY comes out with the first output program that turns out to be a correct solution for *insert*:

P_3 :

```
insert(A,nil,[A,nil,nil,0],1).
insert(A,[H,L,R,B],Y,Inc) :- A<H,B<0,insert(A,L,NewL,IncL),
                             Inc=0,IncL=0,tree(H,NewL,R,-1,Y).
insert(A,[H,L,R,B],Y,Inc) :- A<H,B<0,insert(A,L,NewL,IncL),Inc=0,IncL=1,
                             reball(H,NewL,R,[NH,NL,NR]),tree(NH,NL,NR,0,Y).
insert(A,[H,L,R,B],Y,Inc) :- A<H,B>0,insert(A,L,NewL,IncL),
                             Inc=0,IncL=1,tree(H,NewL,R,0,Y).
insert(A,[H,L,R,B],Y,Inc) :- A<H,B=0,insert(A,L,NewL,IncL),
                             Inc=1,IncL=1,tree(H,NewL,R,-1,Y).
insert(A,[H,L,R,B],Y,Inc) :- A>H,B<0,insert(A,R,NewR,IncL),
                             Inc=0,IncL=1,tree(H,L,NewR,0,Y).
```

```
insert(A,[H,L,R,B],Y,Inc) :- A>H,B>0,insert(A,R,NewR,IncL),
                              Inc=0,IncL=0,tree(H,L,NewR,1,Y).
insert(A,[H,L,R,B],Y,Inc) :- A>H,B>0,insert(A,R,NewR,IncL),Inc=0,IncL=1,
                              rebalr(H,L,NewR,[NH,NL,NR]),tree(NH,NL,NR,0,Y).
insert(A,[H,L,R,B],Y,Inc) :- A>H,B=0,insert(A,R,NewR,IncL),
                              Inc=1,IncL=1,tree(H,L,NewR,1,Y).
```

Had we used the source file of figure 11.2, resulting in a set of 1368 allowed clauses together with examples $e_1, ..., e_{11}$, the first correct solution for *insert* would have been found in 40,695 seconds! Clearly, the number of used positive examples also affects the speed of the learning task. In our case, 11 examples were used because they were somehow produced "incrementally," and because the initial ones were not chosen very carefully. In fact, TRACY is able to learn all the clauses necessary to derive a given positive example. In the case of *insert*, a very well-chosen example is sufficient to learn the entire program. Obviously, such meaningful examples are difficult to find, unless the target program is known a priori. Finally, although TRACY can output a solution only if the set of possible clauses forms a terminating program, in the above experiments we never paid attention to this constraint. However, the design of the Clause Set was such that a recursive call could take place only on a subtree of the input tree. Normally, a choice of this kind, which is normal when writing logic programs, is a sufficient trick for avoiding endless recursive calls in the hypothesis space. Nonetheless, TRACY has an option that can be used to define the maximum number of allowed recursive calls of the set of possible clauses.

11.2 Testing *Insert*

For testing, the use of the FILP system is normally to be preferred for two reasons. First, we do not know in advance how many examples will be necessary to distinguish the program to be tested from all of the possible alternatives. If many examples are required, it is better to use an extensional method, since it has linear complexity in the number of input examples (that is, the examples in E(T,P)). Second, we would want to define a very large number of alternative programs, i.e., a very large hypothesis space. Again, it is better to use a learning method that is linear in the size of the hypothesis space.[3] Finally, answering the queries of FILP is easy when testing a program, since the program itself is used to produce the answers.

---

[3]In the actual implementation, FILP works with a flattened representation of literals. In the following we will use an unflattened representation to improve the readability of the examples. However, we also recall that turning an unflattened program into a flattened one, or vice versa, requires a linear time with respect to the size of the program.

Suppose the following incorrect program P_e for testing is given:

P_e:

```
1) insert(A,nil,[A,nil,nil,0],1).
2) insert(A,[H,L,R,B],Y,Inc) :- A<H, B<0, insert(A,L,NewL,IncL), IncL=1,
                                Inc=0, reball(H,NewL,R,[NH,NL,NR]),
                                Y=[NH,NL,NR,0].
3) insert(A,[H,L,R,B],Y,Inc) :- A<H, B>=0, insert(A,L,NewL,IncL),
                                IncL=1, Inc=0, Y=[H,NewL,R,-1].
4) insert(A,[H,L,R,B],Y,Inc) :- A<H, insert(A,L,NewL,IncL),
                                IncL=0, Inc=0, Y=[H,NewL,R,B].
5) insert(A,[H,L,R,B],Y,Inc) :- A>H, B>0, insert(A,R,NewR,IncL),
                                IncL=1, Inc=0, rebalr(H,L,NewR,[NH,NL,NR]),
                                Y=[NH,NL,NR,0].
6) insert(A,[H,L,R,B],Y,Inc) :- A>H, B=<0, insert(A,R,NewR,IncL),
                                IncL=1, Inc=1, Y=[H,L,NewR,1].
7) insert(A,[H,L,R,B],Y,Inc) :- A>H, insert(A,R,NewR,IncL),
                                IncL=0, Inc=0, Y=[H,L,NewR,B].
```

The rebalancing procedures *reball* and *rebalr* are given as background knowledge, and are defined as in figure 11.2.

We see that clauses 3 and 6 of P_e are wrong. In fact, instead of clause 3 (6), two different clauses must be used to test separately for the balance factor being equal to or greater (smaller) than 0. Moreover, note that if literal "Inc = 0" in clause 3 is replaced with literal "Inc = 1," then program P_e turns out to be "almost" correct. In fact, it would always output balanced trees, but the balance factor and the increase factor may be wrong. Literal "Inc = 0" is responsible for producing unbalanced trees if an element is inserted as a left leaf and the resulting tree needs rebalancing. In the correct program, clause 3 must be replaced by the following two clauses:

```
insert(A,[H,L,R,B],Y,Inc) :- A<H, B>0, insert(A,L,NewL,IncL),
                             IncL=1, Inc=0, Y=[H,NewL,R,0].
insert(A,[H,L,R,B],Y,Inc) :- A<H, B=0, insert(A,L,NewL,IncL),
                             IncL=1, Inc=1, Y=[H,NewL,R,-1].
```

And, similarly, clause 6 must be replaced by the two clauses:

```
insert(A,[H,L,R,B],Y,Inc) :- A>H, B<0, insert(A,R,NewR,IncL),
                             IncL=1, Inc=0, Y=[H,L,NewR,0].
insert(A,[H,L,R,B],Y,Inc) :- A>H, B=0, insert(A,R,NewR,IncL),
                             IncL=1, Inc=1, Y=[H,L,NewR,1].
```

To test P_e, we follow the method presented in chapter 10. Based on P_e, we define the hypothesis space reported in figure 11.6.

11.2. Testing *Insert*

examples	input pair	Pi-1 output	Pe output	time
| e10(*): | ```
65 -> 50
  / \
 25  75
``` | ```
 +50    1
 / \
25 -75
    /
   65
``` | ```
  50    0
 / \
25 -75
    /
   65
``` | 623 |
| e11: | ```
90 -> 50
  / \
 25  75
``` | ```
  75    0
 / \
50  90
/
25
``` | ```
 +50    1
 / \
25 +75
     \
     90
``` | 919 |
| e12(*): | ```
 5 -> -50
  / \
-25  75
 /
15
``` | ```
 -50    0
 / \
15  75
/ \
5  25
``` | ```
 -50    0
 / \
-25  75
 /
-15
 /
 5
``` | 1171 |
| e13(*): | ```
65 -> -50
  / \
-25  75
 /
15
``` | ```
 +50    1
 / \
-25 -75
 /   /
15  65
``` | ```
 -50    0
 / \
-25 -75
 /   /
15  65
``` | 1327 |
| e14(*): | ```
 5 -> -50
  / \
+25  75
  \
  35
``` | no | ```
 -50    0
 / \
-25  75
 / \
5  35
``` | 1478 |
| e15(*): | ```
 5 -> +50
  / \
 25 -75
 /
65
``` | ```
 -50    0
 / \
-25 -75
 /   /
5   65
``` | ```
 +50    0
 / \
-25 -75
 /   /
5   65
``` | 1810 |

Figure 11.7 (cont.): Input-output pairs for testing *insert*
```

ated in order of growing complexity of the input tree. The first such pair for which P_e and P_0 differ is <50, nil>. For this input, P_0 produces no output, whereas P_e outputs:

$Y = [50, nil, nil, 0]$, $Inc = 1$.

As a consequence, the new test set becomes $T_1 = T_0 \cup \{<50, nil>\}$. $FILP(E(T1,P_e),\mathcal{P})$ is called again, yielding P_1:

P_1:

```
insert(A,T,Y,Inc) :- Y=[A,nil,nil,0], Inc=1.
```

The first enumerated input pair such that P_e and P_1 differ is <25, [50, nil, nil, 0]>. For this input pair P_1 outputs:

$Y = [25, nil, nil, 0]$, $Inc = 1$,

whereas P_e outputs:

$Y = [25, [50, nil, nil, 0], nil, -1]$, $Inc = 0$.

Also, this test case shows one of the errors of P_e, since the increase factor variable Inc should be set to 1 and not to 0. However, this may not be easily noticed, as the output tree is balanced. We set $T_2 = T_1 \cup \{<25, [50, nil, nil, 0]>\}$ and $FILP(E(T_2,P_e),\mathcal{P})$ is called, yielding P_2:

P_2:

```
insert(A,T,Y,Inc) :- null(T), Y=[A,nil,nil,0], Inc=1.
insert(A,T,Y,Inc) :- T=[H,L,R,B], A<H, insert(A,L,NewL,IncL),
                     Inc=0, Y=[H,NewL,R,-1].
```

The test case generation procedure goes on in this way, as was shown in the previous chapter. Figure 11.7 summarizes the obtained results. For each entry i ($1 \leq i \leq 15$), the second column contains the first input pair found (according to the adopted enumeration) for which P_{i-1} and P_e give different outputs. The third column is the output pair of P_{i-1} on the i-th input pair. The fourth column is the output pair of P_e. As before, each test set T_i, used by FILP to learn P_i, is obtained by adding the i-th input pair to T_{i-1}. The fifteen examples e_1, ..., e_{15} represent an adequate test set for P_e. Examples marked with an asterisk show errors of P_e. Fifteen more examples have been added during the learning process by the FILP

11.2. Testing *Insert*

queries. The fifth column reports times (in seconds) required to learn program P_{i-1}. Program P_{15}, reported below, was learned in 1831 seconds. This is the first program equivalent to P_e found by the induction procedure:

P_{15}:

```
1)  insert(A,T,Y,Inc) :- null(T), Y=[A,nil,nil,0], Inc=1.
2)  insert(A,T,Y,Inc) :- T=[H,L,R,B], A<H, B<0,
                         insert(A,L,NewL,IncL), IncL=1 , Inc=0,
                         reball(H,NewL,R,[NH,NL,NR]), Y=[NH,NL,NR,0].
3a) insert(A,T,Y,Inc) :- T=[H,L,R,B], A<H, B=0, insert(A,L,NewL,IncL),
                         IncL=1, Inc=0, Y=[H,NewL,R,-1].
3b) insert(A,T,Y,Inc) :- T=[H,L,R,B], A<H, B>0, insert(A,L,NewL,IncL),
                         IncL=1, Inc=0, Y=[H,NewL,R,-1].
4)  insert(A,T,Y,Inc) :- T=[H,L,R,B], A<H, insert(A,L,NewL,IncL),
                         IncL=0, Inc=0, Y=[H,NewL,R,B].
5)  insert(A,T,Y,Inc) :- T=[H,L,R,B], A>H, B>0,
                         insert(A,R,NewR,IncL), IncL=1, Inc=0,
                         rebalr(H,L,NewR,[NH,NL,NR]), Y=[NH,NL,NR,0].
6a) insert(A,T,Y,Inc) :- T=[H,L,R,B], A>H, B=0, insert(A,R,NewR,IncL),
                         IncL=1, Inc=1, Y=[H,L,NewR,1].
6b) insert(A,T,Y,Inc) :- T=[H,L,R,B], A>H, B<0, insert(A,R,NewR,IncL),
                         IncL=1, Inc=1, Y=[H,L,NewR,1].
7)  insert(A,T,Y,Inc) :- T=[H,L,R,B], A>H, insert(A,R,NewR,IncL),
                         IncL=0, Inc=0, Y=[H,L,NewR,B].
```

It is easy to check that programs P_e and P_{15} are equivalent (in P_{15} we have just reordered learned clauses and literals to make the comparison easier). In particular, clauses 3a and 3b (6a and 6b) of P_{15} are equivalent to clause 3 (6) of P_e. In fact, clause 3 (6) merges the two tests "B=0" and "B>0" ("B<0") made separately in 3a and 3b (6a and 6b). However, the testing procedure has tested P_{15} and P_e for equivalence on all possible insertion cases into balanced trees, from the empty tree up to trees of maximum depth 3. As the outputs are the same, P_{15} is removed from $\mathcal{P}$ (by means of the "forbidden clause" option of the Clause Sets language) and no new test case is generated. Again, a few more programs equivalent to P_e are found and then no other program consistent with T_{15} can be found, and FILP fails. Of the fifteen examples generated, examples e_2, e_5, e_6, e_8, e_9, e_{10}, e_{12}, e_{13}, e_{14}, and e_{15} demonstrate the errors of P_e. Of particular interest are examples e_6 and e_{12}. For the input pairs of these two examples, P_e outputs unbalanced trees. This is the consequence of the error in clause 3 of P_e, as discussed above.

Appendix A

How to FTP Our Software

The FILP and TRACY systems (chapters 7 and 8) are free software and are made available through ftp. Both systems are written in C-Prolog (interpreted). The expansion generator that turns a clause set into an actual set of clauses (modified, as described in section 8.4, in order to be used in conjunction with TRACY) is written in C. The software has been developed and tested on Sun workstations running the SunOS operative system, but are likely to run on any other platform supporting C-Prolog and C. The two systems can be used with any kind of non-graphical terminal. However, TRACY also has a graphical interface, developed under Openwin, that makes it easier to use the system.

The software can be retrieved at the ML-archive at ftp.gmd.de, in the directories "MachineLearning/ILP/public/software/filp" and "MachineLearning/ILP/public-/software/tracy," accessible through anonymous login.[1] The wanted file must be uncompressed and untared (when ftping compressed files — those with the ".Z" extension — remember to use binary mode for retrieving the files). In every package are included instructions about the installation and use of the software. Also, a whole set of sample files is provided, including the source files used in chapter 11. Each file is written using the Clause Set notation. In the TRACY package the set of clauses of figure 8.3 is also included, as produced by the expansion generator. Queries about the use of FILP and TRACY can also be sent to gunetti@di.unito.it.

---

[1] The exact path is subject to change. For any problem or question about the use of the ml-archive site, you can send an E-mail to ml-archive@gmd.de. If available, it is more comfortable to use WWW-pages: ftp://ftp.gmd.de/MachineLearning.

Bibliography

[1] I. Adé, L. DeRaedt, and M. Bruynooghe. Declarative Bias for Specific-to-General ILP Systems. *Machine Learning*, 1995. To appear.

[2] D. Aha, C. Ling, S. Matwin, and S. Lapointe. Learning Singly Recursive Relations from Small Datasets. In F. Bergadano, L. DeRaedt, S. Matwin, and S. Muggleton, editors, *Proc. of the IJCAI-93 Workshop on Inductive Logic Programming*, pages 47–58. Chambéry, France, 1993, IJCAII.

[3] D. W. Aha, S. Lapointe, C. X. Ling, and S. Matwin. Learning Recursive Relations with Randomly Selected Small Training Sets. In William W. Cohen, editor, *Proc. of the Int. Conf. on Machine Learning*, pages 12–18. New Brunswick, NJ, 1994, Morgan Kaufmann.

[4] H. Andreka and I. Nemeti. The Generalized Completeness of Horn Predicate Logic as a Programming Language. *Acta Cybernetica*, 4:3–10, 1978.

[5] D. Angluin. Learning Regular Sets from Queries and Counterexamples. *Information and Computation*, 75:87–106, 1987.

[6] D. Angluin, W. Gasarch, and C. Smith. Training Sequences. *Theoretical Computer Science*, 66:255–272, 1989.

[7] S. Arikawa, T. Shinohara, and A. Yamamoto. Learning Elementary Formal Systems. *Theoretical Computer Science*, 95:97–113, 1992.

[8] M. Bain and S. Muggleton. Non-monotonic Learning. In S. Muggleton, editor, *Inductive Logic Programming*, London, 1992, Academic Press.

[9] R. B. Banerji. Learning Theoretical Terms. In S. Muggleton, editor, *Inductive Logic Programming*, London, 1992, Academic Press.

[10] J. M. Bardzin. Prognostication of Automata and Functions. In B. Gilchrist, editor, *Information Processing*, pages 81–84. New York, 1972, North Holland.

[11] M. A. Bauer. Programming by Examples. *Artificial Intelligence*, 12:1–21, 1979.

[12] F. Bazzichi and I. Spadafora. An Automatic Generator for Compiler Testing. *IEEE Trans. on Software Engineering*, 8(4):343–353, 1982.

[13] S. Bell and S. Weber. On the Close Logical Relationship Between FOIL and the Frameworks of Helft and Plotkin. In S. Muggleton, editor, *Proc. Third Int. Workshop on Inductive Logic Programming*, pages 1–10. Ljubljana, Slovenia, 1993, Jozef Stefan Institute.

[14] F. Bergadano. The Problem of Induction and Machine Learning. In *Proc. Int. Joint Conf. on Artificial Intelligence*, pages 1073–1079. Sydney, Australia, 1991, IJCAII.

[15] F. Bergadano. Inductive Database Relations. *IEEE Trans. on Data and Knowledge Engineering*, 5(6):969–972, 1993.

[16] F. Bergadano. Test Case Generation by Means of Learning Techniques. In *Proc. ACM SIGSOFT*, Los Angeles, 1993, ACM.

[17] F. Bergadano and A. Giordana. A Knowledge Intensive Approach to Concept Induction. In J. Laird, editor, *Proceedings of the Fifth International Conference on Machine Learning*, pages 305–317. Ann Arbor, MI, 1988, Morgan Kaufmann.

[18] F. Bergadano, A. Giordana, and S. Ponsero. Deduction in Top-down Inductive Learning. In *Proc. of the Sixth Int. Conf. on Machine Learning*, pages 23–25. Ithaca, NY, 1989, Morgan Kaufmann.

[19] F. Bergadano, A. Giordana, and L. Saitta. Automated Concept Acquisition in Noisy Environments. *IEEE Transactions on Pattern Analysis and Machine Intelligence*, 10(4):555–578, 1988.

[20] F. Bergadano, A. Giordana, and L. Saitta. Biasing Induction by Using a Domain Theory: An Experimental Evaluation. In *Proc. European Conf. on Artificial Intelligence*, pages 363–368. Stockholm, 1990, Pitman.

[21] F. Bergadano and D. Gunetti. An Interactive System to Learn Functional Logic Programs. In R. Bajcsy, editor, *Proc. 13th Int. Joint Conf. on Artificial Intelligence*, pages 1044–1049. Chambéry, France, 1993, IJCAII.

[22] F. Bergadano and D. Gunetti. Learning Clauses by Tracing Derivations. In S. Wrobel, editor, *Proc. IV Int. Workshop on Inductive Logic Programming*, pages 11–30. Bad Honnef/Bonn, Germany, 1994, GMD-Studien.

[23] F. Bergadano, D. Gunetti, and U. Trinchero. The Difficulties of Learning Logic Programs with Cut. *Journal of Artificial Intelligence Research*, 1:91–107, 1993.

[24] F. Bergadano and S. Varricchio. Learning Behaviours of Automata from Multiplicity and Equivalence Queries. *SIAM J. on Computing*, 1995, to appear.

[25] A. Biermann. The Inference of Regular LISP Programs from Examples. *IEEE Trans. on SMC*, 8(8):585–600, 1978.

[26] L. Birnbaum and G. Collins, editors. *Proc. of the 8th Int. Conference on Machine Learning, Part VI: Learning Relations*. Evanston, IL, 1991, Morgan Kaufmann.

[27] L. Blum and M. Blum. Toward a Mathematical Theory of Inductive Inference. *Information and Control*, 28:125–155, 1975.

[28] Henrik Bostrom and Peter Idestam-Almquist. Specialization of Logic Programs by Pruning SLD-trees. In S. Wrobel, editor, *Proc. IV Int. Workshop on Inductive Logic Programming*, pages 31–48. Bad Honnef/Bonn, Germany, 1994, GMD-Studien.

[29] I. Bratko and M. Grobelnik. Inductive Learning Applied to Program Construction and Verification. In S. Muggleton, editor, *Proc. Third Int. Workshop on Inductive Logic Programming*, Ljubljana, Slovenia, 1993, Jozef Stefan Institute.

[30] I. Bratko and R. King. Applications of Inductive Logic Programming. *ACM SIGART*, 5:63–49, 1994.

[31] I. Bratko, I. Mozetič, and N. Lavrač. *KARDIO: A Study in Deep and Qualitative Knowledge for Expert Systems*. Cambridge, MA, 1989, MIT Press.

[32] I. Bratko, S. Muggleton, and A. Varsek. Learning Qualitative Models of Dynamic Systems. In S. Muggleton, editor, *Inductive Logic Programming*, pages 437–452. London, 1992, Academic Press.

[33] P. Brazdil and A. Jorge. Exploiting Algorithm Sketches in ILP. In S. Muggleton, editor, *Proc. Third Int. Workshop on Inductive Logic Programming*, Ljubljana, Slovenia, 1993, Jozef Stefan Institute.

[34] F. P. Brooks. No Silver Bullet: Essence and Accidents of Software Engineering. *IEEE Computer*, 20:10–19, 1987.

[35] T. A. Budd and D. Angluin. Two Notions of Correctness and Their Relation to Testing. *Acta Informatica*, 18:31–45, 1982.

[36] W. Buntine. Induction of Horn Clauses: Methods and the Plausible Generalization Algorithm. *Int. Journal of Man-Machine Studies*, 26:499–519, 1987.

[37] W. Buntine. Generalized Subsumption and Its Applications to Induction and Redundancy. *Artificial Intelligence*, 2(36):149–176, 1993.

[38] R. M. Cameron-Jones and J. R. Quinlan. Avoiding Pitfalls When Learning Recursive Theories. In R. Bajcsy, editor, *Proc. 13th Int. Joint Conf. on Artificial Intelligence*, pages 1050–1055. Chambéry, France, 1993. IJCAII.

[39] C. L. Chang. The Unit Proof and the Input Proof in Theorem Proving. *Journal of the ACM*, 17:698–707, 1970.

[40] C. L. Chang and R. C. Lee. *Symbolic Logic and Mechanical Theorem Proving*. New York, 1973, Academic Press.

[41] J. C. Cherniavsky and C. H. Smith. A recursion Theoretic Approach to Program Testing. *IEEE Trans. on Software Engineering*, 13(7):777–784, 1987.

[42] N. Choquet. Test Data Generation Using Prolog with Constraints. In *Proc. Workshop on Software Testing*, pages 132–141. Los Alamitos, CA, 1986.

[43] L. A. Clarke, J. Hassell, and D. J. Richardson. A Close Look at Domain Testing. *IEEE Trans. on Software Engineering*, 8(4):380–390, 1982.

[44] W. F. Clocksin and C. S. Mellish. *Programming in Prolog*. Berlin, 1981, Springer-Verlag.

[45] H. Coelho and J. C. Cotta. *Prolog by Example: How to Learn Teach and Use it*. Berlin, 1988, Springer-Verlag.

[46] W. Cohen. Pac-learning a Restricted Class of Recursive Logic Programs. In S. Muggleton, editor, *Proc. of the Third Int. Workshop on Inductive Logic Programming*, pages 73–86. Ljubljana, Slovenia, 1993, Jozef Stefan Institute.

[47] W. Cohen. Rapid Prototyping of ILP Systems Using Explicit Bias. In S. Matwin F. Bergadano, L. DeRaedt and S. Muggleton, editors, *Proc. of the IJCAI-93 Workshop on Inductive Logic Programming*, pages 24–35. Chambéry, France, 1993, IJCAII.

Bibliography

[48] W. Cohen. Gramatically Biased Learning: Learning Logic Programs Using an Explicit Antecedent Description Language. *Artificial Intelligence*, 68(2):303–366, 1994.

[49] W. Cohen. Recovering Software Specifications with Inductive Logic Programming. In K. Ford, editor, *Proc. of the AAAI Conference*, pages 142–148. Seattle, WA, 1994.

[50] A. Colmerauer. Metamorphosis Grammars. In L. Bolc, editor, *Natural Language Communication with Computers*, Berlin, 1978, Springer.

[51] T. M. Cover. Learning in Pattern Recognition. In S. Watanabe, editor, *Methodologies of Pattern Recognition*, New York, 1969, Academic Press.

[52] A. P. Danyluk. The Use of Explanations for Similarity-Based Learning. In J. McDermott, editor, *Proc. of the IJCAI*, pages 274–276. Milan, 1987, IJCAII.

[53] R. A. DeMillo. Test Adequacy and Program Mutation. In *Proc. Int. Conf. on Software Engineering*, pages 355–356. Washington, 1989. IEEE Comp. Soc. Press.

[54] R. A. DeMillo, R. J. Lipton, and F. G. Sayward. Hints on Test Data Selection: Help for the Practicing Programmer. *IEEE Computer*, 11(April):34–41, 1978.

[55] R. A. DeMillo and A. J. Offutt. Constraint-Based Automatic Test Data Generation. *IEEE Trans. on Software Engineering*, 17(9):900–910, 1991.

[56] R. Denney. Test Case Generation from Prolog-based Specifications. *IEEE Software*, 8(2):49–57, 1991.

[57] L. DeRaedt. *Interactive Concept Learning*. Ph.D. thesis, Katholieke Univ. Leuven, 1991.

[58] L. DeRaedt and M. Bruynooghe. CLINT: A Multistrategy Interactive Concept-Learner and Theory Revision System. In R. S. Michalski and G. Tecuci, editors, *Proc. Workshop on Multistrategy Learning*, pages 175–190. Harpers Ferry, VA, 1991.

[59] L. DeRaedt and Maurice Bruynooghe. Belief Updating from Integrity Constraints and Queries. *Artificial Intelligence*, 53:291–307, 1992.

[60] L. DeRaedt and S. Džeroski. First-order jk-clausal Theories Are PAC-learnable. *Artificial Intelligence*, 70(1-2):375–392, 1994.

[61] L. DeRaedt, N. Lavrač, and S. Džeroski. Multiple Predicate Learning. In R. Bajcsy, editor, *Proc. 13th Int. Joint Conf. on Artificial Intelligence*, pages 1037–1042. Chambéry, France, 1993, IJCAII.

[62] L. DeRaedt and S. Muggleton. Inductive Logic Programming: Theory and Methods. *Journal of Logic Programming*, 19/20:629–680, 1994.

[63] L. DeRaedt, G. Sablon, and M. Bruynooghe. Using Interactive Concept Learning for Knowledge Base Validation and Verification. In M. Ayel and J. P. Laurent, editors, *Validation, Verification and Testing of Knowledge Based Systems*, pages 177–190. London, 1991, John Wiley and Sons.

[64] L. Devroye. Automatic Pattern Recognition: A Study of the Probability of Error. *IEEE Trans. on PAMI*, 10(4):530–543, 1988.

[65] B. Dolsak, I. Bratko, and A. Jezernik. Finite Element Mesh Design: An Engineering Domain for ILP Applications. In S. Wrobel, editor, *Proc. IV Int. Workshop on Inductive Logic Programming*, pages 305–320. Bad Honnef/Bonn, Germany, 1994, GMD-Studien.

[66] S. Džeroski and B. Dolsak. Comparison of ILP Systems on the Problem of Finite Element Mesh Design. In *Proc. 6th ISSEK Workshop*, Ljubljana, Slovenia, 1991, Jozef Stefan Institute.

[67] S. Džeroski, S. Muggleton, and S. Russell. Pac-learnability of Determinate Logic Programs. In *Proc. of the Fifth ACM Workshop on Computational Learning Theory*, Pittsburgh, PA, 1992, ACM.

[68] S. Džeroski and L. Todorovski. Discovery Dynamics: from Inductive Logic Programming to Machine Discovery. In F. Bergadano, L. DeRaedt, S. Matwin, and S. Muggleton, editors, *Proc. of the IJCAI-93 Workshop on Inductive Logic Programming*, Chambéry, France, 1993, IJCAII.

[69] A. Cornuejols, editor. *Proc. of the Spring Symposium Workshop on Training Issues in Incremental Learning*. Stanford, CA, 1993, AAAI.

[70] T. Ellman. Explanation-Based Learning: A Survey of Programs and Perspectives. *Computing Surveys*, 21(2):163–222, 1989.

[71] W. Emde, C. U. Abel, and C. R. Rollinger. The Discovery of the Equator or Concept Driven Learning. In A. Bundy, editor, *Proc. of the 8th Int. Joint Conf. on Artificial Intelligence*, pages 455–458. Karlsruhe, Germany, 1983, IJCAII.

Bibliography

[72] M. H. Van Emdev and R. A. Kowalski. The Semantics of Predicate Logic as a Programming Language. *Journal of the ACM*, 23(4):733–742, 1976.

[73] F. Esposito, D. Malerba, and G. Semeraro. Classification in Noisy Environments Using a Distance Measure Between Structural Symbolic Descriptions. *IEEE Trans. on Pattern Analysis and Machine Intelligence*, 14(3):390–402, 1992.

[74] R. Fairley. *Software Engineering Concepts*. New York, 1987, McGraw-Hill.

[75] C. Feng. Inducing Temporal Fault Diagnostic Rules from a Qualitative Model. In S. Muggleton, editor, *Inductive Logic Programming*, pages 471–493. London, 1992, Academic Press.

[76] M. Fulk. Saving the Phenomena: Requirements That Inductive Inference Machines Not Contradict Known Data. *Information and Computation*, 79(3):193–209, 1988.

[77] A. Ginsberg. Theory Revision via Prior Operationalization. In *Proc. AAAI Conference*, pages 590–595. San Mateo, CA, 1988, Morgan Kaufmann.

[78] A. Giordana, L. Saitta, F. Bergadano, F. Brancadori, and D. Demarchi. ENIGMA: A System That Learns Diagnostic Knowledge. *IEEE Trans. on Knowledge and Data Engineering*, 5(1):15–28, 1993.

[79] M. E. Gold. Language Identification in the Limit. *Information and Control*, 10:447–474, 1967.

[80] L. Goldschlager and A. Lister. *Computer Science: A Modern Introduction*. London, 1988, Prentice-Hall.

[81] M. M. Gorlick, C. F. Kesselman, D. A. Marotta, and D. S. Parker. Mockingbird: A Logical Methodology for Program Testing. *Journal of Logic Programming*, 8:95–119, 1990.

[82] G. Gottlob. Subsumption and Implication. *Information Processing Letter*, 24(2):109–111, 1987.

[83] G. Gottlob and C. G. Fermuller. Removing Redundancy from a Clause. *Artificial Intelligence*, 61(2):263–289, 1993.

[84] M. Grobelnik. MARKUS, an Optimized Model Inference System. In C. Rouveirol, editor, *Proc. ECAI Workshop on Logical Approaches to Machine Learning*, Vienna, 1992, John Wiley and Sons.

[85] D. Gunetti. Efficient Proofs in Propositional Calculus with Inverse Resolution. In P. Dewilde and J. Vanderwalle, editors, *Proc. of the CompEuro*, The Hague, 1992, IEEE Comp. Soc. Press.

[86] D. Gunetti. Linear Time Proofs of Propositional Horn Formulas with Inverse Resolution. In S. Costantini, editor, *Proc. of the seventh Italian congress on Logic Programming*, Milan, 1992, CittaStudi.

[87] D. Gunetti. Proofs in Propositional Calculus with Inverse Resolution: Completeness and Complexity. Technical Report, Dept. of Computer Science, Univ. of Turin, 1994.

[88] R. Hamlet. Special Section on Software Testing. *Communications of the ACM*, 31:662–667, 1988.

[89] R. G. Hamlet. Reliability Theory of Program Testing. *Acta Informatica*, 16:31–43, 1981.

[90] I. I. Hayes. Specification Directed Module Testing. *IEEE Trans. on Software Engineering*, 12(1):124–133, 1986.

[91] F. Hayes-Roth and J. McDermott. An Interference Matching Technique for Inducing Abstractions. *Communications of the ACM*, 21:401–411, 1978.

[92] D. M. Hoffman and P. Strooper. Automated Module Testing in Prolog. *IEEE Trans. on Software Engineering*, 17(9):934–943, 1991.

[93] R. C. Houghton. Software Development Tools: A Profile. *IEEE Computer*, 16:63–70, 1983.

[94] W. E. Howden. Reliability of the Path Analysis Testing Strategy. *IEEE Trans. on Software Engineering*, 2:208–215, 1976.

[95] W. E. Howden. Functional Program Testing. *IEEE Trans. on Software Engineering*, 6(2):162–169, 1980.

[96] W. E. Howden. Weak Mutation Testing and Completeness of Test Sets. *IEEE Trans. on Software Engineering*, 8(4):371–379, 1982.

[97] W. E. Howden. The Theory and Practice of Functional Testing. *IEEE Software*, 2(5):6–17, 1985.

[98] M. Huntback. An Improved Version of Shapiro's Model Inference System. In E. Shapiro, editor, *Proc. of the Int. Conf. on Logic Programming*, London, 1986, Springer-Verlag.

Bibliography

[99] P. Idestam-Almquist. *Generalization of Clauses*. Ph.D. thesis, Stockholm University, 1993.

[100] P. Idestam-Almquist. Generalization under Implication by Recursive Anti-unification. In P. Utgoff, editor, *Proc. of the Int. Conf. on Machine Learning*, pages 151–158. Amherst, MA, 1993, Morgan Kaufmann.

[101] P. Idestam-Almquist. Generalization under Implication by Using Or-introduction. In P. Brazdil, editor, *Proc. of the European Conf. on Machine Learning*, pages 56–64. Berlin, 1993, Springer-Verlag, LNAI 667.

[102] P. Idestam-Almquist. Recursive Anti-unification. In S. Muggleton, editor, *Proc. of the Third Int. Workshop on Inductive Logic Programming*, pages 241–253. Ljubljana, Slovenia, 1993, Jozef Stefan Institute.

[103] J. P. Joaunnaud and Y. Kodratoff. Characterization of a Class of Functions Synthesized from Examples by a Summers-like Method Using a BMW Matching Technique. In *Proc. of the 6th Int. Joint Conf. on Artificial Intelligence*, pages 440–447. Tokyo, 1979, IJCAII.

[104] G. F. Jones. *Software Engineering*. New York, 1990, John Wiley and Sons.

[105] M. Kearns and U. Vazirani. *Topics in Computational Learning Theory*. Cambridge, MA, 1994, MIT Press.

[106] J. U. Kietz. Some Lower Bounds for the Computational Complexity of Inductive Logic Programming. In P. Brazdil, editor, *Proc. of the European Conf. on Machine Learning*, pages 115–123. Berlin, 1993, Springer-Verlag, LNAI 667.

[107] J. U. Kietz and S. Wrobel. Controlling the Complexity of Learning in Logic Through Syntactic and Task-Oriented Models. In S. Muggleton, editor, *Inductive Logic Programming*, London, 1991, Academic Press.

[108] P. Kilpelainen and H. Mannila. Generation of Test Cases for Simple Prolog Programs. *Acta Cybernetica*, 9(3):235–246, 1990.

[109] K. N. King and A. J. Offutt. A Fortran Language System for Mutation-based Software Testing. *Software Practice and Experience*, 21(7):685–718, 1991.

[110] R. King, S. Muggleton, R. Lewis, and M. Sternberg. Drug Design by Machine Learning: The Use of Inductive Logic Programming to Model the Structure-Activity Relationships of Trimethoprim Analogues Binding to Dihydrofolate Reductase. *Proc. National Academy of Sciences, USA*, 89:11322–11326, 1992.

[111] R. King, S. Muggleton, and M. Sternberg. Protein Secondary Structure Prediction Using Logic-based Machine Learning. *Protein Engineering*, 5(7):647–657, 1992.

[112] R. King and M. Sternberg. Machine Learning Approach for the Prediction of Protein Secondary Structure. *Journal of Molecular Biology*, 216:441–457, 1990.

[113] M. Kirschenbaum and L. Sterling. Refinement Strategies for Inductive Learning of Simple Prolog Programs. In j. Mylopoulos and R. Reiter, editors, *Proc. Int. Joint Conf. on Artificial Intelligence*, pages 757–761. Sydney, Australia, 1991, IJCAII.

[114] D. E. Knuth. *The Art of Computer Programming (3)*. Reading, MA, 1973, Addison-Wesley.

[115] Y. Kodratoff and J. Fargues. A Sane Algorithm for the Synthesis of LISP Functions from Example Problems: The Boyer and Moore Algorithm. In *Proc. of the AISB Meeting*, pages 169–175. Hamburg, Germany, 1978.

[116] S. Lapointe and S. Matwin. Sub-unification: a tool for efficient induction of recursive programs. In D. Sleeman and P. Edwards, editors, *Proc. of the Int. Conf. on Machine Learning*, pages 273–281. Aberdeen, Scotland, 1992, Morgan Kaufmann.

[117] N. Lavrač and S. Džeroski. *Inductive Logic Programming: Techniques and Applications*. London, 1994, Ellis Horwood.

[118] N. Lavrač, S. Džeroski, V. Pirnat, and V. Krizman. Learning Rules for Early Diagnoses of Rheumatic Diseases. In *Proc. 3rd Scandinavian Conf. on Artificial Intelligence*, pages 138–149. Amsterdam, 1991, IOS Press.

[119] P. LeBlanc. BMWk Revisited. Generalization and Formalization of an Algorithm for Detecting Recursive Relations in Term Sequences. In F. Bergadano and L. DeRaedt, editors, *Proc. European Conference on Machine Learning*, pages 183–198. Berlin, 1994, Springer-Verlag, LNAI 784.

[120] C. Lee. *A Completeness Theorem and a Computer Program for Finding Theorems Derivable from Given Axioms*. Ph.D. thesis, University of California, Berkeley, 1967.

[121] X. C. Ling. Learning and Inventing of Horn Clause Theories - A Constructive Method. In Z. W. Ras, editor, *Methodologies for Intelligent Systems 4*, pages 323–331. 1989, North Holland.

[122] X. C. Ling. Inventing Necessary Theoretical Terms. In *Proc. of the IJCAI-91 Workshop on evaluating and changing representation in ML*, Sydney, Australia, 1991, IJCAII.

[123] X. C. Ling. Learning from Good Examples. In *Proc. Int. Joint Conf. on Artificial Intelligence*, pages 751–756. Sydney, Australia, 1991, IJCAII.

[124] X. C. Ling and M. A. Narayan. A Critical Comparison of Various Methods Based on Inverse Resolution. In L. A. Birnbaum and G. C. Collins, editors, *Proc. of the 8th Int. Workshop on Machine Learning*, pages 168–172. Evanston, IL, 1991, Morgan Kaufmann.

[125] J. Lloyd. *Foundations of Logic Programming*. Berlin, 1984, Springer Verlag.

[126] D. W. Loveland. *Automated Theorem Proving: A Logical Basis*. Amsterdam, 1978, North Holland.

[127] J. Marcinkowski and L. Pacholski. Undecidability of the Horn Clause Implication Problem. In *Proc. 33rd IEEE Symp. on Foundations of Computer Science*, pages 354–362, Pittsburgh, PA, 1992, IEEE Comp. Soc. Press.

[128] R. S. Michalski. Pattern Recognition as Rule-Guided Inductive Inference. *IEEE Trans. on PAMI*, 2:349–361, 1980.

[129] R. S. Michalski. A Theory and Methodology of Inductive Learning. *Artificial Intelligence*, 20:111–161, 1983.

[130] R. S. Michalski, J. G. Carbonell, and T. Mitchell, editors. *Machine Learning: An Artificial Intelligence Approach*, vol. 1. Palo Alto, CA, 1983, Tioga Publishing Co.

[131] R. S. Michalski, J. G. Carbonell, and T. Mitchell, editors. *Machine Learning: An Artificial Intelligence Approach*, vol. 2. Palo Alto, CA, 1985, Morgan Kaufmann.

[132] R. S. Michalski, J. Hong, N. Lavrač, and I. Mozetic. The AQ15 Inductive Learning System: An Overview and Experiments. In *Proc. of the First Int. Meeting on Advances in Learning*, Les Arcs, France, 1986.

[133] R. S. Michalski and Y. Kodratoff, editors. *Machine Learning: An Artificial Intelligence Approach*, vol. 3. Palo Alto, CA, 1988, Morgan Kaufmann.

[134] S. Minton. Quantitative Results Concerning the Utility of Explanation-Based Learning. *Artificial Intelligence*, 42:363–392, 1990.

[135] T. M. Mitchell. Generalization as Search. *Artificial Intelligence*, 18:203–226, 1982.

[136] T. M. Mitchell. The Need for Biases in Learning Generalizations. In *Readings in Machine Learning*. 1991, Morgan Kaufmann.

[137] T. M. Mitchell, R. M. Keller, and S. Kedar-Cabelli. Explanation-Based Generalization: A Unifying View. *Machine Learning*, 1:47–80, 1986.

[138] L. J. Morell. Theoretical Insights into Fault-based Testing. In *Proc. Workshop on Software Testing, Verification and Analysis*, pages 45–62. Banff, Canada, 1988.

[139] K. Morik. Balanced Cooperative Modeling. In R. S. Michalski and G. Tecuci, editors, *Proc. Workshop on Multistrategy Learning*, pages 65–80. Harpers Ferry, VA, 1991.

[140] K. Morik, F. Bergadano, and W. Buntine, editors. Special Issue of the Journal "Machine Learning" on Evaluating and Changing Representation, 14. 1994.

[141] S. Muggleton. DUCE: An Oracle Based Approach to Constructive Induction. In *Proc. of the IJCAI*, pages 287–292. Milan, 1987, IJCAII.

[142] S. Muggleton. Inductive Logic Programming. *New Generation Computing*, 8(4):295–318, 1991.

[143] S. Muggleton. Inverting Implication. In S. Muggleton and K. Furukawa, editors, *Proc. of the Second Int. Workshop on Inductive Logic Programming (ILP92)*. ICOT Technical Memorandum TM-1182, 1992.

[144] S. Muggleton and W. Buntine. Machine Invention of First Order Predicates by Inverting Resolution. In *Proc. of the Fifth Int. Conf. on Machine Learning*, pages 339–352. Ann Arbor, MI, 1988, Morgan Kaufmann.

[145] S. Muggleton and C. Feng. Efficient Induction of Logic Programs. In *Proc. of the First Conf. on Algorithmic Learning Theory*, Tokyo, 1990, OHMSHA.

[146] C. Nédellec. *APT, apprentissage interactif de règles de résolution de problèmes en présence de théorie du domaine*. Ph.D. thesis, Université de Paris Sud, 1994.

[147] C. Nédellec and C. Rouveirol. Specifications of the HAIKU System. Orsay, France, 1994. Deliverable D.LRI.2b Univ. de Paris Sud.

[148] T. Niblett. A Study of Generalization in Logic Programs. In *Proc. European Working Sessions on Learning*, London, 1988, Pitman.

Bibliography

[149] P. Odifreddi. *Classical Recursion Theory, vol. 2*. Amsterdam, 1996, North Holland.

[150] A. Offutt. The Coupling Effect: Fact or Fiction? In *Proc. Workshop on Software Testing, Analysis and Verification*, pages 131–140. 1989.

[151] D. Osherson, M. Stob, and S. Weinstein. A Universal Inductive Inference Machine. *Journal of Symbolic Logic*, 56(2):661–672, 1991.

[152] D. Osherson, M. Stob, and S. Weinstein. A Universal Method of Scientific Inquiry. *Machine Learning*, 9(2/3):261–271, 1992.

[153] D. Osherson and S. Weinstein. Paradigms of Truth Detection. *Journal of Philosophical Logic*, 18:1–42, 1989.

[154] M. Pazzani, C. A. Brunk, and G. Silverstein. A Knowledge-Intensive Approach to Learning Relational Concepts. In L. A. Birnbaum and G. C. Collins, editors, *Proc. of the 8th Int. Conf. on Machine Learning*, pages 432–436. Evanston, IL, 1991, Morgan Kaufmann.

[155] M. Pazzani and D. Kibler. The Utility of Knowledge in Inductive Learning. *Machine Learning*, 1:57–94, 1992.

[156] G. Plotkin. A Note on Inductive Generalization. In B. Meltzer and D. Michie, editors, *Machine Intelligence 5*, pages 153–163. Edinburgh Univ. Press, 1970.

[157] G. Plotkin. A Further Note on Inductive Generalization. In B. Meltzer and D. Michie, editors, *Machine Intelligence 6*, pages 101–124. Edinburgh, 1971, Edinburgh Univ. Press.

[158] G. Plotkin. *Automatic Methods of Inductive Inference*. Ph.D. thesis, Edinburgh University, 1971.

[159] R. Quinlan. Induction of Decision Trees. *Machine Learning*, 1:81–106, 1986.

[160] R. Quinlan. Learning Logical Definitions from Relations. *Machine Learning*, 5:239–266, 1990.

[161] R. Quinlan. Knowledge Acquisition from Structured Data. *IEEE Expert*, 6(6):32–37, 1991.

[162] L. Rendell. A General Framework for Induction and a Study of Selective Induction. *Machine Learning*, 1(2):177–226, 1986.

[163] L. Rendell. Learning Hard Concepts. In *Proc. of the 3rd European Working Sessions on Learning*, pages 177–200. Glasgow, Scotland, 1988.

[164] B. L. Richards and R. J. Mooney. Learning Relations by Pathfinding. In *Proc. of the AAAI conference*, pages 50–55. San Jose, CA, 1992, AAAI Press.

[165] J. A. Robinson. A Machine-Oriented Logic Based on the Resolution Principle. *Journal of the ACM*, 12:23–41, 1965.

[166] C. Rouveirol. Extension of Inversion of Resolution to Theory Completion. In S. Muggleton, editor, *Inductive Logic Programming*, London, 1992, Academic Press.

[167] C. Rouveirol. Flattening and Saturation: Two Representation Changes for Generalization. *Machine Learning*, 14(2):219–232, 1994.

[168] C. Rouveirol, H. Adé, and L. DeRaedt. Bottom-up Generalization in ILP. In F. Bergadano, L. DeRaedt, S. Matwin, and S. Muggleton, editors, *Proc. of the IJCAI-93 Workshop on Inductive Logic Programming*, pages 59–70. Chambéry, France, 1993, IJCAII.

[169] C. Rouveirol and J. F. Puget. Beyond Inversion of Resolution. In Porter and Mooney, editors, *Proc. of the Int. Conf. on Machine Learning*, pages 122–130, 1990.

[170] S. Russell. Tree-Structured Bias. In *Proc. of the AAAI Conference*, pages 641–645. San Mateo, CA, 1988, Morgan Kaufmann.

[171] L. Saitta and F. Bergadano. Pattern Recognition and Valiant's Learning Framework. *IEEE Trans. on Pattern Analysis and Machine Intelligence*, 15(2):145–154, 1993.

[172] C. Sammut and R. Banerji. Learning Concepts by Asking Questions. In R. S. Michalski, J. G. Carbonell, and T. Mitchell, editors, *Machine Learning: An Artificial Intelligence Approach*, volume 2, pages 167–192. Palo Alto, CA, 1986, Morgan Kaufmann.

[173] M. Schmidt-Schauss. Implication of Clauses Is Undecidable. *Theoretical Computer Science*, 59:287–296, 1988.

[174] M. Sebag and C. Rouveirol. Induction of Maximally General Clauses Consistent with Integrity Constraints. In S. Wrobel, editor, *Proc. IV Int. Workshop on Inductive Logic Programming*, pages 195–216. Bad Honnef/Bonn, Germany, 1994, GMD-Studien.

[175] E. Y. Shapiro. *An Algorithm That Infers Theories from Facts*. Tech Report 192, Yale University, Department of Computer Science, 1981.

[176] E. Y. Shapiro. *Algorithmic Program Debugging.* Cambridge, MA, 1983, MIT Press.

[177] I. Shemer. System Analysis: A Systemic Analysis of a Conceptual System. *Communications of the ACM*, 30:507–512, 1987.

[178] G. Silverstein and M. Pazzani. Learning Relational Cliches. In F. Bergadano, L. DeRaedt, S. Matwin, and S. Muggleton, editors, *Proc. of the IJCAI-93 Workshop on Inductive Logic Programming*, Chambéry, France, 1993, IJCAII.

[179] G. Silverstein and M. J. Pazzani. Relational Cliches: Constraining Constructive Induction During Relational Learning. In L. A. Birnbaum and G. C. Collins, editors, *Proc. of the 8th Int. Workshop on ML*, pages 203–207. Evanston, IL, 1991, Morgan Kaufmann.

[180] E. Sommer. Rulebase Stratification: an Approach to theory restructuring. In S. Wrobel, editor, *Proc. IV Int. Workshop on Inductive Logic Programming*, pages 377–390. Bad Honnef/Bonn, Germany, 1994, GMD-Studien.

[181] E. Sommer. Fender: An approach to theory restructuring. In S. Wrobel and N. Lavrač, editors, *Proc. of the European Conf. on Machine Learning*, Berlin, 1995, Springer-Verlag.

[182] A. Srinivasan, S. Muggleton, R. King, and M. Sternberg. Mutagenesis: ILP Experiments in a Non-determinate Biological Domain. In S. Wrobel, editor, *Proc. IV Int. Workshop on Inductive Logic Programming*, pages 217–232. Bad Honnef/Bonn, Germany, 1994, GMD-Studien.

[183] I. Stahl. Predicate Invention in ILP - an Overview. In P. Brazdil, editor, *Proc. European Conference on Machine Learning*, pages 313–322. Berlin, 1993, Springer-Verlag.

[184] I. Stahl. On the Utility of Predicate Invention in Inductive Logic Programming. In F. Bergadano and L. DeRaedt, editors, *Proc. European Conference on Machine Learning*, pages 272–286. Berlin, 1994, Springer-Verlag, LNAI 784.

[185] I. Stahl and I. Weber. The Arguments of Newly Invented Predicates in Inductive Logic Programming. In S. Wrobel, editor, *Proc. IV Int. Workshop on Inductive Logic Programming*, pages 233–245. Bad Honnef/Bonn, Germany, 1994, GMD-Studien.

[186] P. Strooper and D. Hoffman. Prolog Testing of C Modules. In V. Saraswat and K. Ueda, editors, *Proc. Int. Symposium on Logic Programming*, pages 596–608. Cambridge, MA, 1991, MIT Press.

[187] P. D. Summers. A Methodology for LISP Program Construction from Examples. *Journal of the ACM*, 24:161–175, 1977.

[188] S. A. Tarnlund. Horn Clause Computability. *BIT*, 17:215–226, 1977.

[189] Birgit Tausend. Biases and Their Effects in Inductive Logic Programming. In F. Bergadano and L. DeRaedt, editors, *Proc. European Conference on Machine Learning*, pages 431–434. Berlin, 1994. Springer-Verlag, LNAI 784.

[190] Birgit Tausend. Representing Biases for Inductive Logic Programming. In F. Bergadano and L. DeRaedt, editors, *Proc. European Conference on Machine Learning*, pages 427–430. Berlin, 1994, Springer-Verlag, LNAI 784.

[191] W. T. Tsai, D. Volovik, and T. F. Keefe. Automated Test Case Generation for Programs Specified by Relational Algebra Queries. *IEEE Trans. on Software Engineering*, 16(3):316–324, 1990.

[192] L. G. Valiant. A Theory of the Learnable. *Communications of the ACM*, 27(11):1134–1142, 1984.

[193] V. Vapnik. *Estimation of Dependencies Based on Empirical Data*. New York, 1982, Springer Verlag.

[194] V. N. Vapnik and Y. A. Chervonenkis. On the Uniform Convergence of Relative Frequencies of Events to Their Probabilities. *Theory of Probability and Its Applications*, 16:264–280, 1971.

[195] V. N. Vapnik and Y. A. Chervonenkis. Necessary and Sufficient Conditions for the Uniform Convergence of Means to Their Expectations. *Theory of Probability and Its Applications*, 26:532–553, 1981.

[196] G. Viviani. *Inferenza induttiva di classi di funzioni ricorsive*. Master's thesis, University of Turin, 1993.

[197] E. J. Weyuker. Assessing Test Data Adequacy Through Program Inference. *ACM Trans. on Programming Languages and Systems*, 5(4):641–655, 1983.

[198] G. Widmer. An Incremental Version of Bergadano and Giordana's Integrated Learning Strategy. In K. Morik, editor, *Proc. of the 4th European Working Sessions on Learning*, London, 1989, Pitman.

[199] R. Wiehagen. Characterization Problems in the Theory of Inductive Inference. In G. Ausiello and C. Bohm, editors, *Fifth Coll. on Automata, Languages and Programming*, pages 494–508. Berlin, 1978, Springer-Verlag, LNCS 62.

[200] P. H. Winston. Learning Structural Descriptions from Examples. In P. H. Winston, editor, *The Psychology of Computer Vision*, New York, 1975, Mc-Graw Hill.

[201] N. Wirth. Program Development by Stepwise Refinement. *Communications of the ACM*, 14:221–227, 1971.

[202] R. Wirth. Completing Logic Programs by Inverse Resolution. In *Proc. European Working Sessions on Learning*, pages 239–250. Montpellier, France, 1989, Pitman.

[203] R. Wirth and P. O'Rorke. Constraints on Predicate Invention. In L. A. Birnbaum and G. C. Collins, editors, *Proc. of the 8th Int. Workshop on ML*, pages 457–461. Evanston, IL, 1991, Morgan Kaufmann.

[204] J. Wogulis and M. J. Pazzani. A Methodology for Evaluating Theory Revision Systems: Results with Audrey II. In R. Bajcsy, editor, *Proc. 13th Int. Joint Conf. on Artificial Intelligence*, pages 1128–1134. Chambéry, France, 1993, IJCAII.

Index

$\mathcal{V}$ function, 58
θ-subsumption, 61
"V" operators, 47
"W" operators, 51

absorption, 47, 55
accuracy, 26
adaptive strategy, 83, 163
adequate test set, 185, 187, 190
ADG, 124
algebraic testing, 186
ambivalent clauses, 61
ambivalent literals, 70
analytic learning, 118
Antecedent Description Grammars, 122
anti-unification (recursive), 74
APT, 126, 129

background knowledge, 4, 13, 17, 38
Bernoulli's Theorem, 110
bias, 109
  language, 109
    generative, 111, 117
    static, 117
  search, 109, 129
  semantic, 127
  shift of, 127
  validation, 129
BMWk methodology, 67
bottom-up methods, 199
bottom-up systems, 125

CIGOL, 47, 54
class, 16
CLAUDIEN, 136

clause schematas, 115
Clause Sets, 115, 129, 140, 172, 191, 200
clause templates, 115, 116, 182
CLINT, 57, 126
compilation, 170
completeness, 12, 15, 25, 89, 142, 149, 154
computation of least general generalization, 36
concept, 16
connection paths, 117
connection, divisors of, 74
connection, factors of, 74
consistency, 12, 142
constructive learning, 18
contradiction backtracing, 80, 81
coupling effect assumption, 187
create operator, 53
cross connection, 76
cross-validation, 26
CRUSTACEAN, 62, 66, 147
cut, 160

deductive learning, 118
Definite Clause Grammars, 111
demand-driven approach, 52
detectability, 31
determinate clause, 41
determinate literal, 41
determinations, 82, 116
domain testing, 186
domain theory, 118
  imperfect, 119

dream operator, 53
dropping condition rule, 57

eager strategy, 83, 111, 163
embedding term, 64
equivalence relation under
    θ-subsumption, 36
equivalence under generalized
    subsumption, 44
EX-identification, 27, 188
example, 11
  negative, 12
  positive, 12
examples, ground, 12
explanation-based learning, 118
extensionality, 77, 80, 140
external connection, 73
extralogical predicates, 179

fault-based methods, 187
FILP, 77, 125, 128, 137, 175, 182, 189, 200
flattening, 15, 53, 54, 68, 83, 209
FOCL, 77, 120
FOIL, 77, 85, 113, 128, 138, 140
functionality, 137

Gencol, 127
generalization, 33
generalization under implication, 61
generalize operator, 48
generating term, 64
GOLEM, 38, 58, 60, 71, 126
greatest common divisor, 76
green cut, 179
Grendel, 122

h-easy programs, 29
HAIKU, 127
heuristic measure, 23
heuristics, 135
hypothesis space, 13
hypothesis space, expansion
    of, 171

identification, 48
identification by enumeration, 28, 29
identification in the limit, 24, 27, 110
  parallel, 30
  postponed, 30
  sequence, 30
ij-determinism, 41
implication, 33
incremental systems, 22, 23
indirect power of a clause, 68
indirect root of a clause, 68
INDUCE, 113
inductive compilation, 171
inductive inference, 170
inductive inference machine, 14
Inductive Logic Programming
    languages, 171
inductive program, 170, 171, 174
inductive programming, 170, 177
inductive programming language, 171
inductive software process, 174
inference-adequate test set, 188
input refutation, 92
input/output modes, 134
inputs
  instantiated, 134
  used, 134
interconstruction, 53
internal connection, 72
intraconstruction, 53, 55, 57
invented predicate, 53
inverse implication, 147
inverse resolution, 45, 60
inverse substitution, 48
inversion-complete inductive rule, 50
IRES, 49, 51, 53, 54, 57, 126
ITOU, 51, 53, 54, 57, 126, 129

language bias, 171
lazy macros in ADGs, 124
lazy strategy, 83, 163
least general generalization, 35, 54, 60, 67, 74, 76
LFP2, 49

Index

linear resolution, 62
linkedness, 30
literal degree, 41
literal depth, 41
literals, ground, 12
logic programming, 199
logical consequence, 61
logical implication, 33, 60
LOPSTER, 62, 68, 72, 73, 76, 147

Machine Learning, 26
MARKUS, 84, 112
MARVIN, 55
minimal Herbrand model, 40
minimally general generalization under implication (MinGGI), 72
minimally unsatisfiable set of clauses, 91
MIS, 77, 79, 111, 113, 128, 163
MISST, 114
ML-SMART, 77, 113, 115, 120, 128, 140
MOBAL, 115, 125
mode restrictions, 116
model inference system, 79
monotonicity, 154
most general subunifier, 64
most specific generalization, 45
most specific V operators, 57
multiple predicate learning, 16, 137, 160
mutation analysis testing, 189
mutual recursion, 17

necessary term, 51
negation, 154, 160
NINA, 126, 127, 129, 136

object program, 174
one-step systems, 22
operationality, 119
outputs
  instantiated, 134
  used, 134

PAC-learning, 188
parent clauses, 45

partial model, 39
path testing, 190
pattern recognition, 17, 26, 109, 110
postprocessing step, 84
power of a clause, 68
predicate invention, 18, 19, 51, 160
  necessary, 21
predicate sets, 115
predicate variables, 115
preference criterion, 109
presentation for an interpretation, 28
PROGOL, 134
program adequate test set, 188
program equivalence, 190
program induction, 170
Prolog, 13
proof tree, 80
proper indirect nth power of a clause, 68
proper indirect nth root of a clause, 68

queries, 24
query
  clause equivalence, 25, 54
  equivalence, 25
  existential, 24, 111
  existential, type I, 24, 80, 81
  existential, type II, 24, 78, 83, 138
  ground, 24
  membership, 24, 81
  program equivalence, 25

range restrictedness, 30
RDT, 115
recursive anti-unification, 72
red cut, 179
reduced clause, 36
redundancy algorithm, 55
redundancy of a clause, 84
redundant literal, 36
refinement, 111
refinement graph, 82
refinement operator, 82, 111, 117
reformulation approach, 52

relational cliché, 90
relative least general generalization, 38, 57, 60
reliable test set, 186, 190
resolution, 33, 45
resolvent of two clauses, 45
reverse engineering, 169
root of a clause, 68
rule models, 115

saturation, 48, 50, 57, 59, 126
schema, second-order, 115
search, breadth first, 82
selective learning, 18
separability assumption, 49
skeletons, 114
software debugging, 169, 175, 191
software development, 174
software maintenance, 168, 175, 177
software reusability, 177
software reuse, 168
software testing, 168
soundness, 15, 24, 154
specialization of a clause, 111
specification adequate test set, 188
speed-up learning, 119
star methodology, 129
starting clause, 125
stepwise refinement, 114
stopping criterion, 25, 109, 128
strongly generative clause, 58
subconcept, 17
substitution, irrelevant, 53
subsumption theorem, 62
 generalized, 43
subterm, 63, 72
subunification, 64
subunifier, 64
syntactically generative, 40
syntactically generative clause, 58

term substitution, 75
test data adequacy, 188
test set adequacy, 189

testing, 185
 fault-based, 189, 191
 functional, 186, 190, 194
 random, 26, 194
 specification-based, 186
 syntax-direct, 186
 weak mutation, 187
theory restructuring, 52
theory revision, 21
top-down methods, 199
TRACY, 125, 138, 200
truncation operator, 51, 54, 57
type restrictions, 116

unfolding algorithm, 163
unfolding problem, 117
unification, 33, 35
unit clause assumption, 49
unit refutation, 92
useful term, 51

Vapnik-Chervonenkis dimension, 110

Logic Programming

Ehud Shapiro, editor
Koichi Furukawa, Jean-Louis Lassez, Fernando Pereira, and David H. D. Warren, associate editors

The Art of Prolog: Advanced Programming Techniques, Leon Sterling and Ehud Shapiro, 1986

Logic Programming: Proceedings of the Fourth International Conference (volumes 1 and 2), edited by Jean-Louis Lassez, 1987

Concurrent Prolog: Collected Papers (volumes 1 and 2), edited by Ehud Shapiro, 1987

Logic Programming: Proceedings of the Fifth International Conference and Symposium (volumes 1 and 2), edited by Robert A. Kowalski and Kenneth A. Bowen, 1988

Constraint Satisfaction in Logic Programming, Pascal Van Hentenryck, 1989

Logic-Based Knowledge Representation, edited by Peter Jackson, Han Reichgelt, and Frank van Harmelen, 1989

Logic Programming: Proceedings of the Sixth International Conference, edited by Giorgio Levi and Maurizio Martelli, 1989

Meta-Programming in Logic Programming, edited by Harvey Abramson and M. H. Rogers, 1989

Logic Programming: Proceedings of the North American Conference 1989 (volumes 1 and 2), edited by Ewing L. Lusk and Ross A. Overbeek, 1989

Logic Programming: Proceedings of the 1990 North American Conference, edited by Saumya Debray and Manuel Hermenegildo, 1990

Logic Programming: Proceedings of the Seventh International Conference, edited by David H. D. Warren and Peter Szeredi, 1990

The Craft of Prolog, Richard A. O'Keefe, 1990

The Practice of Prolog, edited by Leon S. Sterling, 1990

Eco-Logic: Logic-Based Approaches to Ecological Modelling, David Robertson, Alan Bundy, Robert Muetzelfeldt, Mandy Haggith, and Michael Uschold, 1991

Warren's Abstract Machine: A Tutorial Reconstruction, Hassan Aït-Kaci, 1991

Parallel Logic Programming, Evan Tick, 1991

Logic Programming: Proceedings of the Eighth International Conference, edited by Koichi Furukawa, 1991

Logic Programming: Proceedings of the 1991 International Symposium, edited by Vijay Saraswat and Kazunori Ueda, 1991

Foundations of Disjunctive Logic Programming, Jorge Lobo, Jack Minker, and Arcot Rajasekar, 1992

Types in Logic Programming, edited by Frank Pfenning, 1992

Logic Programming: Proceedings of the Joint International Conference and Symposium on Logic Programming, edited by Krzysztof Apt, 1992

Concurrent Constraint Programming, Vijay A. Saraswat, 1993

Logic Programming Languages: Constraints, Functions, and Objects, edited by K. R. Apt, J. W. de Bakker, and J. J. M. M. Rutten, 1993

Logic Programming: Proceedings of the Tenth International Conference on Logic Programming, edited by David S. Warren, 1993

Constraint Logic Programming: Selected Research, edited by Frédéric Benhamou and Alain Colmerauer, 1993

A Grammatical View of Logic Programming, Pierre Deransart and Jan Małuszyński, 1993

Logic Programming: Proceedings of the 1993 International Symposium, edited by Dale Miller, 1993

The Gödel Programming Language, Patricia Hill and John Lloyd, 1994

The Art of Prolog: Advanced Programming Techniques, second edition, Leon Sterling and Ehud Shapiro, 1994

Logic Programming: Proceedings of the Eleventh International Conference on Logic Programming, edited by Pascal Van Hentenryck, 1994

Logic Programming: Proceedings of the 1994 International Symposium, edited by Maurice Bruynooghe, 1994

Logic Programming: Proceedings of the Twelfth International Conference, edited by Leon Sterling, 1995

Inductive Logic Programming: From Machine Learning to Software Engineering, Francesco Bergadano and Daniele Gunetti, 1996